SUPER BOWL XX

Anniversary Handbook

St. Martin's Press
New York

Super Bowl XX Anniversary Handbook
Copyright © 1985 by Associated Features Inc.
All rights reserved.
Printed in the United States of America.
No part of this book may be used
or reproduced in any manner whatsoever
without written permission except
in the case of brief quotations
embodied in critical articles or reviews.
For information, address St. Martin's Press,
175 Fifth Avenue, New York, N.Y. 10010.

ISBN 0-312-90350-2 (USA)
ISBN 0-312-90351-0 (CAN)

ACKNOWLEDGMENTS

High fives are in order for the super Super Bowl team that made the *Super Bowl XX Anniversary Handbook* happen. Each an MVP in his specialty, Peter Alfano of The *New York Times* wrote the game roundups, Martin Lader of United Press International did the player profiles, David Schulz created the trivia quiz, and Lee Stowbridge compiled the massive all-time Super Bowl player directory.

The editor acknowledges with appreciation their contributions.

—ZANDER HOLLANDER

CONTENTS

INTRODUCTION

In January 1986, one of the biggest sporting events in the United States, and for that matter in the world, will celebrate a landmark birthday in New Orleans. There will be Dixieland jazz, crawfish pie and chicken gumbo, and partying to dawn's early light on Bourbon Street as the Super Bowl becomes twenty years old. And it seemed like only yesterday that this championship football game with the pretentious name was just a babe in a sports world that included such American traditions as the World Series, Kentucky Derby, and Indianapolis 500.

The Super Bowl is still a youngster in comparison to these other famous American classics, but it has surpassed all of them as the single most watched event. The World Series may draw more fans and television viewers over the course of its best four-of-seven series, but for one day, nothing brings activity in the United States to a halt like the Super Bowl.

The game is a product of public relations and the television age, and is packaged and sold to reach a mass audience. Sixty seconds of commercial time cost sponsors a million dollars for Super Bowl XIX in 1985, as more than 100 million viewers tuned in to see the game and endure the commercials.

The third Sunday in January is known as Super Sunday, and even a casual or non-sports fan may take a peek at the game just to see who's winning. During the two weeks of buildup, stars get brighter and even obscure players become household names.

If the Super Bowl were judged as a television series, it would be a smash hit, outdistancing the old *Ed Sullivan Show*, *M*A*S*H*, *All in the Family*, and miniseries such as *Roots*. It is the Super Bowl that has the highest television rating of all time.

On Super Sunday, streets, parks, and playgrounds are virtually deserted. Movie houses are near empty, and restaurants report business is slow. Many groups postpone weekly meetings or delay them until the game is over. Some performers cancel their shows.

Because the 1985 Super Bowl was on January 20—Inauguration Day—President Reagan took the oath of office as required by law but postponed until Monday the inauguration parade and ball. Instead, he joined his constituents in front of a television set and watched the Miami Dolphins play the San Francisco 49ers.

Super Sunday has become a day for parties, rivaled only by Christmas and New Year's Eve parties. People invite neighbors, relatives, and friends to enjoy cocktails, canapés, pretzels, and potato chips while watching the lengthy pregame show and the game itself. Gambling may be illegal everywhere except in Nevada and Atlantic City, New Jersey, but millions of dollars are gambled on the game, from handshake bets between friends to the more lucrative wagers at the casinos.

The Super Bowl is a phenomenon; it is remarkable to think that at its inception the National Football League regarded it as an unwanted child, part of the settlement in the merger war between the established league and the upstart American Football League. A championship game between the best teams in each league was something the aloof NFL owners had wanted to avoid. Little did they anticipate this would grow into an unrivaled sports spectacle.

The game was given its name indirectly by the young daughter of Lamar Hunt, the owner of the Kansas City Chiefs of the AFL. Pete Rozelle, the commissioner of the NFL, who would become the commissioner of all pro football, and the owners in both leagues were having a difficult time thinking of an ingenious name that would convey the importance of the championship game.

Hunt's inspiration came after he had arrived home

one night with a ball made of Silly Putty that bounced crazily. His daughter called it a "super ball," and her father attended the next owners' meeting and suggested, "Super Bowl."

Perhaps no game could consistently live up to the title, but super or not, the Super Bowl has captured the imagination of American sports fans from the beginning—from that first Super Sunday when the Green Bay Packers played the Kansas City Chiefs on January 15, 1967.

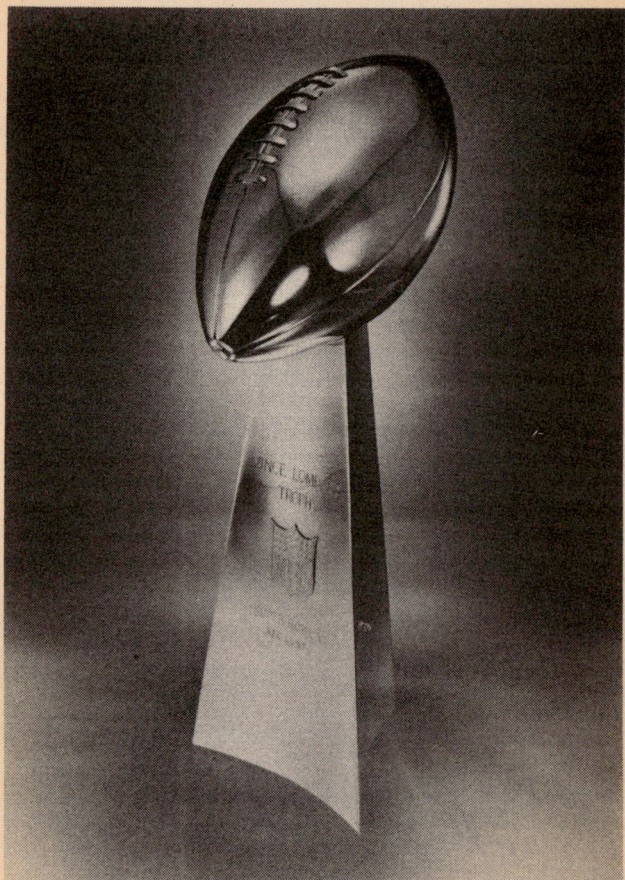

SUPER BOWL I

SHOWDOWN

Only a seventeenth-round draft pick, Green Bay quarterback Bart Starr came full circle in Super Bowl I.

UPI

Participants—Kansas City, champions of the American Football League, and Green Bay Packers, champions of the National Football League.

Date—January 15, 1967.

Site—Memorial Coliseum, Los Angeles, California.

Time—1:05 P.M. PST.

Attendance—63,036.

Radio and Television—National Broadcasting Company (TV and radio), Columbia Broadcasting System (TV and radio).

Regular-Season Records—Kansas City, 11–2–1; Green Bay, 12–2.

Playoff Records—Kansas City defeated Buffalo Bills, 31–7, for AFL title; Green Bay defeated Dallas Cowboys, 34–27, for NFL title.

Players' Shares—$15,000 to each member of winning team; $7,500 to each member of losing team.

Coaches—Hank Stram, Kansas City; Vince Lombardi, Green Bay.

SUPER BOWL I

SHOWDOWN

The first Super Bowl game was a lot like space travel—a voyage into the unknown. As members of rival leagues, the Green Bay Packers and the Kansas City Chiefs were mysteries to one another. They were scouted by word of mouth and hearsay as much as by what the respective coaching staffs had seen on film.

"Films are deceiving," Herb Adderley, the Packers' all-pro defensive back, said after spending an afternoon at the movies. "I still can't tell how fast Otis Taylor is, because I don't know how fast the men covering him are."

But the element of the unknown only made more suspenseful the most anticipated professional football game in history. For two weeks preceding Super Bowl I, the networks televising the game, CBS and NBC, trumpeted its coming with a widespread advertising campaign that would have been surpassed only if they'd been promoting the end of the world.

"Thirteen more days to Super Sunday," the networks said. "Only twelve, eleven, ten, nine, eight."

And so on. It was a countdown just like before a space launch. If the various owners and officials in the upstart American Football League seemed to be sounding and acting a bit more apprehensive than their National Football League counterparts, it was simply because the Green Bay Packers were representing the establishment. For the first time, owners such as George Halas of the Chicago Bears, Wellington Mara of the New York Giants, and Art Rooney of the Pittsburgh Steelers were rooting for "the Pack" and its taskmaster coach, Vince Lombardi.

The Packers were held in awe by pro football fans

and in equally high esteem in the NFL. Lombardi had left the Giants—where he was an assistant coach—to become head coach at Green Bay in 1959. He transformed a perennial losing team located in a tiny frost-bitten midwest city into a dynasty. Green Bay became "Titletown," and its citizens found warmth and camaraderie in the success the Packers had under Lombardi.

They had won four NFL championships since he took over, and when Super Bowl I became a reality, there was widespread relief around the league that the Packers would be carrying the NFL flag into the Los Angeles Memorial Coliseum on January 15, 1967.

Fred Williamson had heard all about the Packers, but the cocky defensive back of the Chiefs wasn't in awe of anyone. He was called "The Hammer" because of the lethal forearm blow he used like a karate chop on unsuspecting receivers. Indeed, Williamson was a black belt in karate, and it made him as intimidating as some of the burly defensive linemen and reckless linebackers he played alongside.

Williamson also was as boisterous as he was tough. He spoke his mind and did not care whom he offended. He sensed that many of his teammates seemed afraid to be playing the Packers.

So Williamson decided he would single-handedly try to give them a boost in confidence. On the first morning at their practice site in Long Beach, California, "The Hammer" gave reporters an earful about the so-called mighty Packers.

Bart Starr, the cerebral Green Bay quarterback, wasn't so hot, he decided. Jim Taylor and Boyd Dowler, heck, there were players better than them in the AFL. On and on Williamson talked as reporters hungrily jotted down every word, filling their appetites for outlandish remarks.

In contrast, the other Chiefs on the practice field were being properly respectful of the Packers, who were still working out in cold Green Bay, out of range of the reporters and circus-like atmosphere surrounding the first Super Bowl. Still, the news spread fast, and Williamson's boasts and taunts were headlines around the country the next morning. But it wasn't the Packers who were annoyed—in fact, they found Williamson amusing. Instead, it was the Chiefs who were upset.

Coach Hank Stram called Williamson into his office for a meeting as the Super Bowl countdown continued. "Fred, a lot of the guys are unhappy about some of the things you're saying. They feel you're giving the Packers impetus. Didn't we warn the entire team back in Kansas City to watch what was said to writers, to avoid making any statements that would fire the Packers up?"

Williamson listened, but he was unmoved. Instead, he was more convinced that the Kansas City Chiefs were going to lose. "I know we're going to get whipped unless something drastic happens to wake us up," he maintained.

The Chiefs' trepidation even extended to the top of the organization. One day, Lamar Hunt, the Kansas City owner, was telling a story about how he had taken his son to see the Packers practice in Dallas five years earlier and how his son had asked why the Chiefs never played Green Bay.

"We're in different leagues and can't play each other," Hunt told his son then.

"My son is ten years old now, and we'll finally have this meeting against the Packers in the Super Bowl," Hunt said. "Frankly, he's worried to death."

On January 8, in Green Bay, the Packers broke camp like a battalion of marines preparing for combat. Lombardi was the drill instructor, a gruff, demanding, no-nonsense coach who made players almost twice his size fearful when he became angry. Super Bowl I was more than a game to Lombardi—it was a test of the superiority of the NFL. The image of the league rested on the Packers' performance, and Lombardi carried the responsibility like a burden.

"A week from today," he told the players just before they departed for their training camp in Santa Barbara, California, "nobody is going to leave that stadium until the job is done. I'll keep you all day, all night, all week if necessary, until you win. There is no way the Green Bay Packers are going to lose this football game."

When the Packers arrived in California, it was as if Air Force One had landed. In Kansas City, fans may sing "Hail to the Chiefs," but it was the Packers who were treated like dignitaries.

They exhibited a kind of unspoken resolve characteristic of movie heroes such as Gary Cooper. When they spoke about the game, they were confident but not shrill, as Fred Williamson was.

"We've made winning a habit," said Jerry Kramer, the Packers' all-pro guard. "We never consider the possibility of losing."

As game day approached, each team buried itself in preparation, trying to ignore the large contingent of reporters and television crews, the Super Bowl parties and fans. Back in Kansas City, a university choir canceled its scheduled performance on Super Bowl Sunday because of a lack of interest. In Green Bay, a policeman who was assigned to work that day said he would be suspicious of any driver or pedestrian who was on the street during the game.

But oddly enough, not everyone seemed infatuated by the game. Burglars broke into the Chiefs' offices in Kansas City and stole several thousand dollars but did not take 2,000 Super Bowl tickets. And in Los Angeles, ticket sales were moving slowly. It was doubtful that the Coliseum would be filled to its capacity of 93,000 when game day arrived.

If the air was filled with tension on Super Bowl Sunday, there was also a feeling of relief among the players on both teams. The two-week ordeal preceding the game had thankfully come to an end. No more films to watch, reporters to talk to, or sleepless nights spent worrying about just how good your opponent was.

Of course, the sideshow was not quite over when the players arrived at the Coliseum on a warm, sunny day. On the field there were marching bands, baton twirlers, floats, and glee clubs stretching from end zone to end zone. As a gesture of goodwill between the leagues, four hundred pigeons disguised as doves were released into the air. Finally, with only 63,036 seats filled, it was time to begin.

The Packers won the coin toss and elected to receive. They were a smaller team than the Chiefs and not as fast, but observers were sure their experience, winning tradition, and status in the NFL would make up for any physical shortcomings. On the first series, however, Bart Starr was sacked twice and the Packers were forced to punt.

Each team was overly cautious in the opening minutes, feeling each other out like boxers in the first round. But when Starr felt he had spotted a weakness in the Chiefs' defense later in the quarter, he wasted no time exploiting it.

Except for Williamson, Green Bay thought the Chiefs' secondary was weak. So Starr went to work from his own 20-yard line, completing passes to tight end Marv Fleming, running back Elijah Pitts, and wide receiver Carroll Dale to move Green Bay into scoring range. With a first down on the Kansas City 37-yard line, Starr dropped back and flipped an 18-yard pass to veteran Max McGee, who had eluded the secondary. McGee then raced untouched into the end zone for the historic first Super Bowl touchdown. The Packers led, 7–0.

McGee was thirty-four years old and a substitute who wasn't expected to play. His roommate was Paul Hornung, and both were famous for their late night antics off the field as well as for what they could do on it. "I don't know about my legs," McGee had told Hornung the night before the game. "I don't know if they'll hold up."

When Boyd Dowler was injured on the second play of the game, McGee had an opportunity to find out just how strong his legs were.

The Chiefs, however, were not dispirited by the Packers' early success. Len Dawson was an NFL cast-off, but in the AFL he developed into a poised and accomplished quarterback the equal of Starr, some experts said. Using a multiple offense that reminded the Packers of the Dallas Cowboys, the Chiefs struck back, scoring on a 7-yard pass from Dawson to Curtis

Old man Max McGee snags a pass in the end zone for the second of his 2 touchdowns.

UPI

McClinton, a fullback. The play had been set up by a 31-yard completion from Dawson to Taylor, the tall, strong, and fast wide receiver.

Now, neither team held anything back. The Packers moved methodically downfield after the next kickoff, traveling 73 yards in thirteen plays to their second touchdown. Nothing fancy was involved, just short passes from Starr to his wide receivers and Taylor's power running on the famous Green Bay sweep. It was Taylor who scored on a 14-yard ramble that put Green Bay ahead, 14–7.

Kansas City came right back but had to settle for a field goal by Mike Mercer. Still, at halftime, the Packers' lead was just 14–10, and some NFL boosters were feeling uneasy.

What made the Packers a great team, however, was their ability to make the big play on defense as well

Fuzzy Thurston (63) and Jerry Kramer lead Elijah Pitts on a Packer power sweep.

UPI

Coach Vince Lombardi: "Winning isn't everything. It's the only thing."

UPI

as offense. Early in the third quarter, with the Chiefs on the march again, Dawson confidently dropped back at his 49-yard line. This time, though, the Packers blitzed their linebackers, and Dawson's hurried toss to Fred Arbanas, the husky tight end, was intercepted by Willie Wood, the nimble defensive back, who returned it 50 yards to the 5-yard line.

The stunned Chiefs could only clutch and grab as Pitts took a handoff from Starr on the next play and went into the end zone to put the Packers ahead, 21–10.

It was not an insurmountable deficit, but Wood's interception seemed to take the heart out of the Chiefs. Starr moved the Packers into scoring range again as the third quarter was coming to a close and found McGee, the old man, open in the end zone for a 13-yard touchdown pass to make the score 28–10.

The fourth quarter was merely icing for Green Bay. The defense harried Dawson and shut down the Chiefs, and the offense whittled away the clock with its ball-possession drives. Once more, the Packers scored, this time on a 49-yard drive culminating in a 1-yard touchdown run by Pitts.

And on a play that was more important for its symbolism than the effect it had on the game, Williamson—"The Hammer"—was knocked unconscious when he tried to stop a Green Bay sweep.

Thus Starr, voted Most Valuable Player, and the Packers prevailed, 35–10, saving the NFL potential embarrassment and giving the young Chiefs and the AFL a lesson in pro football at its best.

"Kansas City is a good football team," Lombardi said in the winning locker room, grinning and clutching the game ball awarded him by his players. "But their team doesn't compare with the top National Football League teams. That's what you wanted me to say, isn't it? There. I've said it."

BART STARR
The First MVP

As diverse as their personalities may have been, the player and the coach fitted together like two pieces of a jigsaw puzzle and brought out the champion in each other.

Bart Starr, quiet and unassuming, a leader by example rather than command, was the intelligent quarterback who executed the designs of the master architect, Vince Lombardi, a blustery firebrand.

Together they turned a woeful Green Bay franchise into the most feared team in football. In the eight-year period from 1960–67, Starr's record was 82–24–4, and the Packers won six division and five NFL titles as well as the first two Super Bowl championships.

Starr was voted the MVP of both those winning Super Bowl games.

The son of an air force sergeant, Starr had been a high school All-American quarterback in Montgomery, Alabama. But he had played little in his final two years at the University of Alabama because of injury, and in the 1956 NFL draft almost two-hundred players were called before Starr was selected in the seventeenth round.

It would be another 2½ years before Starr was given the starting job at Green Bay. The Packers were riding a five-game losing streak in 1959 when Lombardi, then in his first season as coach, told Starr the quarterback job was his. Green Bay won its last four games, and the Starr-Lombardi legend was started on its swift rise to the top.

Explaining the biggest impact Lombardi had made

on him, Starr once said, "A quest for excellence. I feel that probably I had that desire and that identification within me, but I think he was able to extract it."

Although beset by injuries, Starr played sixteen years for Green Bay and later took over as coach. He didn't possess an outstanding arm, but he had a reputation for remaining orderly and cool regardless of the circumstances. He was the NFL's leading passer in 1962, 1964, and 1966 and was named the league's MVP in 1966.

Starr's style of play was conservative, and he was often overshadowed by his more flamboyant teammates. Yet he has been called a "model hero" for his demeanor, and the Columbus, Ohio, Touchdown Club honored him as the Pro Football Player of the Decade for the 1960s.

Scoring Summary

Kansas City Chiefs (AFL)	0	10	0	0—10
Green Bay Packers (NFL)	7	7	14	7—35

Green Bay—McGee, pass from Starr 37 (Chandler kick)

Kansas City—McClinton, pass from Dawson 7 (Mercer kick)

Green Bay—Taylor, run 14 (Chandler kick)

Kansas City—Mercer (FG) 31

Green Bay—Pitts, run 5 (Chandler kick)

Green Bay—McGee, pass from Starr 13 (Chandler kick)

Green Bay—Pitts, run 1 (Chandler kick)

SUPER BOWL II

A FAREWELL
FOR VINCE

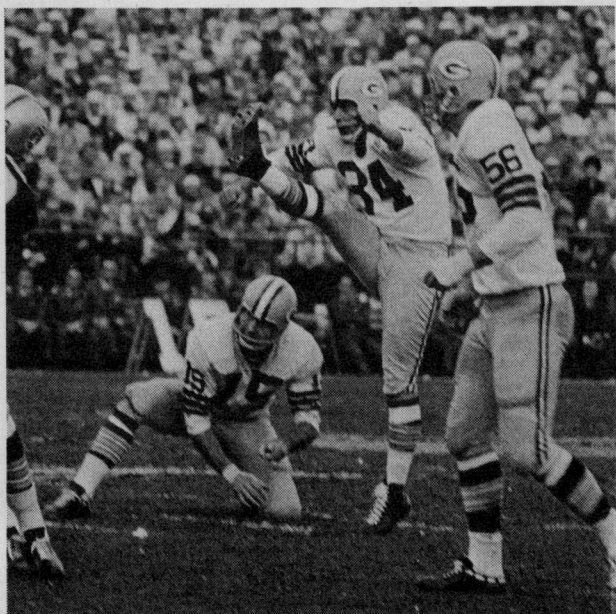

**Super Bowl II was kicker Don Chandler's vale-
dictory, and he made the most of it.**

UPI

Participants—Oakland Raiders, champions of the American Football League, and Green Bay Packers, champions of the National Football League.

Date—January 14, 1968.

Site—Orange Bowl Stadium, Miami, Florida.

Time—3:05 P.M. EST.

Attendance—75,546.

Radio and Television—Columbia Broadcasting System (TV and radio).

Regular-Season Records—Oakland, 13–1; Green Bay, 9–4–1.

Playoff Records—Oakland defeated Houston Oilers, 40–7, for AFL title; Green Bay defeated Dallas Cowboys, 21–17, for NFL title.

Players' Shares—$15,000 to each member of winning team; $7,500 to each member of losing team.

Coaches—John Rauch, Oakland; Vince Lombardi, Green Bay.

SUPER BOWL II

A FAREWELL
FOR VINCE

The news from Green Bay was reassuring and brought a smile to the faces of those who knew all about Vince Lombardi and the Packers' mystique. The Oakland Raiders, champions of the American Football League, were already in Florida rehearsing for Super Bowl II in the warm sunshine, but the Packers were in Green Bay as they were a year earlier, shoveling four inches of snow off their practice field, working out in temperatures of four degrees above zero.

Oddly enough, this seemed like the way it should be. The grizzly old Packers had not been changed by the success brought about by winning five National Football League championships in eight years, including three in a row and Super Bowl I. Lombardi would not allow them to rest on their accomplishments or rely on their reputations to intimidate the opposition. It would be business as usual no matter what the elements.

But there was other news that preceded the Packers to Florida, where Super Bowl II would be played in Miami. And it was disturbing, because there were signs that the Packer dynasty was about to end. Several popular players had already retired, among them Paul Hornung and Jim Taylor; others, such as Bart Starr, who was thirty-four years old, were in the autumn of their careers. But what upset Packer fans the most were reports that Lombardi was going to retire as coach and concentrate on his other job as general manager. Phil Bengtson, Lombardi's trusted defensive coach, was rumored to be his successor.

All during Super Bowl week, talk revolved around
what Lombardi was planning to do. The air of mystery
about the game had disappeared after the first meeting between the leagues in 1967 reaffirmed the superiority of Lombardi's Green Bay teams.

Some football experts felt the Raiders might be a
better team than the Kansas City Chiefs, and certainly their 13–1 record was to be respected in any
league. But the odds makers had made the Packers a
heavy favorite despite a season in which they struggled and finished with just a 9–4–1 record. The Packers won when they had to and finished with a flourish,
defeating Dallas, 21–17, in the NFL championship game,
played in subzero cold in Green Bay.

"Imagine us, the little ol' Raiders, on the same field
with the Green Bay Packers," said Al Davis, the
wisecracking, acerbic managing general partner of the
Raiders, who scuttled Houston in the AFL title game,
40–7.

Lombardi tried to pretend it was business as usual.
But he was smiling more, the players noted, and he
had allowed them to bring their wives to Florida. That
would have been unthinkable a year earlier. There
were also a number of Lombardi's former players and
assistant coaches in Fort Lauderdale, where the team
trained, leading to the speculation that they all wanted
to be on hand for the "old man's" last game. Among
them was Hornung, the free spirit whom Lombardi
treated fondly like a headstrong son.

Bengtson discounted the speculation of a coaching
change as the work of idle reporters and columnists
with space to fill. He and Lombardi were associates
who had an excellent working relationship, but they
were hardly close friends who spent all their free time
together, he said.

Lombardi, who was fifty-four years old and in his
thirtieth year in football, also tried to discourage the
rumors, telling reporters that he would take a "long,
hard look at Vince Lombardi" when the season ended.
At one point, he decided not to answer retirement
questions at all.

But on the Friday before the game, when the Packers had practiced for the last time, the coach called his team together for a talk. "We all know we can win on Sunday," he began. "We are old hands at this game, but we also know that we will have to work harder than ever.

"I want to tell you how very proud I am of all of you," Lombardi continued, "I have told you before that you are the finest team in all of professional football. It's been a long season, and Sunday may be the last time we are all together. Let's make it a good game, a game we can all be proud of."

There were more than a few tears shed at the end of the speech by those big, bad, tough Packers and their coaches.

Not that the Packer's needed any extra incentive to play their best. But Lombardi's pep talk sounded like a farewell speech and only added to their determination. "I owe my career to that man," said Don Chandler, the punter and placekicker. "I owe him everything."

Davis wasn't going to fuel the fire the way Fred Williamson of the Chiefs had a year earlier, either. The Raiders' owner was a shrewd man who came to Oakland as the head coach in 1963 and made the Raiders an AFL power. He also resigned to become the league commissioner for several months in 1966, when he deftly organized a raiding war to sign the NFL's best players and forced a merger.

He returned to Oakland as the general managing partner and solidified the organization as one of the most successful in sports. Still, the brash, outspoken Davis, known in football circles as a "genius," had only the nicest things to say about the Packers.

For the other AFL owners and players, this was quite a sight to behold. The Raiders' emblem was a skull and crossbone, and they lived up to their image as a fierce and marauding team. Ben Davidson, a six-foot-seven, 265-pound defensive lineman who wore a villainous mustache, had gained a reputation for knocking quarterbacks out of games. He even broke the jaw of the New York Jets' Broadway Joe Namath, the AFL's glamour boy. Davidson had been a Packer castoff.

Daryle Lamonica was the Raiders' quarterback. He had been acquired from Buffalo, where he was a reserve behind Jack Kemp on one of the better teams in the league. In his first year in Oakland, he was named the AFL's Player of the Year by United Press International. Tall and strong, Lamonica was called "The Mad Bomber" because of his penchant for throwing long passes. Ironically, the former Notre Dame quarterback had been a thirteenth-round draft pick of the Packers, who decided he had a better chance in the young league.

A Mad Bomber and a defensive lineman known as Big Bad Ben—yes, it seemed fitting that the Raiders trained for Super Bowl II at a private school in Boca Raton, which was bordered on one end by a swamp populated by alligators and snakes.

Although the novelty of the Super Bowl had disappeared after the first game, there was actually more interest in Super Bowl II. Florida hotels reported doing record business for early January as tourists came in from the cold. In Green Bay alone, ten charter airplanes carried Packer fans to Miami.

Two fans were flown to the game courtesy of Dick Capp. The twenty-three-year-old linebacker from Boston College had chipped in with his sisters to pay for their parents' first vacation. Little did Capp know that the Packers would add him to their active roster the day before Super Bowl II.

"I gave my parents tickets for the game, but I never dreamed that I'd be playing in it," Capp said.

On Sunday, January 14, two thirty-foot-high mechanical men—one dressed like a Raider and the other a Packer—puffed smoke and met at midfield for a ceremonial handshake. With a capacity crowd of 75,546 looking on, Super Bowl II was about to begin.

The Packers once again took the initiative. On their first possession they moved into field-goal range, where Chandler connected from 39 yards out. Green Bay led, 3–0.

The Raiders were a high-scoring team, but Lamonica was not having an easy time penetrating the Packers' defense. What's more, Starr and the offense just wouldn't let him have the ball. Near the end of the first quarter, "The Pack" began another one of their relentless marathon drives, this one starting from their own 3-yard line.

The Oakland defense stiffened at its 13, and Chandler came on again, this time kicking a 20-yard field goal. It was 6–0, but the Raiders were only a touchdown behind.

Teams in the AFL usually played more aggressively in the defensive secondary, a style called the bump and run. Often it would aggravate a receiver and throw

Donny Anderson hurdles over Oakland's Bill Laskey for a touchdown.

UPI

him off stride. But when a defensive back played that
close, there was a chance he would get burned easily,
too.

And that is exactly what happened early in the
second quarter when Boyd Dowler, a strong wide receiver, fought his way past Kent McCloughan and
broke free over the middle. Starr threw a perfect pass
that resulted in a 62-yard touchdown. Suddenly Green
Bay was ahead, 13–0.

The play aroused the Raiders from their lethargy.
They were a proud team and did not want to be routed.

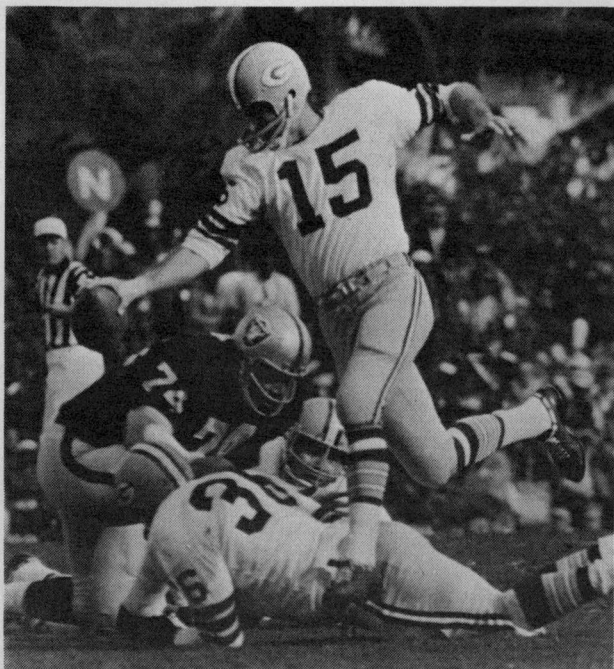

Bart Starr scrambled when he had to . . . on the
way to another MVP award.

UPI

Lamonica led them on a long drive, which he finished with a 23-yard touchdown pass to wide receiver Bill Miller. It was 13–7.

When the Raiders forced the Packers to punt late in the first half, it looked as if they were building momentum for the third quarter. But Roger Bird fumbled that Chandler punt, and Capp, of all people, recovered. After Starr completed a 9-yard pass to Dowler with time ticking away, Chandler rushed on the field to kick a 43-yard field goal, giving his team a 16–7 halftime lead.

The Packers had the ball again in the third quarter when Starr cleverly faked to fullback Ben Wilson, freezing the defense for a split second. He then dropped back and completed a pass to Max McGee, one of the heroes in Super Bowl I. McGee was tackled by Bird at the Oakland 25.

From there, the Packers moved in for the kill, scoring when Donny Anderson carried in from the 2-yard line. The lead was 23–7. By the end of the quarter, Chandler had added his fourth field goal—this one from 31 yards—and the score was 26–7.

A frustrated Lamonica tried to rally the desperate Raiders with some of his long bombs as the final quarter opened, but Herb Adderley intercepted one and returned it 60 yards for a touchdown. The Packers had taken a 33–7 lead, and even a late Oakland touchdown did not dimish the nature of Green Bay's overwhelming victory.

"It was a day of learning," Lamonica said. "I learned an awful lot."

"On paper, I don't think they are any better than us," said Tom Keating, the Raiders' defensive tackle. "But their execution was great."

What Super Bowl II had proven, perhaps, was not that the NFL was superior to the AFL, but that the Packers were just that much better than any team in either league. Starr, the quiet tactician who was Lombardi's coach on the field, was named Most Valuable Player, as in Super Bowl I. He said the players had "a feeling" that Lombardi would be retiring.

The coach, basking in the glow of another victory,

Oakland's Big Ben Davidson is the classic picture of defeat.

UPI

would not give any hints. "It's much too early to do anything," he said.

But a month later, Vince Lombardi indeed retired as coach of the Green Bay Packers.

DON CHANDLER
The Placekicking Packer

The tale has been told of a summer day in 1956 when a discouraged rookie left the New York Giants' training camp, only to be brought back by a club aide named Vince Lombardi.

Don Chandler has said that it didn't happen quite that way, but it is true he was ready to quit before he ever started, and that his career was to become closely entwined with Lombardi's. Chandler returned to enjoy a twelve-year stay in the NFL as one of the game's premier kickers, and in 1963 he led the league in scoring with 106 points.

Chandler, who said he was at his best while kicking under pressure, played with the Giants for nine years, during which time they won six conference titles and one world championship. The Giants suffered through a poor season in 1964, with Chandler contributing little, and it was at this point that Lombardi, then coach of the Green Bay Packers, came to his rescue.

Acquired by Green Bay in 1965, Chandler wound up his career in brilliant style, accounting for 261 points in three championships seasons, and he was a member of the winning team in the first two Super Bowl games.

Although quarterback Bart Starr was voted the MVP of Super Bowl II, Chandler also starred with 4 field goals and 3 conversions for 15 points in a 33–14 victory over Oakland.

Chandler retired after his Super Bowl success and, as fate would decree, this shining moment also marked the final game of Lombardi's career.

Chandler was an outstanding halfback at the Uni-

versity of Florida, but as a senior he also led the
nation's major college punters, and it was this skill
that attracted pro scouts.

A traditional kicker who used the square-toed shoe
and was adept at both punting and placekicking, Chandler likened his craft to that of a golfer.

"That's the only comparison that really means anything," he said. "You have to take your time, keep
your head down, your eye on the ball, and follow
through. It's really very similar to golf."

Scoring Summary

Green Bay Packers (NFL)....	3	13	10	7—33
Oakland Raiders (AFL)	0	7	0	7—14

Green Bay—Chandler (FG) 39
Green Bay—Chandler (FG) 20
Green Bay—Dowler, pass from Starr 62 (Chandler kick)
Oakland—Miller, pass from Lamonica 23 (Blanda kick)
Green Bay—Chandler (FG) 43
Green Bay—Anderson, run 2 (Chandler kick)
Green Bay—Chandler (FG) 31
Green Bay—Adderley, pass interception 60 (Chandler kick)
Oakland—Miller, pass from Lamonica 23 (Blanda kick)

SUPER BOWL III

"I GUARANTEE IT"

Bubba Smith (78) only has eyes for Joe Namath, but the Colts needed more than eye contact to halt Broadway Joe in Super Bowl III.

Vernon Biever

Participants—New York Jets, champions of the American Football League, and Baltimore Colts, champions of the National Football League.

Date—January 12, 1969.

Site—Orange Bowl Stadium, Miami Florida.

Time—3:05 P.M. EST.

Attendance—75,377.

Radio and Television—National Broadcasting Company (TV and radio).

Regular-Season Records—New York, 11–3; Baltimore, 13–1.

Playoff Records—New York defeated Oakland Raiders, 27–23, for AFL title; Baltimore defeated Cleveland Browns, 34–0, for NFL title.

Players' Shares—$15,000 to each member of the winning team; $7,500 to each member of losing team.

Coaches—Weeb Ewbank, New York; Don Shula, Baltimore.

SUPER BOWL III

"I GUARANTEE IT"

It was a time of unrest in the country, a time of violent protest against an unpopular war in Vietnam, of peace signs, long hair, hippies, flower children, and the Beatles. The catch phrase was "generation gap" as young people rebelled against values cherished by their parents. It was the age of the antihero, and in professional football, that role was epitomized by the droopy-shouldered, gimpy-kneed quarterback of the New York Jets—Joe Namath.

"Broadway Joe," he was called, for his affection for the bright lights and the night life offered in an exciting city that, like Namath, rarely slept. In a sport in which teamwork was the first commandment and players became faceless identities hiding in helmets and modern-day suits of armor, Namath wore white shoes and grew a Fu Manchu mustache that infuriated his elders.

Quarterbacks were supposed to be role models for the young—soft-spoken, humble men who wore their hair short and led with a quiet dignity. But here was Namath, a son of the Pennsylvania coal country, holding a glass of Scotch in one hand, with a woman on his arm and mischief in his eyes.

He had a bachelor pad in Manhattan and lived by his own training rules. In Fort Lauderdale, where the Jets were staying before Super Bowl III, Namath stayed in the oceanfront hotel suite that Green Bay coach Vince Lombardi had claimed a year earlier. In typically flamboyant style, the suite was inspected by FBI agents after the Jets arrived because Namath's life had been threatened.

He first caught the public's eye when he played so valiantly in a losing cause for Paul "Bear" Bryant's University of Alabama team against Texas in the 1965 Orange Bowl Game. Namath was signed to an extraordinary four-year, $427,000 contract by Sonny Werblin, the show business magnate who spotted a Hollywood star quality in Namath as well as a rifle-like right arm.

Namath led the Jets from the depths of the American Football League to their first championship in 1968 and a berth in Super Bowl III, to be played on January 12, 1969, Miami's Orange Bowl Stadium.

The Jets' opponents were the Baltimore Colts, the darlings of the National Football league and the establishment in general. The Colts had succeeded the Green Bay Packers as champions, and there were football experts who said that they might be the best team of all time.

On offense, they were led by Earl Morrall, a thirty-four-year-old quarterback who had been acquired from the New York Giants prior to the 1968 season as insurance against injury to John Unitas, the magnificent passer who led the Colts to NFL championships in 1958 and 1959. Unitas was injured in the third game, and Morrall, a quiet, unassuming man who wore his hair in a crew cut and modestly shared praise with his teammates, came off the bench to lead Baltimore to a 13–1 record.

Much like the Packers, the Colts were not a fancy team. Morrall relied on a short, safe passing game and the running of Tom Matte and Jerry Hill, steady but unspectacular runners. On defense, however, the Colts were fearsome and impregnable at times. They posted four shutouts during the season and, in six games, held their opponents without a touchdown.

Their only loss was to Cleveland, and Baltimore avenged that in the title game, trouncing the Browns, 34–0. No wonder the odds makers made them an early 17-point favorite to continue the NFL's domination of the rival league.

"It's a little ridiculous to be a seventeen-point underdog," said Johnny Sample, the Jet's combative defensive back, who had once been a mainstay in the Colts' secondary. "It gives us a psychological advantage."

"I thought we'd be the underdogs," said linebacker Ralph Bakers, "but not by that much. It makes you want to beat them that much more."

It was Namath who helped instill this confidence in the Jets. He felt that the Kansas City Chiefs and Oakland Raiders had treated the Packers with too much reverence in Super Bowls I and II. They actually started believing Green Bay was a much better team, he said.

But Joe Willie—a nickname he concocted at Alabama to give himself a Southern air—was not overly impressed with the Colts, and Morrall in particular.

Several quarterbacks in the AFL, among them Babe Parilli, the Jets' wily old backup, were better than Morrall, Namath said. "I don't have anything against Morrall personally," he said, "it's just that I don't think he's that good a quarterback. That's my opinion. I'm entitled to it, right?"

The Colts were angered by Namath's slight of Morrall, the NFL's Player of the Year. Don Shula, the thirty-eight-year-old head coach, said Namath was out of place. Defensive players such as tackle Bubba Smith and linebacker Mike Curtis could hardly wait to teach the outspoken Jet a lesson. Morrall just shrugged and attributed the remarks to Broadway Joe's craving for the limelight.

"Some guys would say anything or do anything to get their names in the paper," he said. "Maybe Namath represents the new breed of athlete, the kind of athlete the new generation wants. I hope not."

Namath's manner offended most football people, but it did not color their opinion of him as a player. Almost all agreed that he was extremely gifted. In addition to that strong right arm, he had a hair-trigger release, natural leadership qualities that cannot be taught, and rare savvy for a twenty-five-year-old player completing his fourth year.

"A great arm, strong and accurate," Shula said. "He can recognize and pick defenses apart."

Still, Namath's bravado fueled the fire building under Super Bowl III. Though leagues apart, these teams were not entirely strangers. Weeb Ewbank, the Jets' sixty-one-year-old roly-poly coach, had led the Colts to their championships in the late 1950s, nurturing Unitas, then a budding young star. Shula was a defensive back under Ewbank.

The coach was unceremoniously fired in 1962 after Baltimore fell on hard times. A year later, he was hired by Werblin to salvage a floundering franchise initially known as the New York Titans, who played before thousands of empty seats at the crumbling Polo Grounds in New York and who were notorious for writing checks that bounced. Ewbank helped fill the Jets' roster with former Colts such as Sample and Mark Smolinski, a running back.

Werblin renamed the team and moved them into Shea Stadium, located at the site of the 1964–65 New York World's Fair. He gave them respectability, and in 1965, when he signed Namath, he gave them a winner.

Still, it was the AFL, critics claimed, and in Super Bowl III Namath would be playing his first "professional" game. Joe Willie scoffed at that. One night during Super Bowl week, he and teammate Jim Hudson encountered Lou Michaels, the Colts' placekicker and reserve defensive end whose brother Walt was the Jets' defensive coach. Michaels was also from coal country and equally strong-willed.

"You're doin' a lot of talkin', boy," he told Namath. "Haven't you heard of the word 'modesty'?"

Namath didn't back down, though, and maintained that the Jets would win. By the end of the evening, he had bought Michaels a few drinks and driven him back to the Colts' hotel. The local newspaper accounts the next day, painted the restaurant meeting as a near fistfight.

Several days later, however, the newspapers were more accurate in their reporting. Speaking at an awards banquet, Namath said: "We are going to win on Sunday, I guarantee it."

The Colts were flabbergasted. So were some of the Jets, although they didn't mind. The odds makers weren't impressed as the Colts became 18-point favorites.

Jonathan Booth, a neutral observer, concurred with Namath. A professional astrologer who had never watched a football game, Booth said the stars were smiling on the Jets and they would win Super Bowl III.

The week of tumult came to an end on Super Bowl Sunday when 75,377 gathered at the Orange Bowl to see if Namath could back up his boasts. A morning drizzle had given way to sunshine, and the Jets won the coin toss, electing to receive.

With Bill Mathis blocking, Matt Snell picks up yardage on the Colts.

Malcolm W. Emmons

Namath kept his team on the ground, handing off to Matt Snell and Emerson Boozer, trying to establish a running game. Eventually, the Jets were forced to punt.

On the Colts' first possession, Morrall moved easily into field-goal range as fans anticipated still another NFL rout. But Michaels missed the 34-yard attempt.

The Jets took over and quickly gave the ball back when George Sauer, a wide receiver, fumbled after catching a short pass. Baltimore had possession at the New York 12-yard line. Surely the Colts would score now.

When the first quarter ended, they had moved to the 6. However, as Morrall fired into the end zone on the first play of the second quarter, the ball was tipped

Randy Beverly's interception of an Earl Morrall pass proved a turning point for the Jets.
                                             Vernon Biever

by linebacker Al Atkinson and intercepted by defensive back Randy Beverly, who had been beaten by receiver Willie Richardson but was in perfect position to catch the deflected pass. The disbelieving Colts jogged off the field, wondering what had gone wrong.

Now Namath went to work, unlimbering his right arm for the first time. He wasn't the daring young passer who had outdueled Oakland's Daryle Lamonica in the AFL championship game that featured 97 passes, but a more conservative quarterback who mixed his passes well and kept the Colts off-balance with a running game.

The Jets marched to the 4-yard line, where Snell bolted off left tackle into the end zone. For the first time in Super Bowl history, the AFL team led.

Morrall was having difficulty against an aroused Jets' defense, so the Colts called a trick play with 44 seconds remaining in the half. Matte took a handoff and pitched the ball back to Morrall, who failed to see wide receiver Jimmy Orr open in the end zone. He passed instead to Hill, and Hudson intercepted.

Shula fumed at halftime, berating the Colts for their sloppy, uninspired play. But any incentive that might have been gained disappeared when Matte fumbled after the Colts received the second-half kickoff. Baker recovered for the Jets, and Namath conservatively positioned them for a 32-yard field goal by Jim Turner.

On their next series, the Jets moved deep into Colts' territory again, and Turner added a 30-yard field goal. Then, early in the fourth quarter, he connected from the 9-yard line. The Colts and the crowd watched in a state of shock as the lead grew to 16–0. The biggest upset in pro football history was only 13 minutes away.

Shula had become desperate by this time and removed Morrall for Unitas. But the veteran had been idle too long, and the Colts continued to be stymied. They became frustrated, too, as Matte tried to charge Sample after another Beverly interception. "It looks bad, buddy," Sample told Matte, infuriating the running back.

Injured quarterback Johnny Unitas came off the bench to engineer the Colts' final-period touchdown drive.

UPI

With 6:34 remaining in the game, and history waiting in the wings, Unitas finally led the Colts to a touchdown as Hill scored from 1 yard out. It was much too late. When the final gun sounded, the Jets had won, 16–7, and Ewbank was hoisted on the shoulders of his triumphant players.

Namath trotted off in the twilight of the Orange Bowl, his white uniform sullied but holding his index finger on his right hand aloft to say, "We're number one."

The brash young quarterback had kept his word.

Playing well within himself, Namath completed 17 of 28 passes for 206 yards and no interceptions. He was named Most Valuable Player.

In a cool, calculated manner that belied his swinging life-style and outspoken ways, he had given the AFL parity with the NFL. He had more than evened the score for the first two Super Bowl defeats.

Joe Namath was an American folk hero whose place in football history was guaranteed just like the victory he had predicted.

JOE NAMATH
Broadway Forever

For all the notoriety Joe Namath attained as a result of his celebrated off-the-field activities, it is easy to overlook the magnificent accomplishments he recorded during his thirteen-year professional career.

Even his single most spectacular achievement is remembered as much for what he said—"I guarantee it"—as for the deed itself, upsetting the Baltimore Colts in Super Bowl III.

During his glory years with the New York Jets, Namath was easily the most recognizable figure in football. The team had to assign special security men to guard his room on road trips, and his mere presence at a game was said to be worth 10,000 extra ticket sales.

With his flamboyant, showman style, Namath was an instant hit in New York from the day he signed his contract with the Jets. Despite four knee operations and various other ailments, the popular quarterback didn't disappoint, enjoying a career that led to the Hall of Fame.

Namath, who couldn't even earn a regular starting job on his high school team until his senior year, threw for 27,633 yards and 173 touchdowns during a career that ended with the Los Angeles Rams in 1977. In one game against Baltimore in 1972, Namath accounted for 6 touchdowns and 496 passing yards.

"I remember after my first knee operation, right after I signed with the Jets, my doctor told me I'd be lucky to play four seasons with my legs," Namath said. "But I played thirteen seasons. I think I was a

MVP Joe Namath's locker-room flankers: Coach Weeb Ewbank and Joe's dad.

Barton Silverman

helluva entertainer. I think I added some interest to the game."

In the years since he left the game, Namath has remained in the limelight and continued to entertain. First there were TV commercials, and then he turned to acting. His range has been from musical comedy

(*Guys and Dolls*) to drama (*The Caine Mutiny Court-Martial*).

When Broadway Joe, a longtime swinging bachelor, announced his marriage in the winter of 1984, the New York *Daily News* front-paged it with the headline, "Say It Ain't So, Joe."

Scoring Summary

New York Jets (AFL)   0   7   6   3—16
Baltimore Colts (NFL)   0   0   0   7— 7

New York—Snell, run 4 (Turner kick)
New York—Turner (FG) 32
New York—Turner (FG) 30
New York—Turner (FG) 9
Baltimore—Hill, run 1 (Michaels kick)

SUPER BOWL IV

HAIL TO THE CHIEFS

Battling defenders like Minnesota's Jim Marshall was nothing compared to what Kansas City's Len Dawson had to endure before Super Bowl IV.
Darryl Norenberg

Participants—Kansas City Chiefs, champions of the American Football League, and Minnesota Vikings, champions of the National Football League.

Date—January 11, 1970.

Site—Tulane Stadium, New Orleans, Louisiana.

Time—2:35 P.M., CST.

Attendance—80,998.

Radio and Television—Columbia Broadcasting System (TV and radio).

Regular-Season Records—Kansas City, 11–3; Minnesota, 12–2.

Playoff Records—Kansas City defeated Oakland Raiders, 17–7, for AFL title; Minnesota defeated Cleveland Browns, 27–7, for NFL title.

Players' Shares—$15,000 to each member of winning team; $7,500 to each member of losing team.

Coaches—Hank Stram, Kansas City; Bud Grant, Minnesota.

HAIL TO THE CHIEFS

There was an ominous wind blowing in New Orleans during Super Bowl week in 1970. For starters, it was unseasonably cold in the Deep South even for January. Temperatures dipped into the twenties at night, and a strong gale and occasional icy rain made it feel colder, putting a damper on the Bourbon Street festivities, where fans went to eat, drink, ogle scantily clad women, and listen to the sounds of Dixieland jazz.

But what added to the chill preceding Super Bowl IV between the Kansas City Chiefs, the American Football League champions, and the Minnesota Vikings of the National Football League, was an air of scandal involving gambling, the Achilles' heel of sports, and a source of special concern to football commissioner Pete Rozelle.

For the record, the commissioner always tried to minimize the extent to which people legally and illegally bet on pro football, an amount, incidentally, second only to horse racing in sports wagering in this country. But behind the scenes, Rozelle had beefed up his security force to keep tabs on possible player involvement with known gamblers.

Rozelle had forced Joe Namath to sell his interest in an East Side Manhattan bar and restaurant because it was frequented by gamblers. He had previously suspended Alex Karras of the Detroit Lions and Paul Hornung of the Green Bay Packers for one year for gambling on games—even though both had bet on their own teams.

But the news in New Orleans caught Rozelle and

the football world off guard. In a report that appeared
nationally on the NBC-TV *Huntley-Brinkley Report*
on January 6, reporter Bill Matney revealed that a
special Justice Department task force conducting a
wide-ranging gambling investigation was about to call
seven professional football players and one college head
coach to testify about their relationships with known
gamblers. One of the players was Len Dawson, the
quarterback for the Chiefs.

Dawson, the report said, was an acquaintance of
Donald Dawson (no relation), a Michigan restaurateur
who had been arrested by federal agents on New Year's
Day 1970 with $450,000 in checks and gambling rec-
ords on him.

To the average football fan, this news was shocking.
Dawson was the strait-laced type, a thirty-four-year-
old soft-spoken family man who had ridden the bench
for seven years in Pittsburgh and Detroit before going
to the AFL to play for Hank Stram, the Chiefs' head
coach, who had been an assistant at Purdue in Dawson's collegiate days.

Dawson's grace under pressure earned him the nickname "Lenny the Cool." He was modest almost to a
fault. But what had not been made public before the
NBC report was the fact that in 1968 Dawson submit-
ted to a voluntary lie detector test at Rozelle's request,
after the commissioner became suspicious when Las
Vegas bookmakers would not place a betting line on
the Chiefs' games, suspecting perhaps a point-shaving
scam or outright fixes. But Dawson was cleared of any
wrongdoing, and the matter was dropped.

Now, his name had resurfaced on the eve of what
had become one of America's biggest sporting events.
The night of the NBC report, Dawson remained se-
cluded in the hotel room that he shared with teammate Johnny Robinson, who fielded telephone calls
from reporters, telling them to leave Dawson alone.

As luck would have it, however, the quarterback
and Stram had been scheduled to hold a news conference the next morning, presumably to talk about Super Bowl IV and the Vikings. Anticipating the questions
awaiting him, a pale and shaken Dawson told report-

ers: "Yes, I knew Donald Dawson. I met him ten years ago. The only conversations I've had with him in recent years concerned my knee injuries and the death of my father. Yes, I'm shocked by all of this."

With that, Stram asked that all questions deal with the football game at hand.

Earlier that morning, Dawson had read a statement to his teammates during breakfast, essentially saying the same things he told reporters. The Chiefs applauded him and gave him their support. "If there's anybody who can handle this situation, it's Lenny Dawson," Robinson said. "He keeps a lot to himself. He doesn't have a lot of emotion. He keeps his cool."

Back in Kansas City, Jackie Dawson, Len's wife, kept their two children home from school the day after the report, to avoid any unpleasant situations. But Lenny Jr., she said, had reacted badly to developments and did not want to come to the Super Bowl. The children had been stung in the past when they'd heard their father booed, she said, and this was worse.

She explained, however, that this was the biggest game in their father's career and convinced them to go to New Orleans. They stayed at a different hotel, but the Dawsons were reunited after Jackie and the children arrived. "Len wanted to assure them that everything was all right," she said.

"Before we left, I took Len aside and told him, 'Go out and kick the hell out of them.' I'm not as much a lady as he is a gentleman."

Although a Justice Department spokesman said later in the week that none of the witnesses named would be indicted, the gambling investigation remained the topic of conversation in New Orleans. The Vikings, who had defeated the Cleveland Browns for the NFL title, became bit players in this drama.

Although they were in the established league, the Vikings were an expansion team that began play in 1961. Ironically, owner Max Winter had agreed a year earlier to become part of the new AFL but changed his mind and withdrew. The AFL owners were hoping the Chiefs would get revenge for all of them.

Initially, the Vikings were coached by Norm Van

Brocklin, a gruff, hardened coach who never quite understood his quarterback, Fran Tarkenton, the brainy, elusive scrambler who frustrated so many defenses. But after falling on hard times, the management looked north into Canada for help. Bud Grant, a stoic disciplinarian with ten years' experience in the Canadian Football League, was brought in as the new coach.

The quarterback was Joe Kapp, an American who had been successful in the CFL. Kapp was unorthodox to say the least, a linebacker wearing a quarterback's number. He ran with abandon and rarely out of bounds, relishing contact instead. His passes often nosedived like wounded quail, but he was strangely efficient.

Kapp's strength was his competitiveness. He once engaged his teammate Lonnie Warwick, a bruising linebacker, in a fistfight that started when each tried to take the blame for a loss to Green Bay. "He's not afraid of anything," said Clint Jones, a Viking running back.

Thus, the Vikings had cultivated an image of being a physical team from the frigid Midwest, led by Kapp but bolstered by their Purple People Eaters defense, notably linemen Carl Eller and Alan Page. But the only real Viking playing in Super Bowl IV was Jan Stenerud, the Chiefs' placekicker who was from Norway and who had come to the United States to attend Montana State University on a skiing scholarship.

Despite the New York Jets' victory in super Bowl III, the NFL Vikings were a strong 13-point favorite to win this game. Interest in the game in New Orleans was lessened because the Jets' success had proven, the odds makers notwithstanding, the AFL was the equal of the older league.

The continued cold weather and series of tornado warnings during the week also hurt scalpers who found it difficult to give tickets away. On the day of Super Bowl IV, another tornado warning was given in keeping with the spirit of this game.

This was the gaudiest Super Bowl to date. In the pregame show, balloonists dressed as a Viking and an Indian chief were supposed to lift off and float out of the stadium—tornado or no tornado. But Greg Stokes,

The balloon got sacked in pregame ceremonies.
Vernon Biever

a professional balloonist who was dressed as the Viking, had an inexperienced crew that released the balloon too soon. Barely airborne several feet above the ground, the balloon crossed the field and crashed into the end-zone seats, where angry spectators tore gaping holes in it. "I was shocked," Stokes said.

So was Hank Stram when he received a telephone call just before leading his team on the field. The caller was President Richard Nixon, who was wishing the Chiefs luck, especially Dawson, whom the President said he was sure was not guilty of any wrongdoing.

After confetti, balloons, and pigeons were launched to end the pregame extravaganza, the game finally began with the Chiefs receiving the opening kickoff. In contrast to the flashy pregame show, the first quarter was a study in restraint as both teams played conservatively.

It wasn't until late in the quarter that the Chiefs began a sustained drive, with Dawson calling a variety of plays that Stram devised from a multiple set offense that featured the moving pocket—a variation of the rollout pass. When the drive stalled at the 41-yard line of Minnesota, Stenerud kicked a 48-yard field goal to put Kansas City ahead, 3–0.

In the second quarter, Dawson again moved the Chiefs into scoring position, mixing his play-action passes with slashing runs by Mike Garrett. This time Stenerud kicked a 32-yard field goal to make the score 6–0.

Kapp was not having similar success with his Vikings, who found themselves in another punting situation. Once more, Dawson moved the Chiefs, using an end-around play run by Frank Pitts to set up still another Stenerud field goal, a 25-yarder.

When Minnesota's Charlie West fumbled the kickoff, the Chiefs recovered at the 19-yard line. There was no field goal this time. Instead, the Chiefs scored a touchdown in 6 plays—the last a 5-yard scoring run by Garrett. The score at halftime was 16–0, and another Super Bowl upset was in the making.

The halftime show was even more ambitious than the one that preceded the game. After Al Hirt played his trumpet and Marguerite Piazza, an opera singer, fumbled her rendition of "Basin Street Blues," men dressed as American and British soldiers—some on horseback—reenacted the Battle of New Orleans.

Contrary to documented accounts found in any history book, one of which was being read by the public address announcer, the British were winning, as the Americans were backed up inside their 20-yard line. Mercifully, the Chiefs and Vikings reappeared before history was rewritten.

When this latest Battle of New Orleans resumed, the Vikings had new resolve. Kapp drove them 69 yards for a touchdown scored by Dave Osborn on a 4-yard run. The euphoria was short-lived, however. Having advanced to the Vikings' 46 after the ensuing kickoff, Dawson completed a short ball-possession pass to Otis Taylor, the strong and shifty wide receiver

Otis Taylor high-stepped his way to the final score of the game.

Darryl Norenberg

who danced, darted, and ran by the Vikings all the way to the end zone for a touchdown.

The Chiefs led, 23–7, and their defense stopped the Vikings the rest of the game, even sending the combative Kapp to the sidelines with a severe shoulder bruise. Super Bowl IV belonged to the Chiefs, which evened the score between the merging leagues.

In the locker room afterward, President Nixon called again to congratulate Dawson, the quiet hero who had survived a trying and emotionally draining week to become the game's Most Valuable Player, completing 12 of 17 passes for 142 yards.

"The entire week was an ordeal for me," Dawson admitted. "But I didn't win the game, the whole team did. I asked the good Lord to give me the strength and courage to play my best, and asked Him to let the sun shine on my teammates today."

LEN DAWSON
Rocky Road
to the Top

For a self-assured young man who had starred at Purdue and then was a first-round draft choice of the Pittsburgh Steelers, Len Dawson couldn't comprehend the shocking twist his life had taken.

For three years at Pittsburgh, and another two years with the Cleveland Browns, he rode the bench. During those five years, a critical period when he should have been learning and developing, Dawson threw only 45 passes, completing 21 for 204 yards and 2 touchdowns.

That amounts to a single day's work for the average quarterback, and at this point Dawson considered giving it all up. "I'd been in the pros five years and had done nothing," he said.

Instead, he obtained his release from Cleveland and joined the Dallas Texans of the American Football League. In that first year of his new life in 1962, Dawson passed for 2,759 yards and 29 touchdowns.

Moving along with the franchise to Kansas City, Dawson enjoyed a nineteen-year professional career, and when he retired in 1976 his rating was the highest of any passer in NFL history. Some of his numbers included 2,136 completions for 28,711 yards and 239 TDs.

He was the only passer to lead the league four times in the AFL, and he was particularly proud that he also had a career rushing average of 4.5 yards a carry.

After losing to Green Bay in the inaugural Super Bowl, Dawson's proudest moment came in Super Bowl IV, when he led the underdog Kansas City Chiefs, to a 23–7 victory over Minnesota and was chosen MVP.

Thank you, Mr. President.

Malcolm Emmons

Dawson, one of eleven children of a factory worker, was all-state in both football and basketball at Alliance High School in Ohio, and he quickly made a name for himself as a sophomore at Purdue when he threw four TD passes against Notre Dame.

Scoring Summary

Minnesota Vikings (NFL)	0	0	7	0—7
Kansas City Chiefs (AFL)	3	13	7	0—23

Kansas City—Stenerud (FG) 48
Kansas City—Stenerud (FG) 32
Kansas City—Stenerud (FG) 25
Kansas City—Garrett, run 5 (Stenerud kick)
Minnesota—Osborn, run 4 (Cox kick)
Kansas City—Taylor, pass from Dawson 46
(Stenerud kick)

SUPER BOWL V

THE BLOOPER BOWL

Baltimore's Mike ("the Animal") Curtis appears to have the upper hand on Cowboy quarterback Craig Morton in Super Bowl V.

Darryl Norenberg

Participants—Dallas Cowboys, champions of the National Football Conference, and Baltimore Colts, champions of the American Football Conference.

Date—January 17, 1971.

Site—Orange Bowl Stadium, Miami, Florida.

Time—2:10 P.M. EST.

Aattendance—80,055.

Radio and Television—National Broadcasting Company (TV and radio).

Regular-Season Records—Baltimore, 11–2–1; Dallas, 10–4.

Playoff Records—Baltimore defeated Oakland Raiders, 27–17, for AFC title; Dallas defeated San Francisco 49ers, 17–10, for NFC title.

Player's Shares—$15,000 to each member of winning team; $7,500 to each member of losing team.

Coaches—Don McCafferty, Baltimore; Tom Landry, Dallas.

SUPER BOWL V

THE BLOOPER BOWL

There are times when success can be made to feel like failure. The Baltimore Colts and Dallas Cowboys certainly knew what it was like to win often and still face criticism. Good teams are expected to ride impressively to victory, not scratch and claw their way as these teams did in 1970 when they played like a thirsty man on his hands and knees, trying to reach a desert oasis.

Good teams are also expected to win the ultimate game—at least once. The Colts may have been National Football League champions in 1958 and 1959, but those achievements seemed to become footnotes in light of the historic and embarrassing defeat they suffered at the hands of the New York Jets of the much maligned American Football League in Super Bowl III. The Colts were back in Miami for Super Bowl V on January 17, 1971, but all the talk was about the Jets and the day that will live in ignominy.

"No one knows the despair, the abject humiliation we felt that day," said Mike Curtis, the Colts' aggressive middle linebacker. "I felt great anger inside of me that day. The 1968 Baltimore Colts—the first NFL team to lose the Super Bowl."

The Cowboys, on the other hand, managed to avoid Super Bowl embarrassments by losing earlier in the playoffs. They were pro football's uncrowned champions—the team that experts said had the most talent of any and should have been a dynasty. Instead, the Cowboys never could quite make it to the top of the mountain, always losing their grip with the summit in sight.

"It's hard to believe we're here," said Craig Morton, the Dallas quarterback. "But beating San Francisco for the championship ended our frustrations and made us a real proud team. Coach Tom Landry says that adversity brings success. I believe it, and I'm satisfied with the results."

In the year of Super Bowl V, the game had become an American tradition, celebrated with a religiouslike fervor among football fans. In such a short time it rivaled the World Series as an American spectacle. The game was sold out in Miami—where it was being played for the third time—long before it was determined which teams would participate. In 1971, that might have been a blessing.

The irony in this Super Bowl was that it was being played between two NFL teams. After the leagues formally merged for the start of the 1970 season, teams were divided into the American and National conferences, both under the banner of the NFL. Pittsburgh, Cleveland, and Baltimore had been persuaded by Commissioner Pete Rozelle to join the old AFL clubs in the American Conference. In the new alignment, the Colts had defeated the Oakland Raiders for the conference championship and a berth in the Super Bowl.

Thus, many original AFL fans were less than passionate about the outcome. The Colts were not considered part of the club, and they did not feel they were playing to uphold the honor of their adopted conference. "We've been in the AFC for one season—how can the league identify with us, and vice versa?" said Billy Ray Smith, the Colts' veteran defensive end.

"I don't want to win this for the old AFC. I want to win for me and the Colts. To a lot of people in the league, we're still the team the Jets beat."

The Cowboys were simply an enigma. They were coached by Tom Landry, a man called "the Great Stoneface" for his lack of expression on the sideline. Indeed, at times it seemed that the figure standing with his arms folded and wearing a porkpie hat was a cardboard poster and not real.

Landry and the late Vince Lombardi—the Green Bay Packer coach who had died of cancer in September 1970—were assistants under the New York Giants' Jim Lee Howell in the late 1950s. But while Lombardi was loud, imposing, and emotional, Landry was detached and rarely raised his voice. As a head coach, some of his players thought he lacked sensitivity.

What added to this problem of communication was management's clinical approach to building a winner. The Cowboys were football's first computer age team. Player evaluations were based mostly on statistical data that could not measure intangibles such as courage or motivation. Landry approached each game like a mathematician trying to prove the equation "victory equals the sum of offense and defense."

For all the complaints about his lack of personal touch, Landry's knowledge of the game was unquestioned. Few coaches were considered in his class. He also understood enough about human nature to abandon his quarterback shuttle system—which employed Morton and Roger Staubach—after nine confusing games of the regular 1970 season.

The Cowboys were 5–4 when Landry gave the job to Morton, the more experienced of the two. This helped the emotional stability of the quarterbacks as well as the Cowboys' record.

They won their last five games to finish 10–4 and then defeated the 49ers in the NFC title game. Despite the myriad formations and endless shifting in the backfield, the offense was barely adequate at times. Morton had a strong arm and a game-breaking receiver in Olympic gold medal sprinter Bob Hayes, but Landry called all the plays and preferred to be conservative with his erratic quarterbacks. When Calvin Hill, the talented running back, was injured early in the season, the unheralded Duane Thomas stepped in and gave the team another top-flight runner.

But it was the "Doomsday Defense" that Dallas relied upon to keep them in games. All-pro tackle Bob Lilly and linebackers Lee Roy Jordon and Chuck Howley were the cornerstones of a defensive unit that was consistently outstanding.

The Colts were not going to underestimate this defense, not after what had happened against the Jets. Unlike their Dallas counterparts, John Unitas and Earl Morrall were old hands at playing quarterback. Unitas was thirty-seven years old but still capable of winning championships.

Morrall, who stepped in for the injured Unitas and became Player of the Year in 1969, had settled back into a reserve role but was still deeply troubled by his performance against the Jets. To some observers, it seemed that the Colts were more preoccupied with the memory of the Jets than the very real presence of the Cowboys.

"I wanted to dig a hole and hide for six months," said John Mackey, the Colts' tight end of Super Bowl III. "I think of sitting around at halftime of that game two years ago and how bad it was, how unprepared we were."

The Colts were on the verge of being declared the best team ever then. Two years later, there had been player changes and the departure of head coach Don Shula, who went to the Miami Dolphins. Shula was a perfectionist who was demanding and brusque, often openly critical of his players. He was not well liked by many, among them Bubba Smith, the intimidating defensive end.

Shula was replaced by Don McCafferty, a forty-nine-year-old career assistant, who was low key and personable, a player's coach. "He treats you like a man," Smith said. "Not like a dog."

If New Orleans the year before was raucous and a bit on the ribald side, then the return to Miami signaled a more tranquil Super Bowl week for the teams, news media, and fans. There was a crowd of 80,577 in the Orange Bowl Stadium on Super Sunday, but no balloons crashing through the end zone into the stands. It was perhaps the most low-key beginning the game had ever had.

As the first quarter unfolded, however, it became evident that if a screenplay based on Super Bowl V were ever to be written, the Keystone Kops would play the part of both teams. Halfway through the

Linebacker Chuck Howley's interception of Johnny Unitas' pass led to a Dallas field goal in the first quarter.

UPI

quarter, Unitas flipped a pass that was intercepted by Howley, the hard-nosed linebacker who was tackled by Unitas of all people.

With the ball on the Baltimore 46, the Cowboys proceeded to lose 23 yards in 3 plays. At the time, it represented the best Baltimore drive of the game.

When Dallas punted, the Colts' Ron Gardin fumbled, and Cliff Harris of the Cowboys recovered at the 9-yard line.

Morton was unable to move the offense, however, so Mike Clark kicked a 14-yard field goal, giving Dallas a 3–0 lead. With time running out in the period, Morton connected with Hayes on a long pass that resulted in a first and goal inside the Colts' 10-yard line.

Dropping back to pass, Morton was rattled by the Colts' rush and threw to Blaine Nye, a guard and an ineligible receiver. A 15-yard penalty set the Cowboys in reverse again, and they had to settle for another field goal by Clark, giving them a 6–0 lead in the second quarter.

The tomfoolery did not end there. Unitas attempted to move the Colts through the air, but one of his passes sailed above the head of wide receiver Eddie Hinton, who tipped the ball. Mel Renfro, a defensive back, then deflected it again as he tried for an interception. The ball finally came to rest in the arms of Mackey, who raced 75 yards on the volleyball pass to score the game's first touchdown.

In keeping with the spirit of the contest, placekicker Jim O'Brien's conversion attempt was blocked. The score was tied, 6–6.

Later in the quarter, fans were treated to the sight of the aging Unitas, wearing his famous high-top shoes, trying to scramble like Fran Tarkenton. He fumbled, of course, and Dallas recovered. Morton did not squander this opportunity as he took the Cowboys in for the score, the touchdown coming on a 7-yard pass to Thomas. It was now 13–6.

Although there was no further scoring in the first half, the game took on a new perspective when Unitas was hit while throwing still another interception and left the game with bruised ribs. That brought Morrall into the game with an opportunity to avenge the defeat in Super Bowl III.

But after driving to the Cowboys' 2-yard line, the aroused Colts failed to score in 4 plays as the half ended.

By now, it was clear that Super Bowl V might

become memorable for all the wrong reasons. Sure enough, Jim Duncan of the Colts fumbled the opening kickoff in the second half, and Dallas recovered. Several plays later, not to be outdone, Thomas fumbled after reaching the Baltimore 1-yard line. The balloonist in New Orleans would have felt right at home.

The blunders continued unabated into the fourth quarter. An option pass thrown by running back Sam Havrilak of the Colts was caught by Hinton, who was almost in the end zone for a touchdown when Renfro caught him from behind, knocking the ball loose. Players from both teams grappled for it as if it were a greased pigskin until the ball rolled out of the end zone for a touchback.

The Cowboys had possession, but Morton must have figured his team had a better chance to score when the Colts had the ball. Thus, his first-down pass was intercepted by Rick Volk, who returned to the Cowboys' 3-yard line.

From there, even the Colts were able to score as Tom Nowatzke bolted in from the 2-yard line. O'Brien's not-so-automatic conversion tied the score at 13–13 with time running out and sudden-death overtime looming.

With less than 2 minutes remaining, the Cowboys had possession at the Colts' 48-yard line, almost within field-goal range. Morton then attempted to get closer with a short pass to Danny Reeves, which was intercepted by Curtis, who returned the ball to the Dallas 28. Two running plays gained 3 yards, and with 9 seconds to play, Morrall called a time out.

O'Brien jogged on the field. He was the eccentric among the Colts, a long-haired free spirit and a rookie who had dropped out from the Air Force Academy. Now he was the focal point in the most dramatic ending of any Super Bowl. With the Cowboys shouting in an attempt to distract him, O'Brien coolly took aim and kicked a 32-yard field goal.

The game may not have been a work of art, but the Colts defeated the Cowboys, 16–13, to win Super Bowl V, otherwise known as the Blooper Bowl. "Funny thing, my mom is big on astrology and she told me we couldn't lose," O'Brien said. "This is the age of Aquarius, isn't it? And I'm an Aquarius."

Baltimore's Jim O'Brien leaps for joy after his game-winning 32-yard field goal.

UPI

In the final twist of a most unusual game, Chuck Howley, the losers' linebacker, was awarded the Most Valuable Player award.

CHUCK HOWLEY
The Loser
Is a Winner

Two years after he was a number-one draft choice in 1958 of the Chicago Bears, Chuck Howley was back home in Wheeling, West Virginia, pumping gas. His football career had evaporated before it started, and all Howley had left was a quiet opportunity to earn a meager living.

It was at this low point of Howley's life that fate worked its own kind of magic. An expansion NFL franchise in Dallas was desperate for any kind of help it could get, so the Cowboys traded a third-round draft choice to Chicago for Howley.

Twelve years later, Howley had established himself as one of the game's all-time linebackers, earning all-pro honors seven times, and the Dallas Cowboys were recognized as one of the top teams in football.

"I don't even want to think about where I might be if I hadn't come back to football," said Howley, who was neither colorful nor controversial, but always reliable. "When I got out of the game in Chicago, I left without a penny."

It is interesting to consider that the man whose career almost ended before it started was the senior member of the Cowboys at thirty-four, when he was chosen the MVP of Super Bowl V, the first time a player from the losing club was so honored.

Athletics had been all so easy for Howley as a youngster. Big and powerful at six-two and about 225 pounds, he was also gifted with incredible speed for his size. He was an instinctive gambler on defense, known for producing the big play, and in a game against Atlanta, Howley ran 97 yards for a touchdown with a recovered fumble.

At West Virginia, Howley lettered in five sports as diverse as football, track, swimming, wrestling, and gymnastics, and he appeared destined for a prosperous professional career when the Bears made him their number-one draft choice. But a knee injury required surgery, and after sitting out the 1960 season, it all seemed to be over for Howley.

Then came the call from Dallas and a date with destiny.

Scoring Summary

Baltimore Colts (AFC)	0	6	0	10—16
Dallas Cowboys (NFC)	3	10	0	0—13

Dallas—Clark (FG) 14
Dallas—Clark (FG) 30
Baltimore—Mackey, pass from Unitas 75
Dallas—Thomas, pass from Morton 7 (Clark kick)
Baltimore—Nowatzke, run 2 (O'Brien kick)
Baltimore—O'Brien (FG) 32

SUPER BOWL VI

YEAR OF THE COWBOY

The Cowboys' Roger Staubach finally got his chance in Super Bowl VI.

John Biever

Participants—Miami Dolphins, champions of the American Football Conference, and Dallas Cowboys, champions of the National Football Conference.

Date—January 16, 1972.

Site—Tulane Stadium, New Orleans, Louisiana.

Time—2:30 P.M., CST.

Attendance—81,023.

Radio and Television—Columbia Broadcasting System (TV and radio).

Regular-Season Records—Miami, 10–3–1; Dallas, 11–3.

Playoff Records—Miami defeated Baltimore Colts, 21–0, for AFC title; Dallas defeated San Francisco 49ers, 14–3, for NFC title.

Players' Shares—$15,000 to each member of winning team; $7,500 to each member of losing team.

Coaches—Don Shula, Miami; Tom Landry, Dallas.

SUPER BOWL VI

YEAR OF THE COWBOY

The Super Bowl was the kind of public relations stroke of genius that Madison Avenue could appreciate. Pete Rozelle, commissioner of the National Football League, was the consummate salesman and chief architect of this annual extravaganza that made football fans wonder how they ever did without the Super Bowl.

Newspapers and television stations across the country sent at least one reporter and sometimes as many as half a dozen to each Super Bowl game for the privilege of jotting down the same bland, diplomatic, predictable remarks made by players on both teams. Players and coaches who abhorred the idea of being in the same room with a member of the news media graciously sat and repeated their answers as often as asked.

Thus, Super Bowl VI reached a new height in absurdity when the biggest news and most written about player in New Orleans during the second week of January in 1972 was a Dallas Cowboy running back who refused to talk to anyone—reporters and some teammates alike. Duane Thomas was the star of this silent movie.

Thomas was the unheralded runner who stepped in when Calvin Hill was injured the previous season and helped the Cowboys reach Super Bowl V against the Baltimore Colts. Thomas had earned a starting job, and it was the injury-prone Hill who had become disenchanted in the role of a backup during the 1971 season.

But Thomas wasn't too happy, either. During the

summer, the Cowboys' management refused his salary demands, which were based on his newfound value to the team. Thomas was incensed, at one point calling coach Tom Landry "the plastic man," an accurate statement, perhaps, but ill-advised. He was traded to the New England Patriots. But the deal fell through when the Patriots considered him uncooperative and sent him back to Dallas.

It was at that point that Thomas decided to become a monk and take a vow of silence. He was so advised by his confidant Jim Brown, the former Cleveland Browns' fullback and all-time leading rusher in the NFL, and, in retirement, a Hollywood actor.

The glib, witty Thomas who had entertained reporters during Super Bowl week in 1971 refused to even sneeze in their presence in the week of Super Bowl VI. He glowered when they gathered around him on the first day of practice in New Orleans, the traditional press interview and picture day.

Hill, whose job Thomas had taken, became his spokesman. The Yale graduate was a divinity student and eloquent speaker who belied the stereotype of the football player as a Neanderthal. "I never considered Duane unusual or untalkative," Hill said. "I found him cordial and warm. We've even discussed history and philosophy. That's more than you normally get in a discussion with a football player, most of whom prefer to discuss the game or girls."

Not much had changed about the Cowboys since the Super Bowl V debacle in which they and the Baltimore Colts had played like nervous seniors asking girls to the high school prom. It had been duly recorded as another big game the Cowboys couldn't win, which was fast becoming their legacy.

Still, this was a talented and determined team that dusted itself off and came back for more. Landry had allowed the unsettled quarterback situation to fester again in 1971, and after five games the Cowboys were 2–3.

This time, however, Landry decided to bench Craig Morton and go with Roger Staubach, the former midshipman who had joined the Cowboys after five years of active duty following his graduation from Annapolis.

Staubach was a scrambler, an effective runner who would delight any football thrill-seeker. It went against Landry's conservative nature to entrust his offense to this gridiron Houdini, but Staubach led the Cowboys to nine consecutive victories and then another playoff win against the San Francisco 49ers.

Landry exercised some measure of control by calling all the plays, but then he held his breath. "Roger runs when he can't find any open receivers," the coach said. "But I wish he wouldn't."

There was a new element in Super Bowl VI as the Miami Dolphins of the American Conference joined the roster of Super Bowl teams. The Dolphins were an expansion team that had been in existence for only six years, the first four of which bordered on dreadful. In fact, the biggest attraction at home games was Flipper, the purpoise who swam in a pool beyond the end zone and entertained fans who had long since lost interest in the game.

But Joe Robbie, the attorney and sometime politician who owned the majority interest in the team, weathered the losing records and lack of interest in Miami, and it finally paid off when general manager Joe Thomas lured Don Shula from Baltimore in 1970. This was the same Shula the Colts were so happy to see leave, the demanding, whip-cracking coach whose brilliance was forgotten in the Colts' embarrassing loss to the New York Jets in Super Bowl III.

Shula, however, was the proper tonic for the Dolphins, a team becoming too comfortable with the pleasant, unfootball-like climate and losing. He acquired veteran players such as wide receiver Paul Warfield of Cleveland and middle linebacker Nick Buoniconti of New England for leadership, then entrusted the offense to quarterback Bob Griese, a quietly confident young man from Purdue.

To the amazement of Floridians in 1970, the Dolphins made a complete turnabout, finishing with a 10–4 record and a playoff berth. They were eliminated by the Oakland Raiders, but the seeds of success had taken hold. In 1971, they had a 10–3–1 record and defeated the Colts, 21–0, in the American Conference championship, a victory Shula relished.

They relied on the power running of the bullish fullback Larry Csonka and a slow but effective halfback from the University of Wyoming, Jim Kiick. Griese was a conservative passer who set up his tosses with the running game.

Griese, in fact, had a great deal in common with Staubach. Both were modest, unassuming midwesterners, who were All-Americans in college, wore number 12, married former nurses, and worked in real estate during the off-season. Griese, however, did not scramble. Landry would have loved him.

If the Dolphins were not exactly household names on offense, they were even more unknown on defense. As a unit, they played extremely well, although many fans would be hard-pressed to name any starters in addition to Buoniconti.

One fan, however, kept close tabs on Shula's team. Two weeks before Super Bowl VI, the coach was at home studying films when the telephone rang at 1:30 A.M.

"When the phone rang at that hour, I thought it might be some nut calling," Shula said.

Instead, a voice said that it was the President of the United States calling. Shortly, Richard M. Nixon got on the line and warned Shula that Tom Landry was an excellent coach. So just to help out a little, the President suggested a play for the Dolphins.

"I still think you can hit Warfield on that down-and-in pattern against them," he said.

"He also told me," Shula said, "that he was a Washington Redskin fan, but since he is a part-time resident of Miami, he follows the Dolphins closely, too."

The President would be watching on January 16, to see if his play was run. It was otherwise an uneventful time before Super Bowl VI. Spirits were not dampened by the cold and windy weather that plagued New Orleans two years earlier. Hotel rooms were scarce and overpriced, but revelers enjoyed the nights in the French Quarter.

Game day did not dawn brightly for the Cowboys, whose team bus was delayed fifteen minutes in front of the hotel, where it was blocked by three chartered schoolbuses. It was not a good omen.

The pregame show featured air force jets buzzing Tulane Stadium, a marine drill team, and seemingly all of the active men in the United States Armed Forces parading on the field. It might have been a wonderful time for a Soviet invasion. In the stands, 81,023 watched this military show of force.

The pattern of previous Super Bowl games was to play conservatively as teams tried not to lose rather than to win. There was too much glory and money at stake, it was reasoned, to be a riverboat gambler. Thus, invariably, the best offenses looked dull, especially in the early going, and mediocre defenses played as if there were an all-pro at every position.

The teams traded punts in the first quarter until Dallas got the first break when Csonka, a sure-handed ballcarrier, fumbled for the first time all season. Staubach cautiously moved the Cowboys to the Miami 2-yard line, where the Dolphins' cast of thousands stiffened and forced the Cowboys to settle for Mike Clark's 9-yard field goal. The quarter ended with Dallas ahead, 3–0.

Griese, meanwhile, was having difficulty reading the intricate Dallas defense. Time and time again, he was pursued by the front four as he attempted to pass, once being tackled for a 29-yard loss by Bob Lilly.

The defensive showing inspired the offense, which began a time-consuming 76-yard drive late in the first half. Staubach allowed Thomas and Hill to soften the Dolphins with their slashing runs, then he deftly went to the air for the game's first touchdown, connecting with Lance Alworth on a 7-yard pass. It was 10–0 Dallas.

With time running out, Griese frantically drove the Dolphins into field-goal range. With 8 seconds left in the half, Garo Yepremian kicked a 31-yard field goal to narrow the deficit to 10–3 and give Miami a psychological lift.

But their renewed confidence lasted only until the

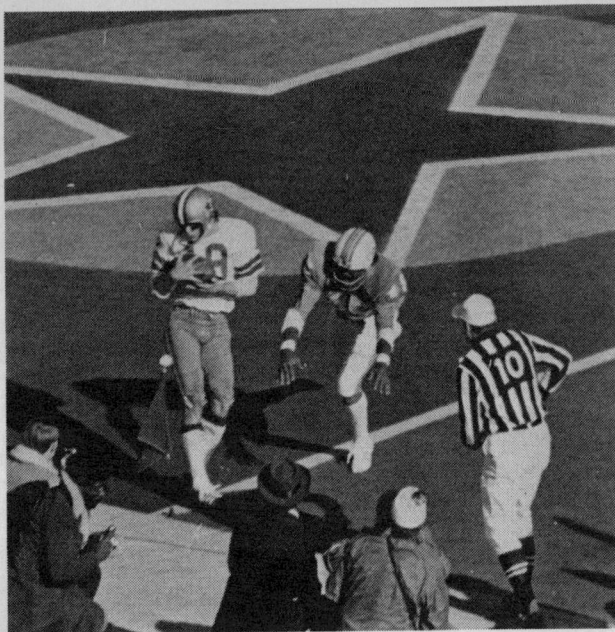

Lance Alworth catches a Roger Staubach pass in the end zone for the first touchdown.

UPI

halftime show—honoring Louis Armstrong and Dixieland jazz—ended. It was lengthy, but not long enough. Dallas took the second-half kickoff and drove 71 yards with Thomas letting his feet do the talking with beautiful cutback runs.

Thomas slashed off tackle for 3 yards and a touchdown, which raised the Cowboys' lead to 17–3. The way the Dolphins had been playing, it already looked as if the game were out of reach.

As the fourth quarter began, the Dolphins were on a modest drive when Griese's attempted pass to Kiick was intercepted by linebacker Chuck Howley, who huffed and puffed down the sideline until he tripped

**Silent Duane Thomas expresses himself into the
end zone to boost the Dallas lead.**

UPI

and fell of his own accord inside the Miami 10-yard
line.

Two plays later, Staubach passed to Mike Ditka in
the end zone from 7 yards out, and Dallas had sealed
its first Super Bowl victory. The score was 24–3, but
more important than the one-sided margin of victory
was the fact that it enabled the Cowboys to shed their
loser's image.

In the locker room, Staubach—voted the Most Valuable Player—accepted a congratulatory telephone call
from the Dolphins' assistant coach, President Nixon.
And Clint Murchison, the Dallas owner, joked that
the victory signaled the "successful end to our twelve-
year plan."

But the most amusing sight was that of Tom Brookshier, the CBS television commentator and former

player, stammering and stuttering as he nervously tried to interview Duane Thomas, who broke his silence with an icy stare and one-word answers for Brookshier's run-on questions.

ROGER STAUBACH
Bull's-Eye for
Straight Arrow

Of all the men who ever played professional football, few achieved stardom in such a roundabout way as Roger Staubach.

A deeply committed and honorable man, Staubach fulfilled an obligation to serve four years in the navy following his graduation from the Naval Academy. His tour included a year in Vietnam during the war.

As a result, when Staubach finally reported to the Dallas Cowboys in 1969, he was a twenty-seven-year-old rookie with a realistic doubt as to whether he'd be able to pick up on what had been a brilliant collegiate career.

His success proved to be beyond expectation. For the next eleven years Staubach was the symbol of the Cowboys, the winningest team in the NFL during the 1970s. Of the ten Super Bowls played during this decade, Dallas appeared in half of them, winning the championship twice. Staubach was the MVP of Super Bowl VI, passing for 2 touchdowns in the 24–3 rout of Miami.

Staubach, a private man who carried his military bearing proudly, was known as a straight arrow who had no vices. He was also an exceptionally gifted all-around athlete, earning seven letters at Navy in football, baseball, and basketball. Some claimed he could have made it in major league baseball.

Staubach, who didn't play quarterback until his senior year of high school in Cincinnati, won the 1963 Heisman Trophy as a junior at Navy, and when he retired from the Cowboys in 1980, he was the top-rated passer in the sixty-year history of the NFL.

His popularity was such that when he announced his retirement, all three TV networks in Dallas carried his tearful farewell speech, and the switchboard in the Cowboys' office was jammed with season ticketholders threatening to cancel their seats.

"If I had it to do all over again, I would want to do it just the way I did it," Staubach said. "I might like to change a few scores, but that's all. I'd just like to be remembered as a darned consistent quarterback."

Scoring Summary

Dallas Cowboys (NFC)	3	7	7	7—24
Miami Dolphins (AFC)	0	3	0	0—3

Dallas—Clark (FG)9
Dallas—Alworth, pass from Staubach 7 (Clark kick)
Miami—Yepremian (FG) 31
Dallas—Thomas, run 3 (Clark kick)
Dallas—Ditka, pass from Staubach 7 (Clark kick)

SUPER BOWL VII

THE PERFECT SEASON

A Bob Griese pass to Howard Twilley put the Dolphins on the scoreboard in the opening quarter of Super Bowl VII.

Participants—Miami Dolphins, champions of the American Football Conference, and Washington Redskins, champions of the National Football Conference.

Date—January 14, 1973.

Site—Memorial Coliseum, Los Angeles, California.

Time—12:30 P.M., PST.

Attendance—90,192.

Radio and Television—National Broadcasting Company (TV and radio).

Regular-Season Records—Miami, 14–0; Washington, 11–3.

Playoff Records—Miami defeated Cleveland Browns, 20–14, and Pittsburgh Steelers, 21–17, for AFC title; Washington defeated Green Bay Packers, 16–3, and Dallas Cowboys, 26–3, for NFC title.

Players' Shares—$15,000 to each member of winning team; $7,500 to each member of losing team.

Coaches—Don Shula, Miami; George Allen, Washington.

THE PERFECT
SEASON

He was Elmer Gantry in football cleats, a fire-and-brimstone coach who would have been very comfortable behind a pulpit in the church of his choosing on Sunday mornings. George Allen had arrived in Washington in 1971 and quickly elevated the Redskins to a contending team. And now the coach who numbered among his friends President Richard Nixon—jokingly referred to as the second most important man in Washington, D.C.—was going to try to deny the Miami Dolphins a perfect season.

Super Bowl VII was returning to Los Angeles for the first time since the game's inception in 1967 when the Green Bay Packers routed the Kansas City Chiefs. It was a homecoming for Allen, too, because he had coached the Rams during the mid and late 1960s, bringing them to within a breath of the biggest game on two occasions.

Allen was one of the more unique men to coach a professional team. He was not a disciplinarian in the Vince Lombardi, Bud Grant, and Don Shula mold. Nor was he the easygoing type in the manner of Don McCafferty and Weeb Ewbank. Allen was a cheerleader who cajoled players with corny sayings, fight songs, and amateur psychology.

He had a reputation for winning fast, and he did so in Washington by making several changes that did not affect the nucleus of the Redskins but added key players on offense and defense. The moves got more attention because Allen traded draft choices for established players, choosing age over beauty. "The future is now," was the Redskins' credo.

Bill Kilmer, a thirty-three-year-old quarterback who threw butterfly passes and ran at three speeds, each one slower than the other, was acquired from the New Orleans Saints as insurance for the popular Sonny Jurgensen. Despite the fans' initial protestations, Kilmer replaced the injured Sonny boy during the 1972 season and led the Redskins to their first Super Bowl berth.

On defense, Allen reinforced his unit by trading for experienced hands such as Ron McDole, Roosevelt Taylor, and Jack Pardee, a thirty-seven-year-old linebacker who had played for Allen in Los Angeles.

"I can't even remember my first eight years in the league," Pardee said. "We didn't win, and that's no fun. But I had the next seven years under the coaching of George Allen. He made winners of us, first as the Rams' coach, and the past two years in Washington. He has made football fun."

The average age of the Redskins was twenty-nine, just one year above the National Football League average, but still the team became known as "The Over the Hill Gang." It only added to the mystique that Allen had created.

But there was more to him than just a cotton candy rapport with his players and inspirational talks before and after games. Allen was meticulous in his preparation, leaving nothing to chance. He was also suspected of spying on his opponents, and Shula, the Miami Dolphins' coach, teasingly said that the old lady who had been watching his team practice during Super Bowl week was about the same height as Charley Winner, one of Allen's assistant coaches.

It was also said that the last light turned out in Washington, D.C., was not in the White House. Allen worked long hours and demanded the same sacrifice of his staff. The day after the Redskins' 26–3 victory against the Dallas Cowboys in the National Conference championship game was the first day off Allen's nine assistants had enjoyed since before training camp had begun.

The Redskins' resurgence under Allen also placed President Nixon in a quandary, The President liked the Dolphins, calling them his second team, and had called Shula to suggest a play before Super Bowl VI. But he'd made it clear before Super Bowl VII that his first allegiance was to Washington's team.

There was a photograph of the President and Allen hanging in the Redskins' offices. The inscription read: "To George Allen—with respect and admiration for his leadership, and with personal wishes. Richard Nixon."

The President's affection for the handsome black-haired, silver-tongued coach transcended the city in which they worked. The President had attended Whittier College in California where Allen was the coach from 1951–56.

Because of his high profile and unorthodox ways, Allen had stolen the spotlight from Shula and the Dolphins in Los Angeles. By January 1973, the Super Bowl was firmly established as an American sports spectacle, but there was nothing particularly intriguing about the last few games.

The Dolphins changed all that with the prospect of an unbeaten season. They had won all fourteen regular-season games, then disposed of Cleveland and Pittsburgh in the American Conference playoffs. Sixteen down and one to go.

But in typical Dolphin fashion, they remained a low-key, relatively unknown team. Individually, fans might be able to single out quarterback Bob Griese, wide receiver Paul Warfield, fullback Larry Csonka, and the newcomer, Eugene (Mercury) Morris, but those were offensive players of whom more is usually known.

The Dolphins, however, had grown fond of their nickname, the "No-Name" defense. It was hung on them inadvertently by Tom Landry, the Dallas Cowboys' coach, a year earlier at Super Bowl VI. "I can't recall their names," Landry said then, "but they are a matter of great concern to us."

The defense had held opponents to an average of 12 points a game during the regular season and then stifled Cleveland and Pittsburgh in the playoffs. Perhaps because the entire team was relatively anonymous, the Dolphins were especially close knit. It was one of the characteristics that Allen was claiming for the Redskins.

"One of the prerequisites of success is that the players play as a unit," said Joe Robbie, owner of the Miami team. "And the Dolphins are as close as a family."

There was still a stigma attached to the team, however. Shula had been the losing coach in Super Bowl III when he was in Baltimore, and the Colts were humbled by the New York Jets. In Super Bowl VI, Shula admitted that his young Dolphins seemed to be in awe of the Cowboys.

So once again, success had led to failure, and there were whispers that Shula could not win the big game. Of course, no other coach had been to as many Super Bowls as he had.

One of his players also enjoyed that distinction. Earl Morrall, the venerable quarterback who had played such an important role with the Colts for four years, was making his third Super Bowl appearance, this time as Griese's understudy.

Morrall had actually played a prominent role in the winning streak during the course of the season when Griese was injured. But during halftime of the AFC championship game against Pittsburgh, Shula decided to make the switch back to Griese.

The score was tied, 7–7, and the Dolphins needed a lift against the aggressive Steeler defense. Griese came off the bench to lead them to a pair of touchdowns and the AFC title. His savvy and leadership belied a boyish face and quiet manner. In the huddle, Griese left no doubt as to who was in charge.

In the closing minutes against Pittsburgh with several players trying to talk at the same time, Griese forcefully said, "Shut up. Let's get this drive going."

"That's the mark of a leader," Mercury Morris said. "That was his way of telling us to be cool."

That poise stood the Dolphins in good stead during Super Bowl week when rain flooded their practice site in Long Beach, California, forcing them to move around like gypsies to a variety of other fields. Shula's easygoing posture—a departure from his more intense style—was a counterpoint to Allen's almost frenzied behavior. One would think it was the Redskins who were unbeaten.

Although the Super Bowl environment was controlled by the league, the number of press and television on hand and the time needed for interviews clearly annoyed Allen. This was time best spent preparing. The Redskins' coach went so far as to have someone chart the angle of the sun as it passed over the Memorial Coliseum during the time of day the teams would be playing Super Bowl VII.

Allen's return to Los Angeles and the Dolphins' unbeaten record had given this game a boost locally that Super Bowl I had failed to achieve. All 90,000 seats in the Coliseum had been sold, and the television blackout of the area within a seventy-five-mile radius of Los Angeles had been lifted. When the Packers played the Chiefs in their historic meeting in 1967, only 63,000 fans were present.

But interest was peaking on press interview day when the reporters and Redskin players at Anaheim Stadium were joined by an unruly crowd of 5,000 young fans who came on the field seeking autographs. "I was frightened that they might step on the players and break their legs," Allen said. "We need an army for security."

Naturally, he was relieved when January 14 arrived. Allen called the Dolphins the best team he had ever seen, but the odds makers were unconvinced. The Redskins were 2-point favorites.

Th teams were similar in style, relying on a conservative ball-control offense. Allen considered passing a necessary evil, while Shula merely tried to take advantage of his team's strengths.

Neither team moved the ball in the early going. The Redskins tried to probe the Dolphins' defense with Larry Brown, their fine running back, but he was running into a wall of resistance led by the burly tackle Manny Fernandez.

Miami finally began to make headway after forcing Washington to punt. Taking possession on their 37-yard line, the Dolphins moved methodically downfield as Griese began to mix the running of Csonka and Jim Kiick with some passing plays. First, he connected with Warfield for a 14-yard gain that brought the ball to the 34-yard line of the Redskins.

Csonka and Kiick pounded the middle for 6 yards before Griese dropped back again, this time spotting Howard Twilley, the slow but wily receiver, open at the 5-yard line. The pass was on target, and Twilley eluded defensive back Pat Fischer to score the game's first touchdown.

The Dolphins clung to their 7–0 lead in the second

Miami's Jake Scott makes one of the 2 interceptions that led to his selection as MVP.

UPI

quarter, thanks to the defense. Jake Scott, a safetyman who had suffered a separated shoulder two weeks earlier, intercepted a pass to halt one Washington drive and middle linebacker Nick Buoniconti intercepted another Kilmer flutterball to end another drive.

Buoniconti returned the ball 32 yards to the Redskins' 27. With less than 2 minutes to play, Griese began moving the Dolphins toward the end zone. The big play in the drive was an 18-yard completion to tight end Bob Mandich, which gave Miami a first down on the 2-yard line. On the second try, Kiick bolted into the end zone and the Dolphins led, 14–0.

The defensive struggle continued in the third quarter, and as the fourth started, the situation was becoming desperate for the Redskins. But now, Kilmer had them on the march, moving from their 11-yard line to the Miami 10. Then the "No-Names" struck again.

Kilmer attempted to hit Charley Taylor in the end zone for a touchdown, but Scott dashed over from his free safety position to make his second interception of the game and run it back 55 yards, The game seemed out of reach, especially when Griese drove the offense into field-goal range, where the reliable Garo Yepremian, a soccer-style kicker from Cyprus, came in to attempt the 3-pointer.

Unfortunately for Yepremian, the next sequence became a nightmare. There was a low snap from center, and his hurried kick was blocked. The ball bounced back to Yepremian, who scooped it up and attempted to pass it to no one in particular,

As he raised his arm, the ball fell from his hands and Dick Bass of the Redskins scooped it up, racing 49 yards for a touchdown. Suddenly the score was 14–7, and there were still more than 2 minutes to play.

A distraught Yepremian stood on the sideline, praying, he said, that his team would overcome his blunder. With 1:14 remaining, the Redskins regained possession, but the "No-Name" defense suffocated Kilmer with a big rush, and time ran out.

The Dolphins had completed the perfect season, defeated the Redskins, 14–7, to finish with a 17–0 rec-

Washington's Dick Bass grabs the ball on the bizarre play that had begun as a kick by Miami's Garo Yepremian and turns it into a 49-yard touchdown.

UPI

ord. Jake Scott was voted Most Valuable Player, and Yepremian could afford to joke about his ill-fated pass attempt.

"Next," a happy and relieved Shula said, "is relaxation and enjoyment. This is the ultimate."

Hail to the victor, Miami coach Don Shula.

UPI

JAKE SCOTT
Great Scott!

On the football field, Jake Scott knew few equals as a free safety. In his conduct as a man, he stood alone as a free spirit.

As much as for the skills he exhibited as a player, Scott is remembered for being one of a kind. He once went skiing with both wrists wrapped in casts, explaining, "As long as you don't fall down you won't have any trouble," and he routinely turned down lucrative requests for endorsements and speaking engagements because he valued his time more than money.

"I'd never be a slave to money or recognition," he said. "I simply want to enjoy myself, and I think I have."

Scott was bitingly honest with his opinions, and he was most comfortable in the outdoors, whether it was skiing, snowmobiling, racing motorcycles, or riding horses.

Although small at six feet and 180 pounds, and with thinning hair even in his youth, Scott was a natural football player. He was an All-American at the University of Georgia and played a year in Canada before joining the Miami Dolphins in 1970. In addition to free safety, he was a fearless punt returner.

Despite numerous injuries and surgery, Scott played every game during his six years with the Dolphins. Following a disagreement with coach Don Shula, he went to Washington for his final three years, starring as a member of George Allen's "Over the Hill Gang."

In his nine years Scott was named to the Pro Bowl

team six times and played in three Super Bowls. It was in Super Bowl VII, concluding Miami's sensational 17–0 season of 1972, that Scott was designated MVP after he intercepted two Billy Kilmer passes, returning the second 55 yards, in the 14–7 victory over the Redskins.

Scott frequently played hurt. He was unable to practice for the two weeks leading up to the Super Bowl because of a separated right shoulder and bone chips in his right wrist, and he played another Super Bowl game with two broken wrists.

"If you're not hurt, you haven't been playing," Scott said. Another time he commented, "Playing football is being able to take a gamble in life. You don't know the outcome, but you risk it."

Scoring Summary

Miami Dolphins (AFC)	7	7	0	0—14
Washington Redskins (NFC)..	0	0	0	7—7

Miami—Twilley, pass from Griese 28 (Yepremian kick)
Miami—Kiick, run 1 (Yepremian kick)
Washington—Bass, fumble recovery return 49 (Knight kick)

DITTO THE DOLPHINS

He was a thirteen-year NFL veteran, but Minnesota's Fran Tarkenton had never been to the Super Bowl before.

Carl Skalak

Participants—Miami Dolphins, champions of the American Football Conference, and Minnesota Vikings, champions of the National Football Conference.

Date—January 13, 1974.

Site—Rice Stadium, Houston, Texas.

Time—2:30 P.M., CST.

Attendance—71,882.

Radio and Television—Columbia Broadcasting System (TV and radio).

Regular-Season Records—Miami, 12–2; Minnesota, 12–2.

Playoff Records—Miami defeated Cincinnati Bengals, 34–16, and Oakland Raiders, 27–10, for AFC title; Minnesota defeated Washington Redskins, 27–20, and Dallas Cowboys, 27–10, for NFC title.

Players' Shares—$15,000 to each member of winning team; $7,500 to each member of losing team.

Coaches—Don Shula, Miami; Bud Grant, Minnesota.

DITTO THE DOLPHINS

The Super Bowl had earned its lofty reputation in part because of the first-class accommodations afforded the teams and the news media. NFL commissioner Pete Rozelle never missed an opportunity to win friends and influence people in the press with a well-timed cocktail party or a dinner that looked like a Roman orgy. And the practice facilities provided the teams were almost as good as those at home.

But what distinguished Super Bowl VIII in Houston from the previous games was the complaint—the strongest of its kind—voiced by Bud Grant, the Minnesota Vikings' coach, about his team's practice site. During Super Bowl week, when players and coaches always say complimentary things about one another and the surroundings, this passed for a major scandal.

Grant was a stern tactician who did not have a lot of rules but expected the players to adhere to the ones he did make. He didn't smile much or crack jokes, but he wasn't the blustery sort that Vince Lombardi was, either. So when Grant complained, he usually had a good reason,

The Miami Dolphins, who were making their third consecutive Super Bowl appearance and were trying to repeat as champions, used the practice facilities of the Houston Oilers, a fellow AFC team. The Vikings, on the other hand, were sent to a high-school field, which among other attractions, offered birds flying through the locker room.

"This is shabby treatment," Grant said, "This is a

Super Bowl game, not a pickup game. The league is responsible, and Pete Rozelle runs the league."

What bothered Grant in addition to the rundown conditions of the field and locker room was that there were no blocking sleds for his team to use. What's more, the Vikings had to take a twenty-minute bus ride to Delmar High School, while the Dolphins were able to walk to their practice field.

Well, Rozelle, America's host, was not happy about Grant's complaints. The commissioner heard the news while still in New York, where the league offices are situated. He informed the Vikings that Grant could be fined if his disparaging remarks continued. That only inflamed the issue, as Grant spent the entire week talking about birds, locker rooms, and a field that looked as if someone had tried to cut the grass with a golf club.

If nothing else, it gave Super Bowl week some needed comic relief. The annual event had lost some of its perspective as people likened it to war. There was no denying that the stakes were high, but football was still a game, not a confrontation between two armies on the field of battle.

That's why Fran Tarkenton was such a refreshing addition to Super Bowl week. This was his thirteenth season as a professional quarterback and his first chance to win a championship. Tarkenton had started his career with the Vikings, was traded to the New York Giants, and then was traded back to Minnesota, which had made its previous Super Bowl appearance with Joe Kapp playing quarterback.

Tarkenton was a glib, outgoing quarterback who enjoyed talking to reporters, a departure from the strong, silent types that football fans felt more comfortable with. He was also unorthodox because he wasn't the prototype pocket passer that coaches preferred. Tarkenton was a scrambler, who did not have a particularly strong arm and who exasperated opposing defenses, and sometimes his teammates, with whimsical dashes around the field, avoiding would-be tacklers.

No, the purist among fans could never quite get accustomed to watching this little six-footer darting

and dashing in the backfield, weaving past players
like a New Yorker walking down a busy Manhattan
street at lunchtime. Other quarterbacks such as Roger
Staubach of the Dallas Cowboys and even Bob Griese
of the Dolphins would run on occasion, but Tarkenton
had the image of a quarterback who would rather run
first, pass later.

His career statistics were unimpressive, as Tarkenton
had begun moving up on the all-time passing leaders.
Still, he was disdainfully called "The Scrambler," which
became synonymous with "The Loser." Tarkenton hoped
that by leading the Vikings to Super Bowl VIII, he
had ended all the negative talk.

"For years I heard that a scrambler couldn't win,"
he said. "And then Roger Staubach and Bob Griese
were quarterbacks on Super Bowl winners. It was the
greatest lie perpetrated on the pro football public."

Football was a team sport, Tarkenton said, and it
was unfair to place the burden of losing and all the
praise for winning on the quarterback's head. But he
understood that the quarterback was perhaps the most
glamorous position in any sport and that he would not
be able to change people's perceptions of him or the
job.

Tarkenton did have at least one strong supporter in
Houston. Oddly, it was Jake Scott, the Dolphins' defensive safety, who grew up in Athens, Georgia, and
was a junior high school student when Tarkenton
quarterbacked the Athens High School team.

"In high school he was just like he is in the pros, a
real leader," Scott said. "I knew his two brothers, his
whole family. We played together."

Before Scott's family moved from Athens to Washington, D.C., his mother taught Tarkenton in a psychology course at the University of Georgia. When
Tarkenton was with the Vikings the first time, he
helped convince Scott—then an outstanding high school
player in Silver Springs, Maryland—to attend Georgia. "He's the only player I ever recruited," Tarkenton
said.

And on Super Bowl Sunday, Scott would be the
defensive quarterback in the Dolphins' secondary who

would try to read Tarkenton's mind. The teams had played twice before—in 1972, when the Dolphins scored an 18–14 come-from-behind victory, and in the 1973 preseason, when the Vikings won.

That victory was not given much consideration by the odds makers, who installed the Dolphins as 6-point favorites. They had successfully repeated as American Conference champions following their unbeaten season in 1972, which was highlighted by a victory against the Washington Redskins in Super Bowl VII.

By now, there were some who speculated that the Dolphins were even better than Lombardi's Green Bay Packer teams in the 1960s. "I think we're better than the Packers," said Larry Csonka, the Dolphins' bull-dozing fullback, "but I'm prejudiced. I think we're a little deeper and we have a better passing attack than the Packers had."

Certainly Csonka, Jim Kiick, and the team's break-away threat, Mercury Morris, gave the Dolphins a running game as formidable as any in pro football. The Packers, in fact, never had a runner with Morris' speed.

"That might be the difference right there," Morris said. "To me, comparing us to the Packers is like comparing Muhammad Ali to Rocky Marciano, two different styles. We're a little more wide open."

Team speed indeed might have been the difference between the great Packer teams and the Dolphins. Although Green Bay had sure-handed, dependable receivers, it did not have anyone who was a deep threat such as Paul Warfield of the Dolphins. So, although Don Shula, the Miami coach, preferred to play a run-oriented conservative game, he knew that Morris and Warfield gave the Dolphins the ability to score quickly.

The Miami players, however, tried to discourage the comparisons to Green Bay or any other NFL dynasties. They had not yet won Super Bowl VIII, and they weren't taking the Vikings lightly. Not when Fran Tarkenton could make any defense look bad with his unconventional ways.

It had been quiet in Houston the week preceding the game. The pregame Super Bowl festivities had become almost low key by now. Business was good for local merchants, and there were plenty of parties. The most celebrated was held in the Astrodome the night before the game, where 2,836 guests attended the world's biggest barbecue. The only people missing were the players and coaches of both teams. They were presumably back in their hotels sleeping. It's just as well that Bud Grant didn't attend. He would have blanched had he seen a perfectly serviceable practice site being used to cook pork and beef and pour drinks for the good-timers.

Super Bowl VIII was not played in the Astrodome, but outdoors in the rickety, old, but larger Rice Stadium. More than 70,000 fans were on hand on a cool, overcast day. The Dolphins won the coin toss and elected to receive.

From the outset, it was clear that Shula intended to use a ball-control offense revolving around the punishing runs of Csonka and his slow but steady running mate, Kiick. Starting from their 38-yard line, the Dolphins moved methodically downfield with Csonka shouldering the load.

He brought the Dolphins into scoring range when he broke through the defense for a 16-yard gain and a first down on the 27-yard line of Minnesota. Csonka was bleeding from the nose after that play. He had broken it again, but by now, it was something he was accustomed to.

Griese connected with Marion Briscoe, a wide receiver, for a short gain, then sent his human tank, Csonka, up the middle again, this time for 5 yards. Miami had a first down on the 15. Csonka gained 8 more yards and Morris added 3, and it was first and goal at the 5-yard line.

It was already clear that the quick but relatively small Vikings' defensive line would have difficulty containing the Miami running game. From the 5-yard line, Csonka bolted over right guard and went into the end zone. The Dolphins led, 7–0.

They soon had possession again on their 44-yard line—excellent field position. And it didn't take long for the Dolphins to move into scoring range. Csonka

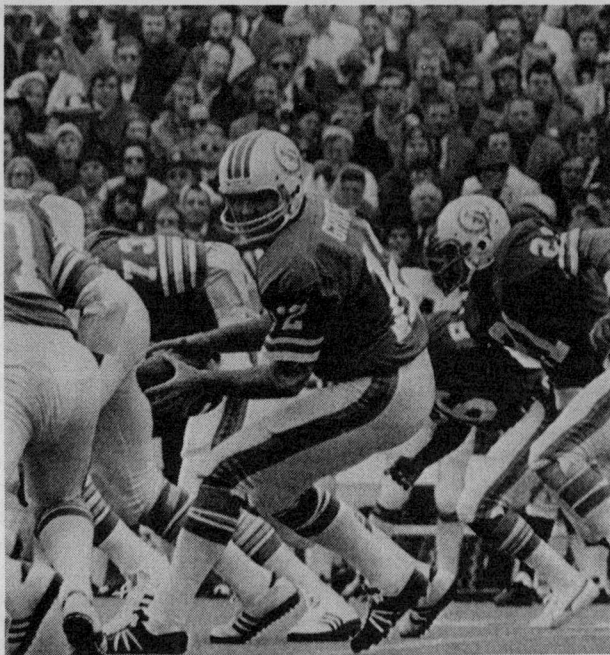

Bob Griese gets ready to hand off during the Dolphins' first touchdown drive.

UPI

showed some quickness this time, circling the end for 12 yards before hammering the middle for 8 more. With the Vikings looking groggy and confused, Griese completed a 13-yard pass to Briscoe for a first down on the 1-yard line.

From there, Kiick gave Csonka a rest and carried for the touchdown. It was 14–0. Although Minnesota's defense became a bit more stubborn, it was not able to keep the Dolphins from controlling the football. In the second quarter, Griese drove them into field-goal range, where Garo Yepremian connected from 28 yards away. The Miami lead was 17–0.

Tarkenton was not getting much of an opportunity to move his team, and when he did late in the first half, Oscar Reed, a running back, fumbled on the Dolphins' 6-yard line to waste a scoring opportunity.

The third quarter was a replay of the first two. So effective were Csonka, Kiick, and Morris, that Griese wasn't even forced to throw the football. He did so only once in the third quarter and hit Warfield for 27 yards, giving the Dolphins a first down on the Vikings' 11-yard line.

Several plays later, Csonka scored from the 2, and the Dolphins had an insurmountable 24–0 lead. Tarkenton salvaged some respect in the fourth quarter when he led Minnesota on a 57-yard drive for the first touchdown scored against Miami's No-Name defense in two Super Bowl games. Tarkenton scrambled 4 yards into the end zone to make the final margin, 24–7. And it was two in a row for the Dolphins.

Super Bowl VIII had not been especially exciting, but it was a testimony to the abilities of the Dolphins, who earned their place as one of the finest teams in pro football history. "They're just a great team that executes well," said Jeff Siemon, the Vikings' middle linebacker.

Csonka was voted the Most Valuable Player, having gained 145 yards in 33 carries. The six-one, 238-pound fullback was an intimidating sight for defensive players who had the unenviable chore of trying to stop him. "It's nice," he said, "to know that you're punishing these guys as much as they're punishing you."

LARRY CSONKA
Zonk!

His running style, in the words of one acute observer, resembled an elephant running downhill. There was no finesse, only brute force, and his favorite move was a forearm to a rival's head and a romp over a fallen body.

Despite a lack of speed, Larry Csonka utilized his strength to rank as one of the all-time great rushers. But he paid painfully for his bullheaded aggressiveness, breaking his nose some dozen times (even he lost count) and enduring a series of other injuries.

"I don't like the idea of people thinking of me as some kind of freak," he said. "I'm just a human being who happens to make a living playing football. I'm no punishment freak. I don't enjoy the pain, and the soreness never seems to go away.

"But the desire to play must come from within. It's based on pride and determination."

The determination was evident early. One summer, while on break from Syracuse University, Csonka returned to the farm in Stow, Ohio, where he was born on Christmas Day 1946, and pounded down a wall of his home as an exercise to strengthen his forearms.

Csonka broke all school rushing records at Syracuse, surpassing even the great Jim Brown, and was the number-one draft choice in 1968 of the Miami Dolphins, then an expansion franchise. Teaming with Jim Kiick in the backfield, Zonk quickly helped establish the Dolphins as an NFL powerhouse. They won four consecutive division titles in the early half of the

Miami's Larry Csonka simply proved too much of a bull for Vikings.

Carl Skalak

1970s, appeared in the Super Bowl three times, and won it twice.

The MVP of Super Bowl VIII played one year in the World Football League and two more with the New York Giants before winding up his career back in Miami in 1979. At the time he retired, Zonk was one of only six players to exceed 8,000 yards in career rushing.

Scoring Summary

Minnesota Vikings (NFC)   0   0   0   7—7
Miami Dolphins (AFC)   14   3   7   0—24

Miami—Csonka, run 5 (Yepremian kick)
Miami—Kiick, run 1 (Yepremian kick)
Miami—Yepremian (FG) 28
Miami—Csonka, run 2 (Yepremian kick)
Minnesota—Tarkenton, run 4 (Cox kick)

SUPER BOWL IX

TIME FOR THE STEELERS

Fullback Franco Harris, the Steelers' 1,000-yard man, rumbles to a touchdown in Super Bowl IX.

Participants—Pittsburgh Steelers, champions of the American Football Conference, and Minnesota Vikings, champions of the National Football Conference.

Date—January 12, 1975.

Site—Tulane Stadium, New Orleans, Louisiana.

Time—2:00 P.M., CST.

Attendance—80,997.

Radio and TV—National Broadcasting Company (TV and radio).

Regular-Season Records—Pittsburgh, 10–3–1; Minnesota, 10–4.

Playoff Records— Pittsburgh defeated Buffalo Bills, 32–14, and Oakland Raiders, 24–13, for AFC title; Minnesota defeated St. Louis Cardinals, 30–14, and Los Angeles Rams, 14–10, for NFC title.

Players' Shares—$15,000 to each member of winning team; $7,500 to each member of losing team.

Coaches—Chuck Noll, Pittsburgh; Bud Grant, Minnesota.

TIME FOR THE STEELERS

By Art Rooney's standards, the Super Bowl was a young upstart, wet behind the ears and lacking in tradition. No matter how big a deal the game had become among Americans—many of whom found it difficult to believe football even existed before the Super Bowl—Rooney knew it represented only the most recent chapter in the sport's history.

Art Rooney, the seventy-four-year-old patriarch of the Pittsburgh Steelers, could have written the history of pro football himself. He was a founding father of the NFL, one of the owners in the days when they were sportsmen whose lives revolved around the game, not businessmen to whom a football team was a toy and tax write-off.

The Rooney family, as well as the Maras in New York and Halases in Chicago, were the foundation of the league, but in recent years none were able to field teams capable of enjoying the rising popularity that the NFL was enjoying. Rooney, especially, had spent forty-two frustrating years without winning a title.

But in 1974, at long last, Rooney had that elusive first championship. The young and aggressive Pittsburgh Steelers culminated a six-year rebuilding plan when they defeated the Oakland Raiders, 24–13, to win the American Conference crown and earn a berth in Super Bowl IX.

"I'm feeling a lot of gratitude toward our players and coaches," Rooney said. "It's the biggest win in my life because it was so long coming. It's like how Halas and Mara and the rest of them must have felt when they were winning."

Super Bowl IX was returning to New Orleans, which had become the fans' favorite site for the game. With its glorious restaurants, Dixieland jazz bands, and notorious nightspots, Super Bowl week was an exciting, if decadent, occasion, marked by twenty-hour days and four hours of sleep.

Even for the teams, the atmosphere seemed more charged. Super Bowl IX was one of the more anticipated games because the Steelers were a fresh face, and their owner was an older but revered one.

Art Rooney had passed on the management of the team to his sons Dan and Art. They had hired Chuck Noll—an assistant to Don Shula—in 1969 after failing to persuade a big-name coach to take the Steelers' job. It wasn't very attractive at the time, given the history of losing and what was considered the Rooney family's old-fashioned ways.

But hiring Noll proved to be stroke of genius. He lost thirteen of fourteen games in his first year but had begun the rebuilding process, discarding many veterans. The Steelers were competitive in the next two seasons, then won a division championship in 1972 and 1973. Still, when they lost in the playoffs, the losers' image clung and it seemed as if fate were teasing Art Rooney.

Finally, after a shaky beginning marked by an unsettled quarterback situation, the Steelers finished with a flourish, dominating their opponents with a stingy defense nicknamed the "Steel Curtain" and an improving offense that had both big-play and ball-control capabilities. The players were also motivated by their fondness for Art Rooney, who treated them like members of his family rather than employees. Rooney often entertained groups of players for dinner.

What made the appearance of the Steelers even more welcome in New Orleans was the fact that their opponents were the Minnesota Vikings, who were in their third Super Bowl game, two in succession. By now the Vikings were becoming somewhat frustrated. Their dominance in the National Conference was unquestioned, yet they were labeled as losers because they had failed in two previous Super Bowl games.

No team that had lost in its first appearance—not Oakland, Kansas City, Baltimore, Dallas, or Miami—failed to win in its second try, except for the Vikings. For Minnesota, it was not a particularly pleasing footnote to Super Bowl history.

What's more, the Vikings were an aging team, with eight of the twenty-two starters on offense and defense having passed their thirtieth birthdays. In comparison, only two of the Steelers' starters were thirty or older. Frank Tarkenton was thirty-four years old, scrambling less than in his younger days, and still labeled a loser. There were those who thought this might be the Vikings' final fling.

Despite their youthful enthusiasm, the Steelers were not a clear-cut choice to win. Only the Green Bay Packers and New York Jets had won the Super Bowl in their first appearance, and in each case, their opponents—Kansas City and Baltimore—were also playing for the first time. Given the circuslike atmosphere and pressure of a big game, the older Vikings seemed to be better prepared for a week of media mania in New Orleans.

The Steelers, like most NFL teams, designed their offense around the running game, especially because their three quarterbacks, Terry Bradshaw, Terry Hanratty, and Joe Gilliam, were inexperienced. Franco Harris, a swift and strong fullback, had gained more than 1,000 yards during the season. Rocky Bleier, a likable Vietnam War veteran, was a dependable blocker and a good running sidekick as well.

But Noll knew that Bradshaw's potential brilliance could make the Steelers a more passing-oriented team. The blond quarterback from Louisiana Tech had a golden arm as well—the strongest, it was said, since Joe Namath. But Bradshaw was inconsistent and had a reputation for not being able to understand the Steelers' playbook.

So it was Gilliam, another strong-arm passer, who was the starter when the season opened. But he, too, struggled, and after six games Noll decided to go with

Bradshaw, despite the fact the Steelers had lost only once.

The fifth-year quarterback was more self-assured this time. The Steelers' offense flourished as Bradshaw began connecting on long passes to Lynn Swann, a small but nimble rookie wide receiver from USC, and John Stallworth, a bigger but equally fast rookie from Alabama A&M. Bradshaw also relied upon veteran wide receiver Frank Lewis and tight end Larry Brown, thus giving Pittsburgh one of the strongest passing games in the NFL.

With Franco on the run and Bradshaw through the air, opposing defenses did not know how to contain the offense. As imposing as the Steelers were when they had the football, they were even more menacing on defense.

Mean Joe Greene, a defensive tackle, was the foundation. Rookie middle linebacker Jack Lambert was the spirit, and outside linebacker Andy Russell was the experience. The Steelers shut down the vaunted Raiders' offense in the AFC championship game as they had stopped opponents all year long.

The Vikings certainly were not going to be intimidated by the Steelers. They were counting on their experience and the law of averages. Tarkenton had capable receivers and a hardworking running back, Chuck Foreman, who was rated as good as any in the NFL. The Purple Gang defense might be getting a little gray, but Carl Eller, Alan Page, Roy Winston, and Paul Krause still formed the nucleus of one of the better defensive units in pro football.

Thus, it was with a great deal of intrigue that football fans awaited this confrontation between the old guard and the young lions in another Battle of New Orleans.

The weather on Super Bowl Sunday was predictably unpredictable for New Orleans. Winds were gusting at twenty-five miles an hour when the teams appeared on the field. The reporters thought that would favor the Vikings, because Tarkenton relied more on a short passing game, while Bradshaw liked to throw deep.

It was more than the wind that played havoc with

each team's offense in the first quarter. Noll and Bud Grant, the Vikings' coach, were conservative, and it was evident from the opening kickoff as both teams relied on the running game. The Steelers had more success moving the football, but neither team could score in the first quarter.

Tarkenton had not been able to do much against the Dolphins' defense in Super Bowl VIII, and now The Scrambler was being stymied again. Midway through the second quarter, the Vikings were on their 10-yard line, but Tarkenton decided it was no time to play safe with straight-ahead running plays.

Instead, he pitched back to Dave Osborn, who would try to get around that impregnable Steel Curtain. But Tarkenton's pitch was off target and rolled into the end zone. He fell on the ball to prevent the Steelers

The Steelers' Steel Curtain came down on Fran Tarkenton.

UPI

from scoring a touchdown, but it did result in a safety. At halftime, the score in Super Bowl IX would have been more fitting for a World Series game: Steelers 2, Vikings 0.

Bill Brown, a reserve running back for the Vikings, picked up a bouncing second-half kickoff and returned it to the 32-yard line but fumbled when he was hit. Marv Kellum of the Steelers recovered on the Minnesota 30.

Now Pittsburgh had its best scoring opportunity of the game. Still, Bradshaw was instructed to be conservative. Bleier took a handoff and was stopped for no gain. Even the Steelers fans were becoming impatient. They had expected Bradshaw to pass, trying for the quick score to discourage the Vikings. On second down, however, the quarterback handed off again, this time to Harris.

And this time with different results. The big fullback rumbled through an opening and ran 24 yards to the Minnesota 6. There was no changing the strategy now. Harris carried again but lost 3 yards.

On second-and-goal from the 9-yard line, with the Vikings looking for a pass, Bradshaw handed off to Harris, who burst into the end zone for the long-awaited first touchdown of the game. Roy Gerela's conversion gave the Steelers a 9–0 lead.

The lead held into the fourth quarter, when the Vikings finally got a break of their own. Harris fumbled and Krause recovered at the Pittsburgh 47-yard line. Tarkenton didn't bother with any running plays. He threw long for John Gilliam, and it resulted in a pass interference penalty against Mike Wagner, the Pittsburgh safety.

The Vikings had a first down on the 5-yard line. Tarkenton now handed off to Foreman, who fumbled, The Steelers recovered, and the Minnesota bench was glum.

Then the Vikings got a second break when Matt Blair blocked a punt by Pittsburgh's Bobby Walden, and Terry Brown recovered in the end zone for a Minnesota touchdown. But the comedy of errors continued as the conversion was missed. Still, the score was 9–6, and the Vikings were very much in the game.

This is when the Steelers' offense asserted itself. Bradshaw led the team on an 8-minute ball-control drive that wasted the clock and put the Steelers in position to score again. With less than 3 minutes to play, Bradshaw rolled out and threw a 4-yard touchdown pass to Larry Brown.

The Steelers' led, 16–6, which was the final score. Franco Harris was the Most Valuable Player, having gained 158 yards in 34 carries, breaking Larry Csonka's record set the previous year.

But the big winner was Art Rooney—at long last.

"The coaches and players were like the fans all week," Rooney said. "They were so confident. And after being with these fellows all year, I thought we could win, too."

FRANCO HARRIS
The Italian Army

When Franco Harris joined Pittsburgh in 1972, there was a good measure of concern on both sides.

Despite impressive credentials at Penn State, Harris left some observers with the feeling that he didn't always put out with his best effort. Harris, for his part, wasn't happy about going to a team that never had won anything.

In the first year of their partnership, both sides had reason to be satisfied. Harris tied an NFL record held by Jim Brown of rushing for more than 100 yards in six successive games, and the Steelers responded by claiming the first playoff berth in their four-decade history.

Reaching the playoffs became an annual affair for the Steelers during Harris' reign, and they won the Super Bowl four times in six years. It was in Super Bowl IX that Harris was chosen MVP after he paced Pittsburgh to its 16–6 victory over Minnesota.

Harris, one of nine children in a family of black-Italian ancestry, was an immediate favorite of the Pittsburgh fans and was the inspiration for Franco's Italian Army, formed during his rookie year.

Although Harris rolled up 12,120 rushing yards (third on the all-time list) by the time he left the NFL in 1984, including eight years when he exceeded 1,000 yards, he never led the league. But he took with him sole ownership or a share of twenty-four NFL records, many of them for postseason and Super Bowl competition.

Harris maintained a low profile and was one of the

most private of the Steelers. This, at times, led to others taking him for granted, yet he was the only NFL player named to the Pro Bowl team every year from 1972 to 1980.

Harris had an unusual running style, blending a fullback's size and a halfback's speed, and he was an excellent blocker.

"I like to think that if you need one or two yards for a first down, I can get it for you, and I have the speed to go outside," he said. "I guess I'm the kind of runner for whatever has to be done."

Scoring Summary

Pittsburgh Steelers (AFC)	0	2	7	7—16
Minnesota Vikings (NFC)	0	0	0	6—6

Pittsburgh—White (safety) downed Tarkenton in end zone

Pittsburgh—Harris, run 9 (Gerela kick)

Minnesota—T. Brown, recovered blocked punt in end zone

Pittsburgh—L. Brown, pass from Bradshaw 4 (Gerela kick)

SUPER BOWL X

AFTERNOON OF A SWANN

Dallas' Ed (Too Tall) Jones confronts Pittsburgh's Terry Bradshaw in Super Bowl X.

UPI

Participants—Pittsburgh Steelers, champions of the American Football Conference, and Dallas Cowboys, champions of the National Football Conference.

Date—January 18, 1976.

Site—Orange Bowl Stadium, Miami, Florida.

Time—2:00 P.M., EST.

Attendance—80,187.

Radio and TV—Columbia Broadcasting System (TV and radio).

Regular-Season Records—Pittsburgh, 12–2; Dallas, 10–4.

Playoff Records—Pittsburgh defeated Baltimore Colts, 28–10, and Oakland Raiders, 16–10, for AFC title; Dallas defeated Minnesota Vikings, 17–4, and Los Angeles Rams, 37–7, for NFC title.

Players' Shares—$15,000 to each member of winning team; $7,500 to each member of losing them.

Coaches—Chuck Noll, Pittsburgh; Tom Landry, Dallas.

SUPER BOWL X

AFTERNOON OF A SWANN

In January 1976 there was more than just another Super Bowl game to celebrate. This was Super Bowl X, a special anniversary, and during the week when the Pittsburgh Steelers talked about trying to repeat as champions and the Dallas Cowboys reflected on their own storied past, the players on those teams shared the spotlight with memories of earlier Super Bowl heroes.

After nine Super Bowls, the championship game actually had something to be nostalgic about, whether it was Joe Namath of the New York Jets guaranteeing victory against the Baltimore Colts in Super Bowl III, "run silent, run deep" Duane Thomas of the Cowboys in Super Bowl VI, Miami Dolphins' placekicker Garo Yepremian's ill-advised pass attempt in Super Bowl VII, or simply the circumstances surrounding the very first Super Bowl when the NFL was represented by the Green Bay Packers and their legendary coach, Vince Lombardi.

The magnitude of the event and the enormous buildup had made it almost impossible for the game itself to live up to expectations, but still the television audience for the Super Bowl was growing. Warm-weather cities lobbied for the chance to play host.

Super Bowl X gave indications that it might be the most memorable since the Jets of the old American Football League upset the Colts in 1969. The Steelers had entered Super Bowl IX touted as the young, relatively inexperienced team that was expected to have difficulty adjusting to the unusual surroundings.

Now, a year later, the Steelers were the old pros—the most formidable team in pro football—having made the playoffs five consecutive times and vying for a second consecutive Super Bowl title, which would enable them to equal the accomplishments of Green Bay and the Miami Dolphins.

The Cowboys were no strangers to this game, having played in Super Bowls V and VI. But in the four-year interval, they had undergone a number of changes in personnel and now were described as a young team that had capitalized on a wild-card berth in the playoffs.

But while the Cowboys roster may have undergone a number of changes, Tom Landry was still the familiar stone-faced visage on the sideline, a respected and highly successful coach. And Roger Staubach, the artful dodger who had led Dallas to victory in Super Bowl VI, had matured into one of the finest signal-callers in the league.

There was also the hope among fans that Super Bowl X would provide the offensive display that had been lacking in previous games. Although the Steelers' defense was perhaps the best ever assembled in NFL history, and the Cowboys' intricate "flex defense" boasted some of the highly regarded young prospects in Harvey Martin, Ed "Too Tall" Jones, and Randy White, people were excited by the daring and resourcefulness of quarterbacks Staubach and Terry Bradshaw.

Staubach often operated out of the shotgun formation, passing to speedy wide receivers such as Golden Richards, Drew Pearson, and the tight ends Jean Fugett and Billy Joe DuPree. Robert Newhouse and Preston Pearson, a former Steeler, were not breakaway runners but dependable backs capable of having a big day.

Bradshaw, in his sixth season, had become the most heralded passer in the NFL. No longer was he criticized for not grasping coach Chuck Noll's offensive philosophy, no longer was he prone to interceptions, a result of relying too much on his strong arm. Bradshaw had suffered only nine interceptions in the 1975 season and completed nearly 58 percent of his passes as the Steelers finished 12–2.

Lynn Swann and John Stallworth had developed into superior receivers, although Noll still counted on the rambling runs by fullback Franco Harris, who rushed for 1,246 yards during the regular season. And Rocky Bleier, the sure-handed, if slow-footed, back whose primary job was to block for Harris, even gained 163 yards in a game against Green Bay.

It would be a shame if those offenses were kept under wraps by the respective coaches, each of whom decided to play the Super Bowl waiting game, which meant waiting for the other team to make a mistake.

But even if the air was filled with passes, there was no guarantee there would be many touchdowns. The Steelers' defense, especially, appeared to have no flaws. Mean Joe Green anchored a front four that hounded opposing quarterbacks unmercifully. Ernie Holmes, L. C. Greenwood, and Dwight White were his partners.

The key to the defensive unit might have been the play of the linebackers. Jack Lambert, Andy Russell, and Jack Ham were not big by NFL standards, but all played as if they weighed twenty-five pounds more. They were lean and mean, especially Lambert, the second-year pro from Kent State who said:

"My favorite thing about football is to hit people and watch them as they lie on the ground."

The linebackers were all quick, which helped them on pass coverages and when they occasionally blitzed. "They are three different types of people off the field," said Woody Widenhofer, the Steelers' linebacker coach, "but they blend together when the game starts. Each one is great."

Obviously, an agile quarterback who can run would be the most effective against the "Steel Curtain." Staubach was just such a quarterback. He was in his seventh year, a veteran on a team that included twelve rookies. The Cowboys had not only remained competitive while rebuilding, they had become NFC champions as well.

"I've enjoyed coaching this season more than any, I believe, since 1966 when we first started winning," said the stoic Landry. "It's been a pleasure working with a team which has such hustle and a good attitude. We've had no serious internal problems, which speaks well for the character of the players."

Staubach provided the leadership on the field as well as the big plays that enabled the Cowboys to win several games that seemed out of reach. "He's done more than ever for us," Landry said.

Staubach played in pain, too, which earned him further respect from his teammates. Because of his penchant for running and the dangers that await a scrambling quarterback, he had suffered cracked ribs, a jammed shoulder, a bruised elbow, and a badly sprained right thumb. And he continued to play, finishing second among the NFC's quarterbacks.

There were more than 80,000 fans in the Orange Bowl on January 18, when Super Bowl X was played. Unfortunately, there were an additional 5,000 fans who had purchased travel packages to Miami, which were to include airfare, hotel room, and tickets for the game, who were left stranded. The tickets never showed up.

Thus, these fans sat in their hotel rooms and watched on television the game they had come many miles to see. In the first quarter there was an unexpected turn of events when Bobby Walden, the Steelers' punter, fumbled a snap and Dallas recovered on Pittsburgh's 29-yard line.

It took only one play for the Cowboys to score as Staubach threw a perfect pass across the middle to Drew Pearson, who trotted into the end zone for a touchdown.

The Steelers' offense began moving later in the quarter as Bradshaw directed a drive from his 33-yard line. It was typical Steeler strategy—Harris and Bleier softening the defense—before Bradshaw connected with the graceful Swann, who caught the ball between two defenders for a 32-yard gain.

Two weeks earlier, the five-eleven, 180-pound Swann had been knocked unconscious in the AFC championship game, against Oakland. He was hospitalized with a concussion. Privately the Steelers worried about how he would react in his next game. Lynn Swann gave them his answer with that pass reception.

The Steelers' Lynn Swann makes a diving catch against the Cowboys' Mark Washington.

UPI

With a first down on the Dallas 16-yard line, two running plays moved the ball to the 7, where Bradshaw threw a scoring pass to tight end Randy Grossman. The score was tied 7–7,

The respective defenses controlled the game in the second quarter, but it was the Cowboys who went into the locker room at halftime with the lead. Staubach drove his team 46 yards in 11 plays, setting up a 36-yard field goal by Toni Fritsch. That made it 10–7 at halftime.

The Steelers had the best opportunity to score in the third quarter, but Roy Gerela missed a field goal attempt, his second miss of the game. Entering the fourth quarter, the game had become another defensive struggle.

The Steelers' special teams provided some needed points early in the final quarter when Reggie Harrison blocked a punt by Mitch Hoopes. The ball rolled out of the end zone, resulting in a safety for Pittsburgh and trimming the Dallas lead to 10–9.

The Steelers retained possession, and Bradshaw marched them into field-goal range, where Gerela was successful from 3 yards out. Pittsburgh led, 12–10, and although the margin was hardly safe, the Steelers had begun to assume control.

Staubach, perhaps sensing a change in the tempo of the game, tried to spark his team with some big plays. But Mike Wagner intercepted a pass and set up an 18-yard field goal by Gerela. With 4:25 to play, the Steelers' lead was now 15–10.

But Dallas was only a touchdown away from reclaiming that lead. The Steelers' offense—despite its respect for the "Steel Curtain"—did not want to place the burden of protecting that slim advantage on the defense. With the offense in possession, Swann asked Bradshaw to forget about trying to run out the clock and throw him a long pass instead.

With third down on his 36-yard line, Bradshaw did just what Swann ordered as he dropped back and spotted Swann streaking downfield toward the end zone. The quarterback never saw the result of his effort. As Bradshaw threw to Swann, he was hit by Cliff Harris on a safety blitz and knocked senseless.

Meanwhile, Swann cut between defenders, and using his great leaping ability, he jumped and caught Bradshaw's pass at the 5-yard line, then spun into the end zone for a touchdown. The conversion attempt failed, but the Steelers led, 21–10.

The Cowboys did not give up, however. Staubach led them on an 80-yard drive in just 5 plays, culminating in a 34-yard touchdown pass to a reserve, Percy Howard. And with 1:22 still to play, Dallas had possession again, trailing 21–17.

Finally, a Super Bowl game worthy of its title. Staubach scrambled for 11 yards and then completed a pass to Preston Pearson for 12 more. Dallas had a first down at the Steelers' 38-yard line with less than 1 minute to play.

Two passes fell incomplete. On third down, Staubach went for the touchdown, trying to hit Drew Pearson near the end zone, But Glen Edwards stepped in front of Pearson for the interception that preserved the

Jubilant fans climbed atop a city bus during the wild celebration in Pittsburgh following the team's Super Bowl triumph.

UPI

Steelers' second consecutive Super Bowl triumph.

Although he caught only four passes, Swann was named Most Valuable Player. In this case, it was not quantity that counted, but the quality of his work.

LYNN SWANN
Born to Leap

In both size and style, Lynn Swann stood out from the typical football player.

At five-eleven and about 175 pounds, he was one of the smaller men to endure the violent world of the NFL, let alone to emerge as a superstar.

He was also strong enough of heart to publicly challenge the unnecessary brutality of the game, and it was Swann's shout of rage in 1976 that led to new regulations protecting the more vulnerable players.

"I'm glad I took a stand," Swann said. "I never played football to prove my manhood."

Suave, gregarious, and self-assured, Swann is a man of many talents, all of which helped establish him as perhaps the game's premier wide receiver on a Pittsburgh Steeler team that won the Super Bowl four times.

From his childhood in San Mateo, California, and through high school, Swann studied dancing, ranging from tap to ballet and modern jazz, and as a USC All-American he won the California long jump championship with a leap of twenty-five feet two inches.

He thus brought a dancer's grace along with great timing and agility to the football field.

"I was always the smallest, so I had to learn to play a smarter game," Swann said, and former teammate Rocky Bleier added, "Lynn is the first receiver who combines the technician's precision and speed."

In Super Bowl X, Swann caught four passes for a then record 161 yards, including the winning touchdown pass, to earn MVP honors in Pittsburgh's 21–17 victory over Dallas.

Swann, who had suffered a concussion two weeks earlier, wasn't even sure until minutes before the game that he would be able to play. He'd been hit by George Atkinson of the Oakland Raiders. Curiously, eight months later, in the opening game of the 1976 season, Swann suffered another concussion on a blow by Atkinson, prompting him to attack "intentional acts of violence." Although he considered retiring then, Swann came back and played until 1982.

Scoring Summary

Dallas Cowboys (NFC)	7	3	0	7—17
Pittsburgh Steelers (AFC)	7	0	0	14—21

Dallas—D. Pearson, pass from Staubach 29 (Fritsch kick)

Pittsburgh—Grossman, pass from Bradshaw 7 (Gerela kick)

Dallas—Fritsch (FG) 36

Pittsburgh—Harrison (safety) blocked Hoopes's punt through end zone

Pittsburgh—Gerela (FG) 36

Pittsburgh—Gerela (FG) 18

Pittsburgh—Swann, pass from Bradshaw 64

Dallas—P. Howard, pass from Staubach 34 (Fritsch kick)

SUPER BOWL XI

A FIRST FOR THE
REBEL RAIDERS

Coach John Madden and his bearded rebel quarterback, Kenny Stabler, personified the irreverant Raider image in Super Bowl XI.

UPI

Participants—Oakland Raiders, champions of the American Football Conference, and Minnesota Vikings, champions of the National Football Conference.

Date—January 9, 1977.

Site—Rose Bowl, Pasadena, California.

Time—12:30 P.M., PST,

Attendance—103,438.

Radio and TV— National Broadcasting Company (TV and radio).

Regular-Season Records—Oakland, 13–1; Minnesota, 11–2–1.

Playoff Records—Oakland defeated New England Patriots, 24–21, and Pittsburgh Steelers, 24–7, for AFC title; Minnesota defeated Washington Redskins, 35–20, and Los Angeles Rams, 24–13, for NFC title.

Players' Shares—$15,000 to each member of winning team; $7,500 to each member of losing team.

Coaches—John Madden, Oakland; Bud Grant, Minnesota.

SUPER BOWL XI

FIRST FOR THE
REBEL RAIDERS

The cynics were having a field day. There was a chance, they said, that Super Bowl XI could end in a tie. Sudden-death overtime made that an impossibility, of course, but when it was determined that the Oakland Raiders and the Minnesota Vikings would be playing for the pro football championship, it was easy to understand why some fans wondered whether either team was capable of winning the ultimate game.

The Raiders and Vikings were actually victims of their extraordinary success. These were two of the winningest franchises in the NFL, but the irony was that success equaled failure. For all the division titles and conference championships between them, neither the Raiders nor the Vikings had won a Super Bowl game. Each was saddled with the reputation for not being able to win the big one.

Only one team does win the big game every year. Still, these two teams were perceived as the NFL's uncrowned champions. The Raiders had won nine divisional titles in ten years in the American Conference West but stumbled in the playoffs every year but one, when they were defeated by the Green Bay Packers in Super Bowl II. Six times the Raiders had lost in the AFC championship game, and all six times the winner was also the Super Bowl champion.

The Vikings had won eight NFC Central Division titles in nine years and advanced to the Super Bowl three times, losing each game. Super Bowl XI was the Vikings' fourth appearance, the most of any team, but all the fans could talk about was their failure to win one of these games with the fancy Roman numerals.

Well, there would be a Hollywood ending for at least one of the teams on January 9, 1977, in Pasadena, California. The Super Bowl had returned to Los Angeles—to the land of sunshine and avocados, freeways and starlets. To the hundreds of reporters covering the game, it would be a time to study their road maps and perhaps hire a tour guide.

The press accommodations were at a hotel near the Los Angeles airport. The Raiders trained in Newport Beach, forty-five miles southeast of the hotel. The Vikings stayed in Costa Mesa, only five miles from the Raiders, but they practiced in Long Beach, which required a twenty-five-mile bus ride every day.

The game would be played in the Rose Bowl, which was situated about forty miles north of the media headquarters. This was indeed the freeway Super Bowl.

Perhaps it was just as well that the reporters were not too close to the Vikings. This was a sullen group that arrived in Los Angeles the week before the game. The players felt that they should be applauded for making the Super Bowl almost one of their regularly scheduled games every year, but they knew that the reporters would be asking about why they had failed to win in the past.

The ornery dispositions and curt remarks were in contrast to the cold statements the Vikings had made after defeating the Los Angeles Rams to win the NFC championship. "Nothing can stop us now," said Carl Eller, the veteran defensive lineman.

"This is the best football team I ever played on," said Fran Tarkenton, the aging but still resourceful quarterback. "I've said that before, and I feel even better about the club now. We're peaking at the right time."

Bud Grant, Minnesota's taciturn coach, was even moved to say, "This team has more firepower and depth than before and a new dimension of emotion."

But once they settled at their hotel and began another week of Super Bowl hoopla, the Vikings became defensive. Tarkenton, always so glib and cooperative with reporters, chided some of them for asking what he felt were dumb questions. At thirty-six years of age, The Scrambler was probably thinking that this would be his last opportunity to win a championship.

The Raiders, on the other hand, never apologized for not winning the Super Bowl. They were considered the black sheep of the NFL, a team whose owner, Al Davis, was once in the forefront of the merger war between the NFL and the old American Football League. Davis was part of the establishment now, but still a plain-talking, street-wise guy from Brooklyn, who enjoyed giving Commissioner Pete Rozelle a hard time. Davis reminded people of what the television character "Fonzie" would have been like as an adult.

The Raiders lived up to their insignia, a skull and crossbones and eyepatch. They were a mix of superbly scouted young players from the college ranks and discarded NFL veterans who were thought to be over the hill or disciplinary problems. All found a home in Oakland, which itself was a city that paled in comparison to its next-door neighbor, San Francisco, the City by the Bay.

Davis and his coaching staff did not care about a player's past or his off-the-field life, as long as he was ready to perform on Sunday. John Madden, the heavy-set and highly emotional coach, was only thirty-three years old when he took over in 1969, and he compiled an 83–22–7 record. There were those who said he was simply Davis' puppet, but Madden ignored such talk.

He might rant and rave and hotly argue a point with a reporter, but behind the bluster he was an engaging and fun-loving man who did not believe in running a football operation as if it were a branch of the military. It was not a system that could work for every team, but the Raiders thrived.

Also contrary to NFL belief, the Raiders built their offense around the passing game. Ken Stabler, nick-named "The Snake" for the way he ran while in high school, did not have the strongest arm in football, but he was one of the more accurate passers in the league. The thirty-year-old Stabler was a left-hander who had completed 66.7 percent of his passes during the regular season to rank second only to Sammy Baugh in

NFL history. In 1945, Baugh completed 70.3 percent of his passes.

Stabler built this impressive record by throwing short- and medium-range passes to running backs Clarence Davis and Mark van Eeghen and to his trusty wide receiver, Fred Biletnikoff, who lacked speed but ran precision patterns. When "The Snake" did throw long, more often than not it was to Cliff Branch, the fastest Raider.

In fact, unlike their previous appearances, the Vikings actually had more game-breaking speed than the Raiders. Ahmad Rashad and rookie Sammy White gave Tarkenton two fast deep threats, and running back Chuck Foreman was regarded as perhaps the best all-around back in the NFL.

Foreman was the catalyst on offense now that Tarkenton was not the mad scrambler of his youth. In the regular season, Foreman rushed for 1,155 yards and caught 55 passes for an additional 567 yards. He scored 14 touchdowns. "He is strong enough to go inside and quick enough to go outside," Grant said. "He does everything well. No one is better at a combination of everything."

"He is the most valuable player in the football world," Tarkenton said.

Thus, in a game that would pit two strong defensive units and quarterbacks who relied more on ball-control passing attacks, Foreman began to look like the difference. And as a relatively quiet Super Bowl week in rainy Southern California came to an end, the Vikings were hoping to bury their losers' image at last.

According to the scripture as written by Pete Rozelle, the sun broke through the clouds on January 9, and the snowcapped mountains made a beautiful backdrop for the Rose Bowl stadium. There were 103,438 fans in attendance to watch one of these teams finally win the big game.

Although the Raiders had earned a reputation for doing the unorthodox, they, too, fell into the Super Bowl trap by playing conservatively early in the game. In the first quarter, they were forced to punt, and Ray Guy's attempt was blocked by Fred McNeill of the

Vikings, who recovered the ball on the Oakland 3-yard line.

Tarkenton clapped his hands and led the offense on the field, confident his team soon would take the lead. But on second down, Brent McClanahan fumbled, and linebacker Willie Hall recovered for the Raiders. A sense of frustration came over the Vikings. Could it be happening again?

Stabler then guided the Raiders 97 yards in a time-consuming drive that resulted in a 24-yard field goal by Errol Mann. Early in the second quarter, Oakland led, 3–0.

When they regained possession, Stabler departed from his season-long game plan and concentrated on the running game. Larry Csonka of Miami and Franco Harris of Pittsburgh had hammered the Vikings' excellent but undersized defensive line and linebackers in previous Super Bowls, and although Oakland did not have a running back in their class, their offensive line was massive and Clarence Davis found the holes.

Midway through the second quarter, Carl Garrett, subbing for Davis, slashed off tackle for 13 yards, then carried twice more for 7 on a Raider drive. With third down and the Vikings looking for another running play, Stabler rolled out and threw a short pass to Biletnikoff, who made a sliding catch on the 1-yard line for a first down.

On the next play, Stabler threw to tight end Dave Casper in the end zone, and Oakland led, 10–0.

After holding the Vikings again, the Raiders took over at the Minnesota 35-yard line following a 25-yard punt return by Neal Colzie. David and van Eeghen carried to the 18-yard line before Stabler found Biletnikoff again, connecting on a 17-yard pass. Once more, it was just a yard short of the end zone.

Pete Banaszak, the dependable backup fullback, scored on the next play, and the Raiders led, 16–0. Super Bowl XI had all the earmarks of a rout.

During halftime, the characters from Disneyland joined 1,400 high school musicians for a spectacular show. Some of the fans wondered whether Mickey Mouse was playing for the Vikings.

Oakland wide receiver Fred Biletnikoff set up 3 touchdowns with catches that twice put him on the 1-yard line and once on the 4.

UPI

Quickly the Raiders increased their lead in the third quarter when Mann kicked a 40-yard field goal. But now Tarkenton came to life, leading the Vikings on a scoring drive that ended when he threw an 8-yard touchdown pass to White. The Raiders' lead was trimmed to 19–7.

The Vikings came right back to threaten again as Tarkenton passed to tight end Stu Voigt for a first down at the Oakland 44-yard line. But misfortune struck again as Tarkenton's next pass was picked off by Hall, who returned it to the Minnesota 46.

Stabler did not waste time with running plays now. He quickly fired a pass to Biletnikoff, who huffed and puffed to the 2-yard line before he was caught. A total of 4 yards had deprived the receiver of 3 touchdowns. Banaszak did the honors again, scoring his second

Raider fullback Pete Banaszak celebrates his second touchdown.

UPI

touchdown to give the Raiders a comfortable 26–7 lead.

Tarkenton began to throw in desperation as the fourth quarter unfolded. And as so often happens in

those circumstances, his pass was intercepted. Veteran
cornerback Willie Brown, a member of the Raiders'
first Super Bowl team, ran 75 yards for a touchdown.
The score was 32–7, and only 5 minutes remained.

   To the Vikings' credit, they did not give up. They
added a consolation touchdown on a Bob Lee pass to
Stu Voigt, making the final score 32–14. But on the
bench in the last 2 minutes, a distraught Foreman
became angered when several Viking fans chastised
the team for losing again.

   "They said all kinds of things that torment a man,"
Foreman said.

   On the other side of the field, several Raiders strained
to lift the 250-pound Madden on their shoulders. One
of football's uncrowned champions had finally won the
Super Bowl. Davis had gained 137 yards rushing, and
Biletnikoff's timely catches had earned him the Most
Valuable Player award. But the happiest man was Al
Davis, the rebel owner who became a member of a
very exclusive club.

FRED BILETNIKOFF
Unlikely Hero

To Fred Biletnikoff, it was simply a question of semantics. His critics said he was too slow to be a standout receiver, and he countered that his supposed lack of speed was deceptive.

"I've always been quick," Biletnikoff would answer. "My moves are faster than my feet, so I have to take advantage of what God gave me."

Take advantage he did. Criticism notwithstanding, Biletnikoff enjoyed a highly successful fourteen-year career with the Oakland Raiders, and by the time he retired in 1978 he was rated among the top five pass receivers in NFL history. He averaged 15.2 yards for 589 career catches, accounting for 8,974 yards and 76 touchdowns.

Although he was the strong, silent type, physically and mentally tough, Biletnikoff suffered inside for his success. He developed an ulcer when he was only twenty-one, he frequently bit his nails until they bled, and it wasn't unusual for him to throw up before a game.

Biletnikoff never took his ability for granted. He drove himself relentlessly and during the early part of his career would become enraged by his mistakes. He spent hours on the practice field catching balls and in his spare time worked out with a punching bag to improve his hand-eye coordination.

"I know what I can do and what I can't do," he said. "My greatest attribute is being consistent. Know what you can do, work on that, and you'll help your team."

That was the way it was at Florida State, where he

was a pass-catching sensation and where, incidentally, he married his first wife under the goalposts. And that was the way it was in the pros.

For ten consecutive years Biletnikoff recorded forty or more catches, and he was chosen to play in the Pro Bowl four times. His finest moment came in Super Bowl XI when the Raiders routed the Minnesota Vikings, 32–14; Biletnikoff was voted the game MVP after he caught 4 passes for 79 yards. Three of the catches set up touchdowns.

"I wouldn't care if the award were a stick of gum," Biletnikoff said. "It's the biggest thing to happen to me as a pro."

Scoring Summary

Oakland Raiders (AFC)	0	16	3	13—32
Minnesota Vikings (NFC)	0	0	7	7—14

Oakland—Mann (FG) 24
Oakland—Casper, pass from Stabler 1 (Mann kick)
Oakland—Banaszak, run 1
Oakland—Mann (FG) 40
Minnesota—S. White, pass from Tarkenton 8 (Cox kick)
Oakland—Banaszak, run 2 (Mann kick)
Oakland—Brown, interception 75
Minnesota—Voigt, pass from Lee 13 (Cox kick)

SUPER BOWL XII

CRUSHING THE ORANGE

The Cowboys' Randy Martin puts the crush on Bronco quarterback Craig Martin in Super Bowl XII.

Participants—Denver Broncos, champions of the American Football Conference, and Dallas Cowboys, champions of the National Football Conference.

Date—January 15, 1978.

Site—Louisiana Superdome, New Orleans, Louisiana.

Time—5:00 P.M., CST.

Attendance—75,804.

Radio and TV—Columbia Broadcasting System (TV and radio).

Regular-Season Records—Denver, 12–2; Dallas, 12–2.

Playoff Records—Denver defeated Pittsburgh Steelers, 34–21, and Oakland Raiders, 20–17, for AFC title; Dallas defeated Chicago Bears, 37–7, and Minnesota Vikings, 23–6, for NFC title.

Players' Shares—$18,000 to each member of winning team; $9,000 to each member of losing team.

Coaches—Red Miller, Denver; Tom Landry, Dallas.

CRUSHING THE ORANGE

Even for the French Quarter, this was a sight to behold. Everywhere you looked, there was orange, orange, and more orange. Every night might as well have been Halloween during the week preceding Super Bowl XII, when the boisterous fans from the "Mile High" city of Denver tried to reach that lofty altitude in the bars and nightspots on Bourbon Street,

When other teams previously earned a Super Bowl berth, there were celebrations and good times to be had by those fans who were lucky enough to purchase tickets to the game. But when the Denver Broncos beat the Oakland Raiders for the right to challenge the Dallas Cowboys in Super Bowl XII, there was no pretense of decorum.

If Dallas represented the sophisticated West, then Denver was the wild, wild West, where the pioneer spirit thrived in the Rocky Mountain setting. And during the 1977 regular season, all that frontier spirit was directed to the Broncos, who fielded their first champion in their eighteen-year existence and won the hearts and color scheme of an entire city.

The Broncos' colors were a reddish orange, but it was the orange that caught the imagination of fans. There was no escaping that color after the Broncos' outstanding defensive unit was nicknamed "The Orange Crush" after the popular soft drink.

It didn't matter that the Denver coach was named Red Miller. By the end of the season, the fifty-year-old career assistant who had won a championship in his first head-coaching job in the pros owned an orange

143

telephone, an orange toilet seat, an orange shower curtain, and an orange Christmas tree. "We are a team of destiny," said Miller.

"Broncomania" was the phrase to describe the passion that Denver felt for its football team, which finished with a 12–2 record in the regular season. On Sunday afternoons, the streets were deserted and even the police patrol cars were equipped with transistor radios so the policemen could listen to the game.

The fanaticism had an ugly side, too. A woman successfully sued a bus company because it left her stranded at a park and ride stop before the season opening game against St. Louis. When a man played the jukebox in a bar in which the patrons were watching a close game against the Baltimore Colts, he was shot to death.

The Broncos had captured imaginations early in the season when they'd trounced the Raiders, the defending Super Bowl champions. But that was considered a fluke around the NFL until the Broncos continued their string of successes. This was a team built on collegiate draft choices, a multitude of free agents, and players acquired in trades. It was a team that was thought to be in a rebuilding cycle under Miller.

Linebacker Bob Swenson was one of those free agents, a player who felt he was scorned by other teams. "The draft is bull," he said. "The scouts for most of the teams are one hundred years old and most of them don't know what they're doing."

On offense, Miller acquired Craig Morton, the thirty-four-year-old former Cowboy and New York Giant who was considered past his prime and prone to injury. The fans thought Morton would be a stopgap until a young quarterback could be groomed. Instead, the man who was the Cowboys' quarterback when they made their first Super Bowl appearance in 1971 had perhaps his most gratifying season and became a folk hero.

Morton still had a strong arm, which he used to complete passes to Haven Moses, a ten-year veteran who was discarded by the Buffalo Bills, and Riley Odoms, a big, fast, and strong tight end. He also had four capable running backs in Otis Armstrong, Lonnie Perrin, Rob Lytle, and John Keyworth.

It was the Orange Crush defense that was the focus of this team, however. The Broncos had no individual stars but were outstanding as a unit, featuring three down linemen and four linebackers. The leader was Randy Gradishar, a six-three 230-pounder from Ohio State who did not have much speed, but made up for it with intelligence and bone-rattling tackles.

The Broncos, however, were not going to be playing another Super Bowl newcomer. The Cowboys were making their fourth visit to pro football's showcase game, tying them with the Minnesota Vikings for the most appearances. Frankly, this might have been the strongest team ever to represent Dallas.

Roger Staubach, who had alternated at quarterback with Morton for several seasons, was now the grand old man of the Cowboys, only a month short of his thirty-sixth birthday. Staubach had cut down on his daring runs that used to make coach Tom Landry squirm with apprehension, but he was still an inspirational leader who retained a boyish enthusiasm for the game.

"When we made the Super Bowl in 1975, we had a young team, and Roger did more to get us there than anybody on the club," Landry said. "This year he had a lot of help. Over the long year, the defense was our main catalyst, but Roger came back strong after a few injuries. I think he's as good as any quarterback playing the game today."

Staubach, who had spent four years in the navy after attending the Naval Academy at Annapolis, played as if he were younger than his years. Perhaps those four years at sea had saved him a lot of punishment. But he also took good care of himself, living a life that made him the all-American boy.

"Right now," Staubach said, "I feel as good physically as I've ever felt. And I still enjoy so much everything about the game—the training, competing, everything."

What made Staubach enjoy the regular season even more was the arrival of Tony Dorsett, the University of Pittsburgh All-American running back, who was

**The thirty-five-year-old Roger Staubach was ready
for the big one after a season marred by injuries.**
UPI

the first real breakaway threat the Cowboys ever had.
The Cowboys gave up their four top draft picks to
Seattle—which had the first pick in the draft—in or-
der to acquire Dorsett.

Because the Dallas offense is complicated, the rookie
struggled during the first half of the season after he
had said he was certain he could step in as a starter.
Instead, he shared playing time with Preston Pearson.

But once he was ready to assume his role in the
starting backfield, Dorsett gave the Cowboys an added
dimension that also helped lessen the burden on
Staubach. "Tony D," as he was called in college, rushed
for 1,007 yards and had touchdown runs of 84 and 77
yards.

The defense, which was young and improving when
the Cowboys lost in Super Bowl X, had now become
fearsome. Ed "Too Tall" Jones, Harvey Martin, and

Randy White were an intimidating force on the defensive line, which often spent as much time in the opponents' backfield as the quarterback.

By now, fans had become accustomed to defensive struggles in the Super Bowl, and they did not expect this one to be any different. Still, it was football's greatest show on earth, and more than 75,000 fans were in attendance at the Louisiana Superdome on January 15, 1978,

Although Craig Morton numbered many of the Cowboys as his friends, they certainly weren't treating him like one once the game began. An early Bronco drive was stopped when Morton—playing on aching knees—was tackled for an 11-yard loss by White.

Later in the first quarter, Morton's pass attempt from his 29-yard line was intercepted by Randy Hughes, the Cowboys' extra defensive back in passing situations. Dallas had a first down on the Denver 25, and Staubach quickly fired a 13-yard completion to Billy Joe DuPree.

With a first down on the 12-yard line, the Cowboys turned to their running game, and Dorsett eventually scored from 3 yards out to make it 7–0.

Morton went back to work and again was under a severe rush from the Dallas front four. A hurried pass was intercepted by Aaron Kyle, who returned 19 yards to the Denver 35-yard line. Robert Newhouse powered for 9 yards, and the darting and dashing Dorsett picked up 18 more for a first down on the 8. But the Orange Crush stiffened, and the Cowboys settled for a 35-yard field goal by Efren Herrera. They now led, 10–0.

Dallas kept up the pressure early in the second quarter as Staubach drove the team back into field-goal range. Herrera connected on a 43-yarder to raise the lead to 13–0. Denver was far from being out of the game, but the Broncos seemed to be suffering from a case of stage fright in their first Super Bowl. The football kept bouncing out of their hands, and every time Morton dropped back to pass, it was like Houdini trying to make another great escape.

In order to avoid the Dallas rush, Morton often threw hurriedly. In the second quarter, his long pass for Haven Moses was intercepted by Benny Barnes. And with time running out before halftime, Morton suffered a fourth interception when Mark Washington picked off a pass. The Cowboys led at intermission, 13–0, but the margin seemed bigger.

The Broncos began to cut into the lead early in the third quarter when they drove into field-goal range for Jim Turner, the former New York Jet whose 3 field goals were the margin of difference in Super Bowl III. Turner kicked a 47-yarder to narrow the deficit to 13–3.

But the Dallas "Doomsday" defense held on the Broncos' next possession when Martin charged in to sack Morton for a 9-yard loss. The play seemed to lift the Cowboys' offense, and Staubach had the team on the move again.

With the ball on the Denver 45-yard line, he threw into the end zone, where Butch Johnson made an outstanding diving catch between two defenders. The Cowboys had struck quickly and now led, 20–3.

Sensing a need to make a dramatic move, Red Miller reluctantly benched Morton and put Norris Weese at quarterback. Weese was not a strong-armed passer, but he was mobile and better able to avoid the Dallas rush.

When Rick Upchurch returned the kickoff 67 yards to the Dallas 26-yard line, Weese rode a wave of momentum into the game. Staying on the ground, the Broncos moved in for a touchdown, which was scored by Lytle on a 1-yard run. Once again they were back in the game, trailing 20–10 as the fourth quarter began.

Landry wasn't at all pleased. This had developed into a sloppy game that reminded the coach of Super Bowl V, when Baltimore beat Dallas in "the Blooper Bowl." The Cowboys fumbled six times in Super Bowl XII but recovered four of them. The Broncos were having less success, losing all four of their fumbles in addition to the four interceptions suffered by Morton.

What also worried Landry was the loss of Dorsett, who left the game in the third quarter because of a knee injury. The coach had too much respect for his former quarterback Morton to believe that a 10-point lead was safe.

So Landry decided to throw away the Super Bowl script and use some razzle-dazzle in the fourth quarter. The Cowboys had driven into scoring range but did not want to settle for another field goal. Besides, Herrera had already missed 3. Landry sent in a rarely used play, which his team executed to perfection.

Staubach took the snap and handed off to Newhouse, the bruising fullback, who started to his left, pulled up, and stunned the Orange Crush when he tossed a 29-yard touchdown pass to wide receiver Golden Richards. "When they called the pass play I was shocked," Newhouse said. "I had stickum all over my hands so that I wouldn't fumble, but then I began to wipe my hands on my jersey and lick them to get rid of it, I never ate so much stickum in my life."

The surprise of the game came when Dallas fullback Robert Newhouse took a pitchout from Roger Staubach and flipped this pass to Golden Richards for a touchdown.

UPI

It was a meal well worth it. The touchdown gave the Cowboys an insurmountable 27–10 lead, which became the final score. It was their second Super Bowl victory. For the Broncos there was disappointment, but it did not diminish the most successful season in the team's history.

HARVEY MARTIN-
RANDY WHITE
The Harvey and
Randy Show

Coming out of high school, neither youngster could envision much of a future in football. Randy White, playing for a team in Wilmington, Delaware, that could win merely five games in two years, was recruited by only three colleges; and Harvey Martin, whose gentle soul dominated a giant's physique, wasn't even a starter until his third game as a high school senior in Dallas.

Their dedication to work and their determination to succeed enabled Martin and White to refine their skills in college, and the good fortune of the NFL draft brought them together on the Dallas Cowboys.

Martin, the right end, and White, the right tackle, stood together for many years on the Doomsday defense, and in 1977 they shared the Most Valuable Player award when the Cowboys crushed the Denver Broncos, 27–10, in Super Bowl XII.

It marked the first and only time that MVP award of the championship game went to more than one player.

There are certain similarities between the two behemoths. At their peaks both were very powerful and yet very quick. White, at six-four and about 265 pounds, was known as the strongest man on the Cowboys, capable of bench pressing 500 pounds. Martin, an inch taller and weighing in the area of 250 pounds, was the perennial team leader in sacks after joining the Cowboys in 1973, enjoying his best season in 1977 when he totaled 85 tackles and a league-leading 23 sacks in fourteen games.

An even closer parallel between the two men could be perceived from their earlier years, when both were heavily influenced toward football by their fathers.

White was an exceptionally good baseball player in high school, but not as notable in football. Yet his father, Guy, told Randy his future was in football and selected the University of Maryland for him.

Although White claims, "Ever since I started playing football I've been afraid I wouldn't be good enough," in 1975 he was the second player chosen in the draft, going ahead of Walter Payton.

Martin was virtually pushed into football by his stepfather, Sylvester Martin. He played college ball at East Texas State, and even after joining the Cowboys he had to push himself to be more aggressive.

Eventually he said, "I found myself getting meaner and looking at the guy across from me as the enemy."

Scoring Summary

Dallas Cowboys (NFC)	10	3	7	7—27
Denver Broncos (AFC).......	0	0	10	0—10

Dallas—Dorsett, run 3 (Herrera kick)
Dallas—Herrera (FG) 35
Dallas—Herrera (FG) 43
Denver—Turner (FG) 47
Dallas—Johnson, pass from Staubach 45 (Herrera kick)
Denver—Lytle, run 1 (Turner kick)
Dallas—Richards, pass from Newhouse 29 (Herrera kick)

BRANDING THE COWBOYS

This was one of only a few bad moments in Super Bowl XIII for Steeler quarterback Terry Bradshaw, stripped of the ball by Cowboy linebacker Thomas Henderson, whose teammate Mike Hegman scooped it up and ran into the end zone.

UPI

Participants—Pittsburgh Steelers, champions of the American Football Conference, and Dallas Cowboys, champions of the National Football Conference.

Date—January 21, 1979.

Site—Orange Bowl Stadium, Miami, Florida.

Time—4:00 P.M., EST.

Attendance—79,484.

Radio and TV—National Broadcasting Company (TV); Columbia Broadcasting System (radio).

Regular-Season Records—Pittsburgh, 14–2; Dallas, 12–4.

Playoff Records—Pittsburgh defeated Denver Broncos, 33–10, and Houston Oilers, 34–5, for AFC title; Dallas defeated Atlanta Falcons, 27–20, and Los Angeles Rams, 28–0, for NFC title.

Players' Shares—$18,000 to each member of winning team; $9,000 to each member of losing team.

Coaches—Chuck Noll, Pittsburgh; Tom Landry, Dallas.

BRANDING THE COWBOYS

Reputations are easy to come by, more difficult to refute. Terry Bradshaw knew what it was like to be typecast and how that first impression was always there in the shadows of a football player's career, waiting to step into the spotlight again. Even as a thirty-year-old quarterback with two Super Bowl victories in as many tries to his credit, Bradshaw had to live with his shadow.

He came out of Louisiana Tech in the 1970 college draft as a first-round pick, a quarterback who had the kind of arm that could turn a franchise around. Bradshaw was "The Louisiana Rifle," and the Pittsburgh Steelers envisioned him as the answer to their quarterback problems for at least a dozen years.

But those weren't only accolades that were heaped upon the shoulders of this six-three, 215-pound talent. Beginning in his rookie year, critics doubted Bradshaw's intelligence, suggesting that he should wear a dunce cap rather than a helmet. That kind of talk stung the quiet young man from Shreveport, Louisiana, who wasn't accustomed to playing in a big city like Pittsburgh and being the focus of the media. He was considered a country boy who was out of his league.

In college, Bradshaw was an aggressive take-charge quarterback who dared defenders to intercept his blue dart passes. He was big, strong, and rawboned—tough to bring down. He could run, too. Although the pro scouts had been to the college town of Rustin, Louisi-

ana, to watch him, the national media did not know
very much about Bradshaw.

Louisiana Tech had a small-college program, and
there was speculation whether Bradshaw would have
been as dominant at a bigger school. Then, in his
rookie year in the NFL, those doubts seemed to have
credence as Bradshaw led the league in interceptions.

"I choked my rookie year," he said. "I felt the pressure so much that I couldn't respond to it. I couldn't
lift up my arm to throw the football without throwing
it into the ground. I was afraid I wasn't going to live
up to my reputation."

The growing pains would last a while. Even at the
start of his fifth season, Bradshaw's future was under-
mined. He began the 1974 season on the bench, before
replacing young Joe Gilliam in the seventh game and
leading the Steelers to their first championship in
Super Bowl IX. A year later they repeated as champs,
and Bradshaw was firmly established as the number-
one quarterback.

But there remained, lurking in the shadows, that
reputation even after nine years. "Bradshaw couldn't
spell 'cat' if you spotted him the C and the A," said the
Dallas Cowboys' extroverted linebacker Thomas "Hollywood" Henderson. He was only half-kidding.

"It haunts you," Bradshaw said. "I don't think you
can ever live it down. In my early years, guys called
me a hillbilly and didn't try to understand me. I began
feeling sorry for myself. Now, I'm prepared for what
people will say."

But by now, in the week preceding the Super Bowl
XIII in Miami between the Pittsburgh Steelers and
Dallas Cowboys, all the talk centered on the notorious
"Steel Curtain" defense that had enabled Pittsburgh
to become one of the dominant teams of the 1970s.
The Cowboys were making their fifth Super Bowl
appearance—the most of any team—and they, too,
were renowned for their defense.

Still, it seemed as if quarterback Roger Staubach,
the former midshipman and naval officer and now one
of the NFL's elder statesmen, was given his share of
credit for contributing to the Cowboys' enviable re-

cord, which included twelve playoff appearances in thirteen years. No one doubted the intelligence of Roger the Dodger, even though coach Tom Landry often called many of the team's plays.

To his credit, Bradshaw did not dwell on his reputation. The Steelers and Cowboys had become pro football's two most glamorous teams, and Bradshaw was happy to have a part in Pittsburgh's success. His blond hair was thinning, a reminder that his career was not going to last forever. Bradshaw did not mind, since he was happiest when back home on his ranch in Louisiana.

He was married now, no longer one of pro football's most eligible bachelors. His wife was figure skater Jo Jo Starbuck, whose professional career helped divert attention from football,

There was a great deal of anticipation in Miami before Super Bowl XIII. The Steelers had finished the regular season with a 14–2 record, while the Cowboys were 12–4 after a customarily slow start. These were the unquestioned best teams in their respective conferences, and the confrontation was expected to provide some offensive highlights as well as the now traditional Super Bowl defensive show.

The Cowboys had followed their victory against Denver in Super Bowl XII with a letdown during the early part of the 1978 season. After losing consecutive games to Minnesota and Miami, their record was 6–4, and people wondered whether Landry's detached, unemotional style was benefiting a team that needed a swift kick in the pants.

But the veteran coach—the only one the Cowboys ever had—did not waver. He had been through slow starts before in 1970, 1971, and 1975. "The first half of the year you kind of jockey for position," Landry said. "Naturally, you don't want to get out of position to win, but you win or lose the title in the second half of the season."

What Landry and the fans in Dallas were not accustomed to, however, was a free spirit in their midst. And Hollywood Henderson was unlike any other player who had worn the Dallas uniform.

He gave himself the nickname "Hollywood," then

proceeded to play the role. Henderson did not need an agent or public relations staff; he was his own best salesman. He had heard the bland remarks made by players during Super Bowl week, comments that were prompted by diplomacy and that old sports axiom, "Never give your foe any added incentive."

That was fine for other players, but not Hollywood. No sooner had he stepped off the airplane in Florida than he began to pick apart the Steelers. Henderson called middle linebacker Jack Lambert "Dracula" because he was missing two front teeth. He also referred to Lambert as a "toothless chimpanzee."

Of Randy Grossman, the Steelers' backup tight end who would be starting because Bennie Cunningham was injured, he said: "He only plays when someone dies or breaks a leg or something."

Henderson did not hide the fact that he wanted to be a big name in football. At Langston University, a small college near Oklahoma City, it was said that he once attended a Sammy Davis, Jr., concert on campus and presented Davis with an autographed picture of Hollywood Henderson.

Henderson had talent to back up his ambition, although he floundered during his first two years with the Cowboys. "I was cocky," he said. "I couldn't count the number of times I fell asleep in meetings. And I had trouble with the Cowboys' system."

He finally settled down in 1977 and won a starting job. He had a daring, if not always well-conceived, style that would result in spectacular plays and missed assignments. But he helped the relatively young Cowboys win Super Bowl XII, and he was threatening to take on the Steelers all by himself this year. All in fun, of course,

On January 21, 1979, the fun ended, and after a hard morning rain, Super Bowl XIII began under clearing, although windy, conditions with 78,656 watching in the Orange Bowl and more than 100 million fans in front of their television sets.

The first touchdown was set up when the Cowboys botched a wide-receiver reverse and Drew Pearson fumbled. The Steelers recovered on their own 47-yard

The Steelers' John Stallworth scores the first of his 2 touchdowns on a pass from Terry Bradshaw. UPI

line. It took Bradshaw just 7 plays to reach the end zone, the touchdown coming on a 28-yard pass to John Stallworth.

But near the end of the first quarter, the Cowboys moved to the 39-yard line of Pittsburgh, where Staubach connected on a 13-yard pass to Tony Hill. The receiver then tiptoed down the sideline as if he were walking a tightrope, going the remaining 26 yards for a touchdown. The score was tied at 7–7.

Early in the second period, Henderson backed up his words when he rushed in from his linebacking position to sack Bradshaw, causing a fumble. Fellow linebacker Mike Hegman picked up the ball and dashed 37 yards for a touchdown. The Cowboys were ahead, 14–7.

Bradshaw did not wait long to atone for his mistake. After lulling the Cowboys' flex defense to sleep with 2 running plays to Franco Harris, the quarter-back connected with Stallworth with a medium-range pass that the wide receiver turned into a 75-yard touchdown run. The score was tied, and for the first time the Super Bowl was an offensive carnival.

Neither team played conservatively as both defenses were hard-pressed to live up to their reputations. Late in the first half, Mel Blount, the Steelers' defensive back, intercepted a pass, giving Bradshaw another good opportunity to score.

Quickly he went to work, completing 2 passes to Lynn Swann. But with just 33 seconds left and the ball on the 7-yard line, Bradshaw could not afford to rely on the running game. He faked to Harris, how-ever, which froze the defense, and lofted a soft pass into the end zone, where Rocky Bleier cradled it for a touchdown. At halftime, the Steelers were ahead, 21–14.

There were adjustments made during intermission, thus yardage was harder to come by in the third quarter. The Cowboys had the only successful drive, resulting in a 27-yard field goal by Rafael Septien. Entering the final quarter, the Pittsburgh lead was 21–17.

Then Bradshaw went to work again, expertly mix-ing his running and passing plays. From their own 15-yard line, the Steelers moved to the Cowboys' 22, where the defense deployed for an expected pass play on third and 9. Instead, Bradshaw handed off to Harris on the draw play, and the fullback charged through the startled Cowboys for a touchdown. It was 28–17.

When the Cowboys fumbled the ensuing kickoff, the Steelers took over on the 18-yard line. Bradshaw wasted little time as he spotted Swann alone in the end zone for a touchdown. With less than 7 minutes to play, the lead was a comfortable 35–17.

The Cowboys were not prepared to make a conces-sion speech, however. Staubach calmly drove them 89 yards in 8 plays, culminating with a 7-yard touch-down pass to Billy Joe DuPree. There was only 2:27 left, however, and the Cowboys still trailed, 35–24.

Dallas tried an onsides kick, and Dennis Thurman, a defensive back, recovered for the Cowboys. With 52 yards standing in the way of a touchdown, Staubach showed all the poise and resourcefulness of a thirty-six-year-old veteran as he guided the offense to a touchdown in just 5 plays—the last a 4-yard pass to Butch Johnson.

With 22 seconds remaining, the score was 35–31, and everyone anticipated another onsides kick. Darkness had enveloped the Orange Bowl, and the excited fans were standing for the dramatic moment. Septien kicked it short again, only this time the Steelers' Rocky Bleier cuddled the ball in his arms as if it were made of fine crystal.

Pittsburgh ran out the final seconds and won its third Super Bowl, 35–31, in what was the most entertaining of them all. Bradshaw, who completed 17 of 30 passes for 318 yards and 4 touchdowns, was voted the Most Valuable Player of the game. At long last, he had earned the respect of the pro football establishment.

Assisted by Mean Joe Greene, Steeler coach Chuck Noll is given the traditional victory hoist.

UPI

TERRY BRADSHAW
Louisiana Smarts

"I guess I can force myself to be smart when necessary," Terry Bradshaw used to say.

This always was in answer to those who responded to the Li'l Abner image he carried from Louisiana to the NFL, where he became one of the game's all-time great quarterbacks, leading the Steelers to an unprecedented four Super Bowl championships in a six-year span.

When an injury to his right arm finally ended his career in 1983, Bradshaw ranked among the all-time top fifteen in four major passing categories, including 2,025 completions for 27,989 yards and 212 touchdowns.

He was probably at his devastating best in Super Bowl XIII, when the Steelers beat the Cowboys, 35–31, as Bradshaw threw 4 touchdown passes and gained the first of two consecutive MVP awards on Super Sunday.

This was a long way from his schoolboy days at Woodlawn High in Shreveport, Louisiana, where he'd not only been a star quarterback but had thrown the javelin 245 feet for a scholastic record.

"Inside of me I always felt different," he remembered. "I wanted to be somebody. I wanted to be good."

Such an incentive inspired Terry to throw a football for countless hours into a bucket he'd set up in his backyard. This was the route that led him to Louisiana Tech and then to the pros.

"I came along at the right time and joined a team of giants," he would say of his Steeler days. "I'm a product of my team. I was a good quarterback because I played on a great football team."

For the modest quarterback who kept insisting he was lucky, off-seasons were spent on his four-hundred-acre horse and cattle ranch back home in Louisiana.

He signed with CBS as a football analyst after his playing days and went a step further to prove he could do more than call a football game. He sought and received nonfootball assignments that took him far afield.

In the winter of 1985 he got to cover an international dog-sled race in Alaska in which the contestants faced ornery moose as linebackers.

Although Bradshaw didn't get to call the signals—his old coach, Chuck Noll, never responded to the moose call, but there were television directors on the sidelines—the battered football veteran of Shreveport came through unscathed.

As one observer remarked, "What's a moose to a guy who has encountered Broncos, Lions, and Rams?"

Scoring Summary

Pittsburgh Steelers (AFC)	7	14	0	14—35
Dallas Cowboys (NFC)	7	7	3	14—31

Pittsburgh—Stallworth, pass from Bradshaw 28 (Gerela kick)

Dallas—Hill, pass from Staubach 39 (Septien kick)

Dallas—Hegman, fumble recovery return 37 (Septien kick)

Pittsburgh—Stallworth, pass from Bradshaw 75 (Gerela kick)

Pittsburgh—Bleier, pass from Bradshaw 7 (Gerela kick)

Dallas—Septien (FG) 27

Pittsburgh—Harris, run 22 (Gerela kick)

Pittsburgh—Swann, pass from Bradshaw 18 (Gerela kick)

Dallas—DuPree, pass from Staubach 7 (Septien kick)

Dallas—B. Johnson, pass from Staubach 4 (Septien kick)

ANOTHER STEEL TRAP

Pittsburgh's Terry Bradshaw (12) pitches out to Franco Harris (32) for an early score in Super Bowl XIV.

UPI

Participants—Pittsburgh Steelers, champions of the American Football Conference, and Los Angeles Rams, champions of the National Football Conference.

Date—January 20, 1980.

Site—Rose Bowl, Pasadena, California.

Time—3:00 P.M., PST.

Attendance—103,985.

Radio and TV— Columbia Broadcasting System (TV and radio).

Regular-Season Records—Pittsburgh, 12–4; Los Angeles, 9–7.

Playoff Records—Pittsburgh defeated Miami Dolphins, 34–14, and Houston Oilers, 27–13, for AFC title; Los Angeles defeated Dallas Cowboys, 21–19, and Tampa Bay Buccaneers, 9–0, for NFC title.

Players' Shares—$18,000 to each member of winning team; $9,000 to each member of losing team.

Coaches—Chuck Noll, Pittsburgh; Ray Malavasi, Los Angeles.

SUPER BOWL XIV

ANOTHER STEEL TRAP

The only reason the Rams should have been in Los Angeles was because this is where they play their home games and where many of the players make their off-season homes. But that was not why the Rams were still in uniform during the third week in January 1980. In a totally bewildering season, with a number of plot twists, the Rams had earned a berth in Super Bowl XIV, opposite none other than the Pittsburgh Steelers, who were making this an annual event.

But were the Rams really the first home team in a Super Bowl game? Geographically, perhaps, but not in the hearts of many fans. Beginning the following season, the Rams were moving thirty miles south to Anaheim, California, where they would infuriate all concerned by continuing to be known as the Los Angeles Rams.

Sound confusing? Well, no one in pro football was quite prepared when the Rams staggered through a mediocre 9–7 regular season in 1979 and somehow won two playoff games to end up in the Super Bowl. This was the Steelers' fourth appearance in football's game of games, and they returned with a 3–0 Super Bowl record. That did not bode well for the Rams, who played their home games in the Memorial Coliseum, only twenty miles from the Rose Bowl in Pasadena, site of Super Bowl XIV.

But in this instance, being home wasn't necessarily an advantage for the Rams. After announcing their move to Anaheim, the team was often booed by the fans at the Coliseum. There was ample reason. Not only were the Rams considered unfaithful, but they were mediocre, too.

Keeping track of their exploits was like watching a television soap opera. There were family feuds, trage- dies, injuries, and rivalries. There was victory and there was defeat, almost in equal proportion.

And it was all rehashed by more than 1,000 report- ers during Super Bowl week, just in case someone missed hearing about the controversies. The first stroke of bad luck occurred in March 1979, when owner Car- roll Rosenbloom drowned while swimming in rough waters in Florida. His wife, Georgia, inherited major- ity ownership, which amounted to 70 percent. Rosen- bloom stipulated, though, that his son Steve become the general manager of the Rams.

From the beginning, Mrs. Rosenbloom and her step- son did not get along, resulting in an ongoing power struggle. Meanwhile, the team suffered setbacks when coach Ray Malavasi underwent treatment for high blood pressure; fullback John Cappelletti, the Ram's most dependable player, was lost for the season with a severely torn groin muscle; and all-pro tackle Doug France left training camp claiming that the black and white players practiced racism.

All this, and the season hadn't even started yet. Some of the problems were resolved in mid-August when Mrs. Rosenbloom fired her stepson Steve and replaced him with Don Klosterman, who had been the general manager. But the Rams remained a jinxed team throughout a vexing season.

Injuries sidelined stars such as defensive backs Rod Perry and Pat Thomas, offensive guards Dennis Harrah and Doug Smith, and wide receivers Ron Jessie and Billy Waddy.

But the biggest blow was suffered when quarter- back Pat Haden, the small but effective quarterback who had attended Southern Cal, broke a finger on his passing hand in early November and was declared out for the season. Haden was extremely popular among the players and fans, and had led the Rams to the NFC championship the past two seasons.

Malavasi had little choice but to use Vince Ferragamo, the tall, dark, and handsome but inexperienced quarterback. Ferragamo grew up near Los Angeles, but when John McKay, the Southern Cal coach, decided to recruit Haden, a disappointed Ferragamo went to the University of California at Berkeley.

Unable to win a starting job there, he transferred to Nebraska and impressed the professional scouts with his strong arm and size. But Ferragamo had played sparingly in his two years with the Rams as Haden led them to a 25–7–1 record. "Let's face it," Ferragamo said, "I haven't played enough to really know if I can complete passes."

Malavasi did not help his young quarterback's confidence when he pulled him out of games on November 26 and December 2. Bob Lee, a journeyman, came off the bench to lead the Rams to victory in those games. Still, Malavasi said, "I have all the confidence in the world in Vince. He's the starter."

Ferragamo returned to the lineup and began to display the kind of long-range passing game that the Rams lacked under Haden. He was prone to mistakes, but the Rams began winning just enough to stay in contention for a playoff berth. Then, against heavily favored Dallas in their first postseason game, Ferragamo threw 3 touchdown passes in a 21–19 victory.

The next week, he played well enough as the Rams defeated the Tampa Bay Buccaneers, 9–0, in a defensive struggle. In a tense game with a Sugar Bowl berth hanging in the balance, Ferragamo played with poise.

Still, Tampa Bay was not Pittsburgh, and during the 1979 season the Steelers continued to be the dominant defense team in the NFL. They had suffered four losses, but these were attributed in part to letdowns rather than a decline. The Steelers were getting older, but Terry Bradshaw was in his prime as a quarterback, and Franco Harris, Lynn Swann, and John Stallworth were still potent offensive players.

On defense, the Steelers allowed opponents just 264 yards a game. Mean Joe Greene, L. C. Greenwood, Jack Lambert, and Mel Blount had become household names. But Malavasi refused to be intimidated. "The

Steelers are good," the Rams' coach said, "but we don't fear them. Like I said before, we don't fear anyone."

Actually, the Rams had an impressive defense of their own, anchored by veteran linemen Jack Youngblood and Fred Dryer, and hard-hitting defensive backs Bob Brudzinski and Jack "Hacksaw" Reynolds. If it weren't for the injuries—particularly the one to Haden—and all the behind-the-scene turmoil, the Rams might have been rated even with the Steelers, instead of being a 10-point underdog.

Thus, Super Bowl XIV was expected to be a tour de force for Pittsburgh, reaffirmation that the Steelers had perhaps surpassed Vince Lombardi's Green Bay Packers and Don Shula's Miami Dolphins to become the best football team in history.

In anticipation of a rout, Super Bowl XIV was being called "the Super Bore." And once the game began, it seemed as if the predictions were right on the mark when the Steelers moved easily into field-goal range on the strength of a 32-yard completion from Bradshaw to Harris. Matt Bahr connected from 41 yards out, and Pittsburgh led, 3–0,

But on their next possession, the Rams showed that their offense had been unfairly maligned. Wendell Tyler, a talented runner who was criticized because he was prone to fumble, caught a 6-yard pass, then scooted around left end on a running play for 39 yards and a first down at the Steelers' 14.

It took 5 plays, but the Rams eventually scored when burly running back Cullen Bryant dove in from the 1-yard line. Quite unexpectedly, the Rams led, 7–3.

What the touchdown did was establish the fact that the Rams had not come this far just to play a supporting role in the coronation of the Steelers. And Ferragamo, despite his season-long ups and downs, appeared to be inspired by the big game.

But Terry Bradshaw had been in many big games, and he wasn't one to get easily flustered. After Larry Anderson returned the next kickoff 45 yards to give his team good field position, the thirty-one-year-old quarterback went to work, In 8 plays, the Steelers moved to the 1-yard line, covering much of the ground through the air as Bradshaw hit tight end Bennie

The Steelers' Lynn Swann gets a ride on the shoulders of Ram defender Pat Thomas after catching a pass.

Wide World

Cunningham and Swann. Harris then took a pitchout and ran into the end zone to put Pittsburgh ahead again, 10–7, in the second quarter.

The lead did not last long. Ferragamo drove Los Angeles downfield on a 5-minute march that showed they could control the ball against the "Steel Curtain." When the drive stalled at the 14-yard line, Frank Corral kicked a 31-yard field goal to tie the score.

Now it was the Rams' defense that made its impact felt. The players felt they were every bit as good as the Steelers' defense, and it showed when Dave Elmendorf intercepted Bradshaw's pass with 3:05 left in the first half, giving the Rams good field position. Patiently using the clock, Ferragamo moved his team to the 13-yard line before he was sacked for a 14-yard loss.

That was still within Corral's field-goal range as he booted a 45-yarder to give the Rams a 13–10 halftime lead. While hundreds of musicians and singers paid tribute to the Big Band era in another one of those Super Bowl halftime extravaganzas, the Steelers sat in their locker room, contemplating.

"I knew it wasn't going to be easy," Bradshaw said. "I told you guys, but no one believed me."

If they didn't believe him before the game, they did now. And the Steelers came out fired up in the third quarter, taking just 5 plays to regain the lead as Bradshaw threw a 47-yard touchdown pass to Swann. The score was 17–13.

Now, perhaps, the Rams were ready to fold. But not quite. Ferragamo was playing as if he were trying to imitate Bradshaw. Anything Terry could do, he would do better. A 50-yard completion to Billy Waddy gave the Rams a first down at the Pittsburgh 24-yard line.

Then Malavasi sent in a play that took the "Steel Curtain" completely by surprise. Ferragamo handed off to Lawrence McCutcheon on what looked like another basic sweep. But McCutcheon stopped and threw a 24-yard scoring pass to Ron Smith for the go-ahead touchdown. The conversion was missed, but the Rams led again, 19–17.

The Steelers entered the fourth quarter staring at

their first Super Bowl defeat and the biggest upset in the game since the New York Jets defeated the Baltimore Colts in Super Bowl III.

"I was scared," Jack Lambert said. "The Rams had the momentum going for them."

The Steelers were champions, and now was the time to show it. Starting on their 25-yard line, Harris gained 2 yards. Chuck Noll, the Steelers' coach, sent in a pass play for Stallworth, a pass that Bradshaw did not have success completing in practice all week. But it was the play the coach felt would work.

Bradshaw dropped back, spotted Stallworth in the

Ram receiver Ron Smith's foot notwithstanding, Steeler linebacker Jack Lambert steals the ball for an important fourth-quarter interception.
Wide World

clear, and threw a perfect pass that the rangy receiver caught on the run and carried 73 yards for a touchdown. In a matter of minutes, the Steelers had regained the lead, 24–19.

Just as the Steelers expected, the Rams moved right back into scoring range behind Ferragamo's accurate passing. But now it was time for the Pittsburgh defense to pitch in. On first down from the Steelers' 32-yard line, Ferragamo's pass for Ron Smith was intercepted by Lambert, who returned it 16 yards.

There was 5:24 to play, and the fans expected the Steelers to try and protect their slim lead. But Bradshaw was not going to play it safe. He completed a 45-yard pass to Stallworth for a first down on the Rams' 22. A pass interference penalty against Pat Thomas gave the Steelers a first down on the 1-yard line.

The proud Los Angeles defense was stubborn, but on the third try, Harris barreled into the end zone. The Steelers took a 31–19 lead, and in just a few minutes the game was over. It was not one of the Steelers' more impressive Super Bowl triumphs, but it was the one that proved their mettle.

Bradshaw, who was intercepted 3 times, still had the poise and perseverance to complete 14 of 21 passes for 309 yards and 2 touchdowns. Once again, "The Louisiana Rifle" was named Most Valuable Player.

JOHN STALLWORTH
Second Banana

For most of his career, John Stallworth has been known as "the other man," and he once was described as the quintessential second banana.

This was the price Stallworth had to pay for joining the Pittsburgh Steelers in the same draft as Lynn Swann in 1974. Although Stallworth eventually earned recognition as one of the premier wide receivers in the NFL, he kept a lower profile than Swann and for the most part was overshadowed by his teammate in the public eye.

It was therefore fitting that even in Super Bowl XIV, when Stallworth put on a dazzling display of acrobatic catching, he was still only the second star behind quarterback Terry Bradshaw, the MVP. The six-two, 190-pound Stallworth made 3 key receptions in the 31–19 victory over the Los Angeles Rams, including a 73-yard touchdown pass to give Pittsburgh the lead, then an over-the-shoulder grab against three defenders to set up the clinching score.

Stallworth went to high school in Tuscaloosa, Alabama, in the shadow of Alabama, but he was overlooked by that school's famed coach, Bear Bryant, and had to play his college ball in virtual anonymity at Alabama A&M. Taking a positive view of the experience, Stallworth said, "There was a lack of publicity, but it just made me a stronger individual."

A series of injuries hampered Stallworth's career, and he didn't become a full-time starter with the Steelers until his fourth year. Still, he was a key ingredient on four Super Bowl championship teams

Pittsburgh's John Stallworth scores the go-ahead touchdown on a 73-yard pass play.

Wide World

and in his quiet but spectacular way has set several team records.

Included are the Steeler marks for career receptions, receiving yards, and touchdown receptions. He also set another team record of at least 1 pass reception in 67 consecutive games between 1977 and 1982.

"Playing in Lynn's shadow never bothered me a whole lot," Stallworth said. "We concentrate on the team effort, and I wouldn't have wanted to play anywhere else."

Scoring Summary

Los Angeles Rams (NFC)   7   6   6   0—19
Pittsburgh Steelers (AFC)   3   7   7   14—31

Pittsburgh—Bahr (FG) 41
Los Angeles—Bryant, run 1 (Corral kick)
Pittsburgh—Harris, run 1 (Bahr kick)
Los Angeles—Corral (FG) 31
Los Angeles—Corral (FG) 45
Pittsburgh—Swann, pass from Bradshaw 47 (Bahr kick)
Los Angeles—Smith, pass from McCutcheon 24
Pittsburgh—Stallworth, pass from Bradshaw 73 (Bahr kick)
Pittsburgh—Harris, run 1 (Bahr kick)

RETURN FROM OBLIVION

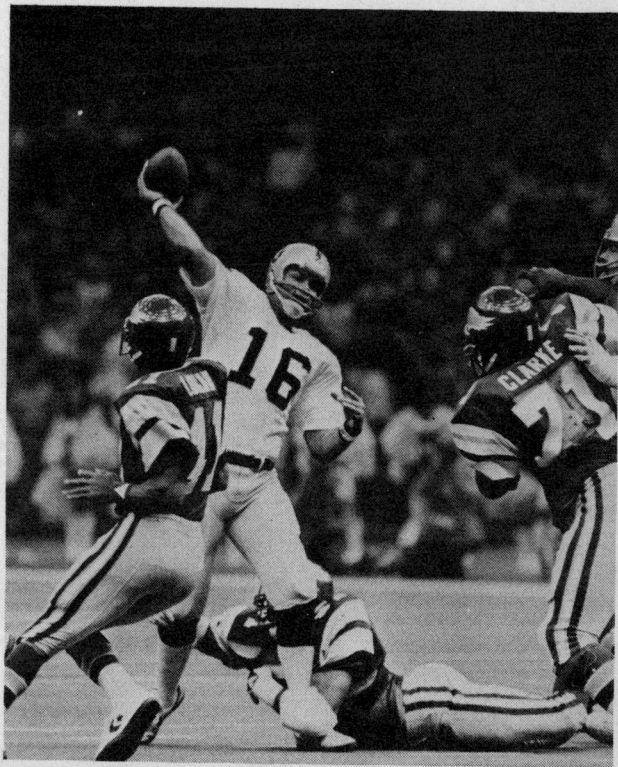

For Oakland's Jim Plunkett, Super Bowl XV meant
long-sought redemption.

UPI

Participants—Oakland Raiders, champions of the American Football Conference, and Philadelphia Eagles, champions of the National Football Conference.

Date—January 25, 1981.

Site—Louisiana Superdome, New Orleans, Louisiana.

Time—5:00 P.M., CST.

Attendance—76,135.

Radio and TV—National Broadcasting Company (TV); Columbia Broadcasting System (radio).

Regular-Season Records—Oakland, 11–5; Philadelphia, 12–4.

Playoff Records—Oakland defeated Houston Oilers, 27–7, Cleveland Browns, 14–12, and San Diego Chargers, 34–27, for AFC title; Philadelphia defeated Minnesota Vikings, 31–16, and Dallas Cowboys, 20–7, for NFC title.

Players' Shares—$18,000 to each member of winning team; $9,000 to each member of losing team.

Coaches—Tom Flores, Oakland; Dick Vermeil, Philadelphia.

RETURN FROM
OBLIVION

Super Bowl XV offered more than a contrast in playing styles. The Oakland Raiders and Philadelphia Eagles represented two totally divergent philosophies that made this a morality play as well as a football game. The Eagles preached pro football's time-honored tenets—discipline and hard work. The Raiders were mischief makers who sometimes delighted in breaking all the rules.

They had a good example in owner Al Davis, whose acid tongue and contrary nature infuriated the NFL establishment. But nothing had upset his fellow owners and commissioner Pete Rozelle more than when Davis said he was moving the Raiders to Los Angeles, despite playing to capacity crowds and widespread support in Oakland.

Pro football was a business, Davis contended, and as a businessman he was pursuing a better deal in Los Angeles, where the Rams had vacated the Memorial Coliseum and gone to Anaheim. A more favorable lease awaited the Raiders in L.A., as well as a potentially lucrative television package. The case was now in court.

It galled some league owners that the Raiders were on the verge of winning their second Super Bowl. There was still resentment over the fact that they were an original American Football League team. Davis was the one who briefly became commissioner of the AFL and forced a merger of the leagues when he led successful raids on several of the NFL's star players.

But the Raiders had also become a haven for castoffs, dropouts, and malcontents, the players no one else wanted. They seemed to thrive in an atmosphere where they were treated as adults and not children or military recruits.

"We're not a bunch of choirboys and Boy Scouts," said Gene Upshaw, the team's veteran offensive guard. "They say we're the halfway house of the NFL. Well, we live up to that image every chance we get."

Coach Tom Flores had taken the same road traveled by John Madden and, before him, John Rauch and Davis himself. He didn't care what the players did in their free time as long as it did not affect their performance on the day of the game. Of course, they were expected to adhere to what few rules existed. When they didn't, there was no ranting or raving or extreme punishment; Flores simply took their money.

It was estimated that Super Bowl week in the madcap city of New Orleans cost Raiders players $15,000 in fines. John Matuszak, the hulking defensive end with a checkered past, was the most celebrated offender, incurring a $1,000 fine for breaking curfew on the Wednesday before the game.

"I broke a rule that I shouldn't have, and I'm paying the fine for it," Matuszak said. "Wednesday night is my normal night to go out, so I went. I walked out the front door. I had nothing to hide."

The Raiders openly scoffed at the suggestion made by Dick Vermeil, the young, by-the-book coach of the Eagles, who said he would have put Matuszak on an airplane home if Big John were playing for him.

"If Tom Flores sent home every guy on this football team who screwed up," Upshaw said, "he'd be the only guy on the sideline."

This is not to say that the Raiders took their professions lightly. The only reason why Davis and his coaches allowed such freedom of thought and expression was because the Raiders won. "Pride and Poise" was the team's slogan, and it had held up through the years as Oakland became one of the most successful franchises in pro football.

And if opposing teams thought the Raiders specialized in roughhouse tactics that bordered on dirty play, they should have seen what went on during practices when the Oakland players often fought among themselves.

Upshaw was a fourteen-year veteran who had seen every type of football player and misfit wear the Raiders' silver-and-black uniform, He had been through hundreds of practices and dozens of big games. Yet on Wednesday and Thursday during Super Bowl week, Upshaw got into shoving matches and fights with his teammates in the spirited practice sessions.

"It was so intense and vicious," said safety Burgess Owens, a former New York Jet, "that I thought Flores would have to call it off."

The Eagles practiced hard, too, but in comparison to the Raiders' barroom brawls, Vermeil ran a boot camp. He was a highly motivated, driven young coach who had made the Eagles respectable, then contenders in a sports-minded city whose fans are demanding and sometimes harsh on the home teams.

Vermeil brought his enthusiasm and twenty-hour days to Philadelphia in 1976 after leaving the head coaching job at UCLA. The system was regimented and stifled the individuality of the players, but it got results, and Eagle fans had gone too long without a winner to question Vermeil's methods.

He may not have been Al Davis' type of coach, but Davis said: "The man is true to what he believes, and that was good enough to get him there."

The Eagles, in fact, were favored to win Super Bowl XV on the strength of an impressive defensive unit that allowed an average of just 14 points a game. Among the Eagles' victories was a 10–7 triumph against the Raiders early in the 1980 season.

The defensive unit was molded by assistant coach Marion Campbell, whose players combined experience and youth. Veterans such as linebackers Bill Bergey and Frank LeMaster, and a thirty-six-year-old defensive end Claude Humphrey, who led the team in sacks with 14½, were the cornerstones of the defense.

Youngsters such as linebacker Jerry Robinson, defensive back John Sciarra, and defensive end Thomas Brown completed the older players. Campbell also employed a variety of defenses that enabled him to use almost everyone on the defensive roster, giving the players a feeling they all were contributing.

"Are we underrated? I guess we are," LeMaster said. "We had the number-one defense in the league, but we don't have any name players. We just have a bunch of tough, hard-nosed guys who love to hit."

On offense, quarterback Ron Jaworski flourished under Vermeil and at twenty-nine years of age was reaching his peak. The Eagles were conservative, as was the custom in the NFL, and Jaworski relied on running back Wilbert Montgomery to make the ball-possession offense successful. Harold Carmichael, the six-seven wide receiver, was Jaworski's favorite target.

But although the Raiders may have had more talent on offense, there was a problem at quarterback. After years of steady leadership under Daryle Lamonica and Ken Stabler, Oakland found itself between quarterbacks. Dan Pastorini had been acquired, but when he was hurt, the Raiders turned to Jim Plunkett, the former Heisman Trophy winner from Stanford who had faded into near obscurity after several brilliant years with the New England Patriots and bitter experience with the San Francisco 49ers.

The Raiders were 2–3 and fading fast when Pastorini broke his leg and Plunkett inherited the starting job. He was thirty-three years old, slowed by damaged knees and years of punishment he took when the hapless Patriots did a poor job of protecting him.

But Plunkett was ready to step in when needed. In the fifteen games that he started—among them playoff games—the Raiders won thirteen. "I think I've been ready for quite a while," he said.

On January 25, 1981, 76,135 fans were in the Superdome in New Orleans to watch this morality play unfold. The odds makers said the Eagles would win again, just as they had during the regular season.

The game was barely under way before the Raiders forced the first mistake. Jaworski's first pass attempt was intercepted by linebacker Rod Martin, who returned 17 yards to the Eagles' 30-yard line. Even a defense as good as Philadelphia's would be hard-pressed to keep the Raiders from scoring.

They initially stayed on the ground as running backs Mark van Eeghen and Kenny King carried to the 19-yard line. Plunkett then attempted his first pass and hit Cliff Branch for 14 yards and a first down at the 5. Van Eeghen carried twice but could only gain 3 yards.

So on third down, Plunkett faked a running play and threw into the end zone to Branch, who scored the first touchdown of the game. Six minutes into the game, the Raiders had struck for a 7–0 lead. Already they had established that this would not be a repeat of the early-season loss to Philadelphia.

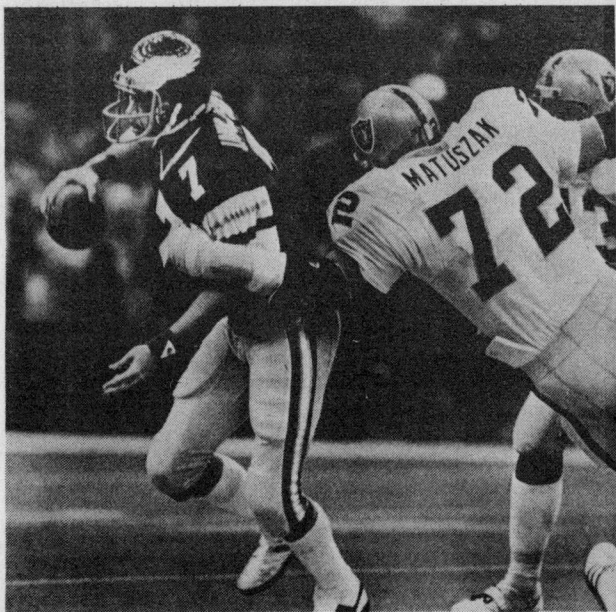

Oakland's John Matuszak puts the arm on scrambling Eagle quarterback Ron Jaworski.

Wide World

Jaworski rallied the Eagles and apparently had evened the score when he threw a 40-yard touchdown pass to Rodney Parker. But Carmichael was penalized for being in motion on the play, and the touchdown was called back. The Eagles were forced to give up the ball.

With just over a minute remaining in the opening quarter, the Raiders had a first down on their 14-yard line. A 2-yard run by King and a 4-yard pass to Branch made it third and 4 at the 20. Plunkett set to pass, looking for a short gain and another first down.

But the Eagles' pass rush forced Plunkett to scramble, and the gimpy-kneed quarterback desperately looked for an open receiver. Downfield, he spotted King and threw a perfect pass that King caught at the 39-yard line behind all the Eagle defenders. King raced the remaining 61 yards to the end zone to complete a Super Bowl record 80-yard touchdown play, which widened the Raiders' lead to 14–0.

The Eagles, who had started strongly, now appeared to sag in disappointment. The offense was able to generate one drive that resulted in a 30-yard field goal by Tony Franklin, but otherwise the team was uninspired.

"We never got into the flow of the game," Jaworski would say later. "I sensed a lack of emotion as the game went on."

The Raiders received the second-half kickoff but were mired on their 14-yard line. Plunkett went to work, mixing the running game with passes to King and a 32-yarder to Bob Chandler. It was first down on the Philadelphia 33.

Van Eeghen gained 4 yards the hard way, then Plunkett took to the air again, hitting Branch for 29 yards and a touchdown. The Raiders led, 21–3, and were in control.

Sensing that he had to do something quickly, Jaworski opened up the passing game when the Eagles reclaimed the ball. But the Raiders feast on another team's adversity, and Rod Martin made his second interception later in the third quarter. This time the Raiders set-

Cliff Branch scores the second of his 2 touchdowns.
UPI

tled for Chris Bahr's 4-yard field goal to raise their
lead to 24–3.

As the fourth quarter started, the Eagles' outlook
was dim. Jaworski led them on their first touchdown
drive of the game, the score coming on an 8-yard pass
to Keith Krepfle. But the drive had wasted precious
time. Trailing 24–10, the Eagles still needed 2 touchdowns to tie.

They wouldn't get a chance to try. Plunkett took the Raiders on a ball-control drive that ended when Bahr kicked a 35-yard field goal to make it 27–10. That is how the game ended as Oakland won its second Super Bowl game and spoiled the Eagles' first appearance in the game. Plunkett, the comeback story of the year, was named Most Valuable Player.

But there was still plenty of tension in the locker room as the Raiders awaited the arrival of commissioner Pete Rozelle for presentation of the Lombardi Trophy to his antagonist, Al Davis. As the players hustled to take snapshots of this meeting of adversaries, Rozelle and Davis were gracious and avoided harsh words.

"It's our finest hour," Davis said.

A Hollywood ending: The embattled NFL commissioner, Pete Rozelle, presents the championship trophy to his greatest challenger, Oakland owner Al Davis (left).

UPI

JIM PLUNKETT
Destiny of a
Quarterback

In 1978 he was unwanted, and for two years after that he was forgotten. In his own mind, his career was as good as finished.

Nevertheless, when an emergency arose and his number was called, Jim Plunkett remembered the way he used to do it and thus produced one of the more courageous comebacks ever seen in football.

"Circumstances dictate the story, and I guess it must be somewhat storybook," Plunkett said once delirium had replaced despair.

The son of Mexican-American parents who were both poor and blind, Plunkett did indeed live a storybook youth, working long hours to help support his family and to pay for school in San José, California. At the age of seventeen he could throw a football 85 yards, and he was an All-American quarterback at Stanford, winning the Heisman Trophy.

Plunkett was the number-one choice in the 1971 draft, and the six-three quarterback played every single offensive down that year for the New England Patriots, earning Rookie-of-the-Year honors.

In 1975 Plunkett asked to be traded, and he was sent to San Francisco, near his hometown of San José, but just as at New England, it was another losing situation. Shortly before the start of the 1978 season Plunkett was released, and he says, "That period is vivid in my mind. It was the most miserable time in my life. I felt like the whole world was caving in on me."

Signed by the Oakland Raiders, Plunkett didn't run

a single play in 1978, and the following year he threw a total of 15 passes in four appearances. But in 1980 Plunkett was given an unexpected chance when Dan Pastorini broke a leg in the fifth game.

The Raiders rallied behind Plunkett to make Super Bowl XV against Philadelphia. Plunkett then climaxed his incredible comeback by throwing 3 touchdown passes, including the 80-yarder to Kenny King, in the 27–10 victory over the Eagles.

"I've dreamt it many times, but I never thought I'd be here. There were times I wanted to throw in the towel," Plunkett said.

Scoring Summary

Oakland Raiders (AFC)	14	0	10	3—27
Philadelphia Eagles (NFC) ...	0	3	0	7—10

Oakland—Branch, pass from Plunkett 2 (Bahr kick)
Oakland–King, pass from Plunkett 80 (Bahr kick)
Philadelphia—Franklin (FG) 30
Oakland—Branch, pass from Plunkett 29 (Bahr kick)
Oakland–Bahr (FG) 46
Philadelphia–Krepfle, pass from Jaworski 8 (Franklin kick)
Oakland–Bahr (FG) 35

SUPER BOWL XVI

49ER GOLD RUSH

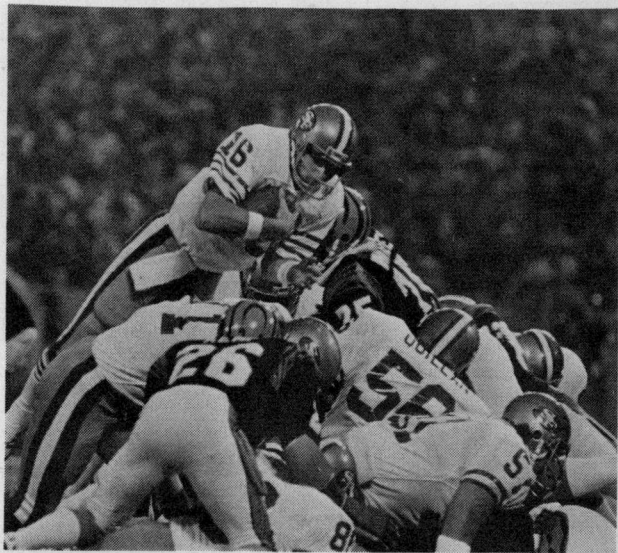

49er quarterback Joe Montana climbs the mountain for the first score in Super Bowl XVI.

UPI

Participants—Cincinnati Bengals, champions of the American Football Conference, and San Francisco 49ers, champions of the National Football Conference.

Date—January 24, 1982.

Site—Pontiac Silverdome, Pontiac, Michigan.

Time—4:00 P.M., EST.

Attendance—81,270.

Radio and TV—Columbia Broadcasting System (TV and radio).

Regular-Season Records—Cincinnati, 12–4; San Francisco, 13–3.

Playoff Records—Cincinnati defeated Buffalo Bills, 28–21, and San Diego Chargers, 27–7, for AFC title; San Francisco defeated New York Giants, 38–24, and Dallas Cowboys, 28–27, for NFC title,

Players' Shares—$18,000 to each member of winning team; $9,000 to each member of losing team.

Coaches—Forrest Gregg, Cincinnati; Bill Walsh, San Francisco.

SUPER BOWL XVI

49ER GOLD RUSH

The man in the bellhop uniform looked familiar. He greeted the buses carrying the San Francisco 49ers to their hotel headquarters in Pontiac, Michigan, and he welcomed the National Conference champions with a bellhop's traditional courtesy and a smile. Then, Bill Walsh, the man in the bellhop uniform and the 49ers' coach, held the hotel door open as his amused players filed into the lobby.

It would be difficult to imagine Vince Lombardi, the late coach of the Green Bay Packers, going to such lengths to surprise the players before a big game. It would also be out of character if Tom Landry, Don Shula, or Dick Vermeil did what Walsh did. But in 1981, the longtime assistant coach and offensive innovator led the 49ers to the Super Bowl as their head coach and was being celebrated around the National Football League as a genius.

It is a word that is used loosely in sports, and Walsh did his best to discourage such talk. He wasn't, after all, a boy wonder among coaches who burst upon the football scene and changed the way the game is played. Walsh was fifty years old and silver-haired, a man who had spent his career serving other masters until he became a head coach at Stanford University at the age of forty-five. Two years later, he took over the floundering 49ers and built them into winners, using many of the same techniques he had as an assistant in Cincinnati and San Diego, where he'd coached quarterbacks such as Ken Anderson and Dan Fouts.

Now, Walsh had led the 49ers to Super Bowl XVI,

where they would play Anderson and the Cincinnati
Bengals in Pontiac, Michigan. This was the first cold-
weather site for the Super Bowl, and commissioner
Pete Rozelle was persuaded to choose Pontiac—the
home of the Detroit Lions— because the game would
be played in the Silverdome. If it snowed, it would not
affect the outcome or the comfort of the fans sitting
indoors in the climate-controlled atmosphere.

Super Bowl XVI promised to be one of the more
offensive-minded games. The teams relied on different
types of passing games—the Bengals throwing long
more often than the 49ers, who utilized the rollout
passes of former Notre Dame star Joe Montana. Still,
there would be a lot of Walsh's influence on both
sides of the line of scrimmage in this game, which
made him the central figure during Super Bowl week.

Walsh and the 49ers did not seem overwhelmed by
all the attention given the game and the hordes of
news media that had descended on icy Pontiac. Football players all had heard about the hype surrounding a Super Bowl game, but the reality never struck
until a player had a firsthand experience.

"I almost have to apologize," Walsh said. "I just
don't feel that great importance to the game. It's just
a football game.

"Football," he added, "is so mundane. The geniuses
are those who have significant endeavors—human progress, medicine, not sports. Not an isolated American
sport."

But the Super Bowl game had transcended American sports to some extent, as it was now seen in
countries all over the world. Walsh, however, was not
going to let the magnitude of the event spoil what he
felt should be an enjoyable time for the players. This
was a time for work and play.

"I think we're loose," said offensive guard Randy
Cross. "We're enjoying this and having fun."

What made the work enjoyable for the 49ers was
that Walsh had a fertile imagination. On the Thursday preceding every game, he would devise a list of 25
plays to use against that week's opponent. Many of
the plays would be new ones that Walsh devised dur-

ing the week. Standing on the sideline the day of the
game, Walsh could be seen referring to his list. The
goal would be to run them all by halftime.

This made it difficult to scout the 49ers. Opposing
teams just did not know what new plays the coach had
implemented. Walsh enjoyed being unpredictable in a
sport in which teams tended to play alike. The Super
Bowl, especially, often had been dull and repetitive
because teams were not willing to take chances.

"I'm supposed to be egocentric," Walsh said, "maybe
because I'm willing to talk instead of saying, 'No com-
ment.' I haven't gotten this far by being a detached,
professorial personality. There is no time or room to
be a white-haired philosopher."

The 49ers had defeated the Bengals, 21–3, in Cincinnati earlier in the season, a defeat that stung the
Bengals. They did not like the way Montana spiked
the ball in the end zone after scoring the third touchdown. Thus, in a departure from the Super Bowl plati-
tudes that teams toss at one another, linebacker Reggie
Williams said the Bengals were looking for revenge.

"Montana did that maliciously," said Williams, an
Ivy Leaguer who attended Dartmouth. "I can't fault
anyone for getting excited, but it was 21–3, and I'm
thinking basically he did it not thinking we would
meet again."

The road to the Super Bowl was not particularly
easy for either team. The 49ers needed a last-second
victory against Dallas in the NFC championship game
to survive, the touchdown coming on a scramble pass
from Montana to Dwight Clark.

The Bengals were more hard-pressed, winning an
overtime game against the Dolphins in severe heat
and humidity in Miami, then beating the San Diego
Chargers at home a week later in arctic conditions in
which the wind chill factor was forty degrees below
zero.

Anderson figured to do much better in the Silverdome, where neither the temperature or wind would
hinder his passing game. The dark-haired thirty-two-
year-old veteran had completed a fine season after a
stumbling start. His receivers were veteran Isaac Cur-

tis, dependable tight end Dan Ross, and the irrepressible rookie Cris Collinsworth.

Collinsworth was a six-five, 195-pound wisp who outran and outleaped defensive backs for the football. He caught 67 passes during the regular season and had emerged as one of the more colorful personalities on the team.

The Bengals relied on Pete Johnson, a 250-pounder, to supply the bulk of their running game, and although Johnson was quick for someone his size, and gained 1,077 yards, the Bengals did not figure to win this game on the ground.

In addition to Clark, Montana had excellent receivers in Fred Solomon and tight end Charle Young, a thirty-year-old veteran who was enjoying a resurgence in San Francisco. The 49ers also lacked a game-breaking runner. Backs Ricky Patton and Earl Cooper were effectively used by Montana as pass receivers.

Each team had a strong defense, although the 49ers boasted the superior pass rush, led by defensive end Fred Dean. Cornerbacks Ronnie Lott and Eric Wright of San Francisco were as good as Anderson had encountered all season.

Because the game was being played in the North for the first time, Super Bowl week had the air of a winter carnival. The city of Pontiac even staged some snowmobile races. The officials did not know how much those snowmobiles would have come in handy on game day.

It was cold and clear on January 24, 1982, and the roads leading to the Silverdome were dry. Still, there was a massive traffic jam leading to the stadium, which delayed fans for several hours. Even one of the buses carrying the 49ers, including Walsh and Montana, was caught in traffic.

The players joked and the coach kidded that the game had already begun and the 49ers were winning, but privately Walsh was concerned. When the bus finally arrived, there was only an hour and thirty-five minutes until kickoff—only twenty-five minutes until the 49ers were supposed to be on the field to warm up.

There were 81,270 fans in the Silverdome to watch

each of these teams make its first Super Bowl appearance. The tension showed right from the opening kickoff when San Francisco's Amos Lawrence fumbled and the Bengals recovered on the 49ers' 26-yard line.

Anderson tried to capitalize in a hurry. He completed a pass to Curtis and another to Ross, giving the Bengals a first down on the 5-yard line. A running play gained no yardage, and Anderson was tackled attempting to pass, for a 6-yard loss. On third down from the 11, he threw to the end zone for Ross, but Dwight Hicks, the safety, cut in front and intercepted, returning the ball to the 32-yard line.

The 49ers played a ball-possession passing game, which meant that Montana rarely threw long but relied on relatively secure tosses to his receivers and backs. On their first series, the shifty quarterback completed passes to Patton, Clark, Solomon, and Young. It was first down on the Bengals' 33-yard line.

Now Cooper hit the middle for 10 yards, and 2 plays later Montana threw a 14-yard pass to Solomon. With a first down on the 1-yard line, Montana dove over for the touchdown, which put the 49ers ahead, 7–0.

The Bengals continued to hurt themselves. Anderson moved the team, but another mistake cost them a scoring opportunity. This time, Collinsworth fumbled after catching a pass at the San Francisco 8-yard line, and the 49ers recovered.

Montana moved the offense effortlessly again, taking small chunks of yardage at a time. A 21-yard pass to Solomon was the big gainer. With a first down on the Bengals' 11-yard line, Montana fired into the end zone for Cooper, who caught the touchdown pass. San Francisco led, 14–0, early in the second period.

The 49ers' defense then began to shut down Cincinnati, and Montana kept the ball away from the Bengals' offense with his long drives. Just before halftime, Ray Wersching kicked a 22-yard field goal to make it 17–0.

On the ensuing kickoff, Wersching booted the ball low, making it difficult to handle. One after another, several Bengals bobbled it but could not gain possession. Milt McColl of the 49ers fell on the ball at the

Cincinnati's Ken Anderson had a 300-yard passing game, but it mattered little in the final count.
UPI

4-yard line with only 2 seconds left, and Wersching kicked a 26-yard field goal. At halftime, the 49ers had a commanding 20–0 lead.

Once again, a Super Bowl game was not living up to expectations. But Walsh was not ready to begin accepting congratulations. Anderson could always score in a hurry. The game was not beyond the Bengals' reach.

Anderson did just that early in the third quarter, ending a long drive with a 5-yard dash into the end zone to cut the deficit to 20–7. Then the Bengals came right back and drove to the 3-yard line. First down and goal to go.

Johnson bulldozed for 2 yards. Now it was second and 1. Again Johnson carried. No gain. On third down, Anderson faked into the line and threw a short pass to Charles Alexander, who was stopped in his tracks. Fourth and goal, still on the 1.

Johnson carried again, using the force of his 250 pounds. But the inspired 49ers' defense stopped him short of the end zone. It was an impressive goal-line stand.

The defense did not have a chance to relax. Early in the fourth quarter, the Bengals scored when Anderson threw a 4-yard touchdown pass to Ross. The 49ers led, 20–14.

San Francisco's Ray Wersching boots the winning field goal, his fourth of the game.

UPI

Now Montana sensed the game slipping away. He led the 49ers' on a 50-yard drive, staying mostly on the ground this time but completing an important 20-yard pass to Mike Wilson. Wersching's 40-yard field goal made it 23–14.

Minutes later, Eric Wright intercepted Anderson's pass, giving the 49ers another scoring opportunity. They played it safe and took Wersching's 23-yard field

A first for the professor, 49er coach Bill Walsh.
George Gojkovich

goal. With 1:57 left in the game, the 49ers led, 26–14.

The Bengals gave it one last try. Anderson completed 6 consecutive passes, the last one a 3-yard touchdown toss to Ross. But there wasn't enough time. The 49ers held on to win Super Bowl XVI, 26–21.

Montana was voted Most Valuable Player and Walsh received a congratulatory telephone call from President Ronald Reagan. "This is the ultimate in my career," the coach said. "I cannot conceive of a more satisfying moment."

JOE MONTANA
Climbing the
Mountain

For a man reserved to the point of shyness, Joe Montana is all passion and fireworks when let loose before a frenzied crowd of football fans.

Although he insists, "I'm just plain Joe," Montana has been the guiding force behind some of the most remarkable comebacks ever seen in football. At Notre Dame his reputation was such that he was the inspiration for a song, "The Ballad of Joe Montana."

Saving his best Houdini act in college for last, Montana concluded his college career with a particularly memorable performance when he led the Irish from a 22-point deficit in the final quarter to a 35–34 victory over Houston in the 1978 Cotton Bowl.

Despite this whirlwind windup to an already exceptional list of accomplishments, Montana carried a reputation for being inconsistent and erratic, and in the 1979 draft he lasted until the third round.

A dedicated worker who frequently stayed late to practice with his receivers and then studied films at night, Montana won the full-time starting job with San Francisco midway through his second year, and the following season, 1981, he helped the 49ers win the Super Bowl.

Before reaching Super Bowl XVI, however, the 49ers had to deal with Dallas in the NFC championship game, and they were trailing by 6 points when they got the ball on their own 11 with only 4:54 remaining. Montana then led San Francisco on a relentless drive, culminating with a 6-yard touchdown pass to Dwight Clark with 51 seconds to play for a 28–27 triumph.

MVP Joe Montana earned a large chunk of the Super Bowl championship trophy.

UPI

Taking a different tack in the Super Bowl, Montana helped San Francisco to a 20–0 halftime lead over Cincinnati, and the 49ers held on for a 26–21 victory. Montana wound up as MVP, the first of two times he would be so honored.

Explaining his ability to accept success without much fuss, Montana said, "I think a lot of it has to do with my nature. I'm a reserved type person, and I don't let a lot of my feelings show. I handle things within myself. I try not to let what's happened change me."

Scoring Summary

San Francisco 49ers(NFC) ..   7 13   0   6—26
Cincinnati Bengals (AFC)   0   0   7 14—21

San Francisco—Montana, run 1 (Wersching kick)
San Francisco—Cooper, pass from Montana 11 (Wersching kick)
San Francisco—Wersching (FG) 22
San Francisco—Wersching (FG) 26
Cincinnati—Anderson, run 5 (Breech kick)
Cincinnati—Ross, pass from Anderson 4 (Breech kick)
San Francisco—Wersching (FG) 40
San Francisco—Wersching (FG) 23
Cincinnati—Ross, pass from Anderson 3 (Breech kick)

SKINNING THE DOLPHIN

**Washington's John Riggins slips from the grasp
of Miami's Don McNeal en route to the winning
touchdown in Super Bowl XVII.**

UPI

Participants—Miami Dolphins, champions of the American Football Conference, and Washington Redskins, champions of the National Football Conference.

Date—January 30, 1983.

Site—Rose Bowl, Pasadena, California.

Time—3:00 P.M., PST.

Attendance—103,667.

Radio and TV—National Broadcasting Company (TV); Columbia Broadcasting System (radio).

Regular-Season Records—Miami, 7–2; Washington, 8–1.

Playoff Records—Miami defeated New England Patriots, 28–13, San Diego Chargers, 31–28, and New York Jets, 14–0, for AFC title; Washington defeated Detroit Lions, 31–7, Minnesota Vikings, 21–7, and Dallas Cowboys, 31–17, for NFC title.

Players' Shares—$36,000 to each member of winning team; $18,000 to each member of losing team.

Coaches—Don Shula, Miami; Joe Gibbs, Washington.

SKINNING THE DOLPHIN

If the Super Bowl is the culmination of the pro football season, then it would have been proper and fitting had Super Bowl XVII been remaned "the Super Cup" on this one occasion. That would have been in keeping with the spirit and theme of the 1982 season when the real world intruded and the NFL season was cut short by the players' strike.

The fifty-seven-day walkout began after the third game of the regular season. There had been rumors and threats of a strike, and negotiations were at an impasse, yet many fans and football officials were stunned when the players made good their threat. For eight weeks, football widows welcomed their reluctant husbands back into the family. For eight weeks, even coach Dick Vermeil of the Philadelphia Eagles locked away his game plans and took the time to be with his family, discovering, he said, the beauty of autumn.

But an autumn without pro football left many fans with an emptiness that could not be filled. And when the season finally resumed, some fans were unforgiving and stayed away from the stadiums. Being a football player was the ultimate fan's fantasy. With the exception of boxing, it seemed like the most macho of all games, played by hulking young men who dressed like knights in armor and jousted in the arena on Sunday afternoons. Football fans could not understand why players would strike.

NFL commissioner Pete Rozelle had always been a master in public relations, putting the sport's best foot forward. But now, gambling and drug scandals were threatening to undermine football's popularity, and the strike added another negative note.

In an attempt to salvage a nine-game regular season and rekindle interest, Rozelle created a one-time Super Bowl Tournament, inviting sixteen teams to the playoffs. Out of this logjam, the Washington Redskins and Miami Dolphins emerged to earn berths in Super Bowl XVII on January 30.

It was as if the playoffs had been staged so that the Redskins and Dolphins could meet on the tenth anniversary of Super Bowl VII, when Don Shula's Dolphins had completed a perfect 17–0 season with a 14–7 victory against the Redskins. That was in more pleasant times for Rozelle—when interest in pro football was peaking.

The Redskins in 1982 were a lot like those perfect Dolphins. Joe Theismann was a nimble quarterback who excelled in the short passing game in the manner of Bob Griese, and in John Riggins the Redskins had a bull-like fullback who reminded fans of Larry Csonka.

The football strike may have dampened enthusiasm in a lot of cities, but Washington, D.C., quickly recovered from the blahs. The nation's capital, where decisions affecting world events are made on a daily basis, had gone hog-wild over the Redskins. A city that would collectively yawn over another presidential inauguration or a visit from a foreign dignitary lost all semblance of decorum over the beloved Redskins.

This was a team that had opened the previous season by losing its first five games under new coach Joe Gibbs, a development that had some fans wondering if President Reagan could step in and do something. But the Redskins won eight of their remaining eleven games in 1981, then took eight of nine in 1982, before sweeping three more playoff games.

In a city of sophistication and reserve, the Redskins won with players who called themselves "The Hogs," "The Fun Bunch" (who had a unique end zone celebration), and "The Smurfs," the crew of small wide receivers. They were carried on the broad shoulders of Riggins, "The Diesel," a thirty-three-year-old eccentric who quit pro football in 1980 when he felt he was not being paid enough.

The holes that Riggins ran through were made by "The Hogs," the Redskins' offensive linemen, who were nicknamed by assistant coach Joe Bugel. The Hogs had become fashionable in Washington, where people sported "Hog Power" T-shirts. George Starke, a veteran tackle, anchored the line, which included four free agents and four draft choices.

Compared to the publicity surrounding the Redskins, the Dolphins came to Super Bowl XVII with relatively little fanfare. They had not played in the Super Bowl in nine years, although they continued to be a playoff team. But the playoffs became a stumbling block as the Dolphins lost nine consecutive postseason games.

That they would break the losing streak in the roulette wheel Super Bowl Tournament was unexpected. Shula still was regarded as a masterful coach, but his team was too young, the experts said. The biggest inconsistency was the quarterback position played by third-year pro David Woodley.

Woodley had attended Louisiana State, where he shared the position. He was an option quarterback in college who lacked the experience to move in as a pro starter in his rookie year. But Shula utilized Woodley's running ability and brought him along slowly in the passing game. Thus, the Dolphins relied on a more conservative attack.

When touchdowns were needed or Woodley was having an especially trying day, Shula turned to veteran backup Don Strock, a capable passer who knew the offense as well as anyone who ever played for Shula. The combination of Woodley and Strock was known as "Woodstrock" in Miami.

The Dolphins were not considered in a class with their Super Bowl predecessors who made three consecutive trips to the big game, but there was ample talent on hand. Tony Nathan and Andra Franklin were dependable, if not flashy runners. Nat Moore and Duriel Harris were fast, sure-handed receivers. On defense, the "No-Names" were replaced by the "Killer B's," the nickname given the unit because the last names of several players on the unit began with the letter B.

"Things fell into place for us," said Shula, who was coaching in his fifth Super Bowl game, four with the Dolphins and one with the Baltimore Colts.

By game time on January 30, any lingering bad feelings in the strike-shortened season were forgotten as 103,667 came to the Rose Bowl for football's showcase game. Many were from Washington and Miami and were dressed in the colors of their favorite teams. It was a beautiful day in Southern California, and tailgate picnics began hours before game time.

There was one particularly big party going on under a candy-striped tent. Dixieland music was played and 800 people in red jackets ate barbecued chicken and drank beer. The sponsor of this affair was the Nissan Motor Company of Japan. The Super Bowl had truly become a worldwide spectacle.

Once the game began, the Dolphins assumed an early lead on a play that exploited the Redskins' zone defense. With the ball on his own 24-yard line, Woodley passed to Jimmy Cefalo, who was open on the sideline between defenders. He caught the ball and sprinted for the end zone as a stunned crowd looked on. Only 7 minutes into the game, the young Dolphins led, 7–0.

"Woodley read that zone perfectly," Cefalo said. "I just caught the ball between them and outran everyone."

The defenses controlled the action for the remainder of the first quarter and early into the second, when Dexter Manley sacked Woodley, causing a fumble. The Redskins recovered on the Miami 46-yard line. Theismann then led into field-goal range, where Mark Moseley converted from 31 yards out. The score was 7–3.

Any advantage the Redskins might have gained from that score was negated when Fulton Walker fielded the ensuing kickoff and ran it back 42 yards to give the Dolphins excellent field position. Woodley maneuvered them downfield another 50 yards in 13 plays before Uwe von Schamann kicked a 20-yard field goal to put Miami ahead, 10–3. There were 6 minutes remaining in the first half, but the action had just begun.

With 1:51 remaining, Theismann completed an 80-yard march when he flipped a 4-yard touchdown pass to Alvin Garrett, one of the Smurfs. The score was tied at 10–10 at halftime.

The Redskins had to figure a way to contain Walker on those kickoffs. He fielded Jeff Hayes' next one on the 2-yard line, broke through the first wave of Redskins, and did not stop running until he had covered 98 yards and scored a touchdown. The opportunistic Dolphins had moved ahead, 17–10.

The Redskins were annoyed. Gibbs was an offensive-minded coach, but in the playoffs he had turned to ball possession and Riggins. His team wasn't playing as he had envisioned.

Early in the third quarter, the Redskins were able to control the football, however, and moved 61 yards into field-goal range. The big play was an end reverse from Riggins to Garrett that gained 44 yards. But when Moseley had to settle for a 20-yard field goal, fans began to wonder whether the Redskins would be able to penetrate the Killer B's for the touchdown they needed.

In fact, the defense very nearly added to the Dolphins' point total when defensive end Kim Bokamper deflected a Theismann pass on the Washington 5-yard line and almost intercepted it for an easy touchdown. Theismann dove for Bokamper, however, and jarred the ball loose from his grasp, saving 7 points. As the period ended, Miami still led, 17–13.

The Redskins' defense was also doing its job. Woodley had become ineffective in the second half and seemed rattled. The Dolphins were not able to even get a first down. Their defense was becoming overworked.

Finally, it cost them. On a fourth and 1 from the Miami 43, Theismann handed off to Riggins, who bolted through a hole, broke several tackles, and rambled into the end zone for the go-ahead touchdown. The Redskins led for the first time, 20–17.

Again, Woodley was unable to move the Dolphins, and Washington took over. With 8:49 to play, the Redskins turned to Riggins, who ate up yardage in short chunks that kept the drive going. The Redskins

**His own pass blocked by Miami's Kim Bokamper,
Washington quarterback Joe Theismann plays the
defender and knocks the ball loose on one of the
big plays of the game.**

UPI

moved to the 6-yard line, where Theismann faked a
handoff, then threw into the end zone for Charlie
Brown. The touchdown made the score 27–17, and
Don Strock could not get the Dolphins closer in the
final minutes.

The final gun started a wild celebration among the
Redskins and the fans in Washington, D.C. There was
another celebratory telephone call from President
Reagan—this time to Gibbs—and Riggins easily won
the Most Valuable Player award, having established a
Super Bowl record with 166 yards gained on 38 carries. But it was easy, he said. All he'd had to do was
follow the "Hogs."

Washington's Charlie Brown scores the insurance touchdown on a pass from Joe Theismann.

UPI

JOHN RIGGINS
"The Diesel"

To best sum up the turbulent times and tantalizing talent of John Riggins, you can start with the word "different."

So different, indeed, that Riggins is unique among football players both as a free spirit and a rambling, awesomely powerful fullback.

Early in his career Riggins demonstrated a propensity for attracting attention when he showed up at the New York Jets' 1973 training camp with a Mohawk haircut (his head was shaved except for a strip of hair down the middle). "I did it for the fun of it," he explained. "I did it to show everyone I was boss of my own destiny."

And to the best that any team player is able, Riggins retained control of his destiny. Disenchanted with the Jets, he left them after becoming the club's first-ever 1,000-yard rusher in 1975. He'd led the Jets in rushing (769 yards) and receiving (231) as a rookie in 1971, and the next year he ran for 944 yards. It was in 1973 that he became a summer holdout when the Jets refused to give him a substantial raise.

After playing out his option in 1975, he signed as a free agent with the Redskins in 1976 and continued to reflect his simple tastes but single-minded manner. He literally gave away $300,000 when he chose to sit out all of 1980.

"I am a man of many different faces," Riggins said. "If you scrape off the outside stuff, down deep inside I don't know who I am, and I guess most people don't."

From the days when he shattered the school records

of Gale Sayers at Kansas, there was never any question about the natural abilities of Riggins, a physical, punishing runner who grew up on a farm.

In the 1982 playoffs he became the first player to rush for more than 100 yards in four consecutive playoff games, totaling 610 yards.

During Super Bowl week in Los Angeles, Riggins— always the individualist—attended Redskins owner Jack Kent Cooke's party dressed in white tails and tophat—a fun prelude to Super Sunday when "The Diesel" was the MVP in the Redskins' 27–17 upset of the Dolphins.

This may have been the biggest thrill for him since he saw his picture on a bubble gum card.

Scoring Summary

Miami Dolphins (AFC)	7	10	0	0—17
Washington Redskins (NFC)..	0	10	3	14—27

Miami—Cefalo, pass from Woodley 76 (von Schamann kick)
Washington—Moseley (FG) 31
Miami—von Schamann (FG) 20
Washington—Garrett, pass from Theisman 4 (Moseley kick)
Miami—Walker, kickoff return 98 (von Schamann kick)
Washington—Moseley (FG) 20
Washington—Riggins, run 43 (Moseley kick)
Washington—Brown, pass from Theismann 6 (Moseley kick)

SUPER BOWL XVIII

RAIDERS ON THE MOVE

The Raiders' Marcus Allen races for the longest touchdown in Super Bowl history.

Participants—Los Angeles Raiders, champions of the American Football Conference, and Washington Redskins, champions of the National Football Conference.

Date—January 22, 1984.

Site—Tampa Stadium, Tampa, Florida.

Time—4:30 P.M., EST.

Attendance—72,920.

Radio and TV—Columbia Broadcasting System (TV and radio).

Regular-Season Records—Los Angeles, 12–4; Washington, 14–2.

Playoff Records—Los Angeles defeated Pittsburgh Steelers, 38–10, and Seattle Seahawks, 30–14, for AFC title; Washington defeated Los Angeles Rams, 51–7, and San Francisco 49ers, 24–21, for NFC title.

Players' Shares—$36,000 to each member of winning team; $18,000 to each member of losing team.

Coaches—Tom Flores, Los Angeles; Joe Gibbs, Washington.

SUPER BOWL XVIII

RAIDERS ON THE MOVE

Against the wishes of commissioner Pete Rozelle and the other owners in the National Football league, Al Davis, the Black Bart of pro football, had moved the Raiders from Oakland to Los Angeles, from a blue-collar city to Tinseltown.

The results during the 1983 regular season, however, were very much the same: by any address, the Raiders were one of the most successful teams in sports history. They were going to the Super Bowl for the third time in eight years and fourth overall.

Black and silver were the colors the Raiders wore, and they looked ominous and out of place in Los Angeles, a city of pastels. The Raiders were not cut in the image of the sun worshippers and surfers who munched on salads and avocados and talked about finding "their own space." The Raiders were more like a lunch-pail crew, aggressive and hardworking. They made their own space even if it infringed on someone else's territory. The NFL was fighting in federal court to send the Raiders back where the league said they belonged —to Oakland—but thus far, Davis was winning the legal fight. It was his team, he said, and he was free to move it wherever he wanted without the permission of his fellow owners.

The Raiders were already known as a team of misfits and malcontents, unwanted by other teams. They played an intimidating style of football. And Davis had been Rozelle's adversary since the merger of the old American Football League and the NFL. But even if the Raiders were not especially well liked around the league, there was grudging respect for the way they performed on the playing field.

Super Bowl XVIII gave them an opportunity to confront America's latest football heroes—the Washington Redskins. John Riggins, Joe Theismann, the Smurfs, the Fun Bunch, and the Hogs were back in the championship game, trying to become the first team since the Pittsburgh Steelers to win consecutive Super Bowl titles.

Ironically, the Raiders played a style that was more along traditional football lines. "We play a two-back offense, we play man-to-man, bump-and-run, pass defense," Davis said. "Our quarterbacks call their own plays. Some of the other teams, well, all the technical stuff they use is getting so technical, I don't think they understand it themselves."

The Redskins were one of those technical teams, in Davis' estimation. Under Joe Gibbs, the Redskins ran some very basic plays but masked them in a variety of formations and shifts that were intended to confuse defenses. Gibbs was an offensive coordinator before becoming a head coach and was considered one of the more innovative coaches in the sport.

Still, it was difficult to characterize any team with a workhorse running back like Riggins as being wide open. In Theismann, though, Gibbs had a quarterback who was small by professional standards and who was most effective when rolling out and throwing on the run. The various formations and shifts helped keep defenses from mounting a big rush that could smother the agile but still vulnerable Theismann.

After Riggins followed the Hogs to glory in Super Bowl XVII, Theismann had emerged during the 1983 season to become a cover-boy quarterback and star of the Redskins. He was not the shy, reserved type that made most quarterbacks comparable to space shuttle commanders. Theismann had become accustomed to publicity when he attended Notre Dame and the sports information director changed the pronunciation of his name from "Theezman" to "Thighsman" in his junior year to rhyme with the Heisman Trophy.

Theismann never won the award, but he was an

All-American who led the fighting Irish to a 20–3–2 record in his starting career. In his senior year, he finished second in the Heisman voting to Jim Plunkett, who would be the quarterback for the Raiders in Super Bowl XVIII.

Because he weighed less than 180 pounds, Theismann was considered too small for the NFL and played in Canada for three years. In 1974, he returned and became a backup to Sonny Jurgensen and Billy Kilmer with the Redskins. Theismann didn't play much at quarterback, but he was a punt returner for two seasons.

Now, he was rated as one of the most intelligent and effective quarterbacks in the NFL even if he lacked size and a strong arm. He was a celebrity in Washington, D.C., good-looking and glib, a person who soaked up the spotlight.

His success made the Redskins favorites to repeat as champions in the first Super Bowl game to be played in Tampa, Florida. The Raiders had been trying to give the starting quarterback position to Marc Wilson, a tall, rangy, strong-armed passer with healthy knees. But injuries kept interfering with Wilson's progress, and Plunkett had stepped in again to lead the team to a 13–3 regular-season record.

The Raiders still had many of the characteristics that defined their teams through the years—the defense was stingy and punishing, the offense was capable of making the big play. But there were two important additions.

Marcus Allen, in his second year, had given the Raiders a breakaway runner, the first one the team ever had. Previously, the Raiders relied on the power running of sturdy backs such as Marv Hubbard, Mark van Eeghen, and Clarence Davis.

Defensively, Al Davis had pulled off a coup late in the season when he acquired Mike Haynes from the New England Patriots. Haynes was disgruntled in New England and had wanted to be traded. For a number-one draft choice, the Raiders acquired an all-pro cornerback to team with their other all-pro on the other side, Lester Hayes.

Hayes and Haynes may have sounded like the name of a vaudeville act, but they toyed with opposing teams' passing games. Quarterbacks rarely challenged either player and tried to beat the Raiders' defense by throwing to the running backs or the tight end.

The Redskins, however, were not conceding anything to the Raiders during Super Bowl week. Alvin Garrett, one of the Smurfs, Charlie Brown, and Art Monk figured they would be able to get open against the cornerbacks, especially when Theismann began to scramble, which would break down the defense. And there was always Riggins to soften that defense—ready, willing, and able to carry the ball 35 times if need be.

It was a consensus among the reporters and NFL officials that the Redskins had too much offense for the Raiders. They had met earlier in the season and Washington had won that offensive show, 37–35. The Redskins did not think there was anything the Raiders had done since then that would make a big difference in the Super Bowl.

The Raiders felt differently. They had played poorly on defense in that first meeting, a result of mistakes rather than deficiencies. "I get up in the middle of the night and run films of that game," said Matt Millen, the Raiders' hard-nosed 250-pound linebacker. "I just can't sleep thinking about this game.

"I lie in bed at three A.M. or four A.M., wishing I could play it right then. If we just don't screw up and overpursue and make mistakes, we'll kill them."

Super Sunday was a clear day, but a strong, swirling wind threatened to make it difficult for either team to throw the long pass. The wind was a factor from the start as Theismann had trouble throwing deep.

Late in the first quarter, after failing to move the ball, the Redskins were forced to punt. But the snap was high, and Jeff Hayes and Derrick Jensen, the captain of the Raiders' special teams, broke up the middle and blocked the punt, then recovered in the end zone for a touchdown. The Raiders led, 7–0.

The game continued to be a defensive contest as the

The Raiders set the tone of Super Bowl XVIII by flattening the Redskins' John Riggins.

UPI

Redskins were stymied by the Raiders' ability to clog the openings in the line and keep Riggins from finding room to run. Millen was especially effective at helping to shut down Riggins before the big fullback could gain any momentum. The Hogs, apparently, had met their match.

On offense, Plunkett was content to play it safe, not risking any unnecessary passes in the tricky wind. With 10:48 to play in the first half, however, with the ball on his own 35-yard line, he decided to open up the attack.

Plunkett spotted Cliff Branch open down the middle, where the wide receiver had split the defense. His pass to Branch was on target, and the receiver wasn't caught until he had reached the Redskins' 15-yard line. Two plays later, Plunkett completed a 12-yard pass to Branch for a touchdown. The Raiders led, 14–0.

Theisman finally began to move the Redskins after the next kickoff. They maneuvered into field-goal range, where Mark Moseley's 24-yarder narrowed the deficit to 14–3.

As the half was coming to a close, the Redskins had the ball again on their 12-yard line. There were 12 seconds remaining, and the fans figured that Washington would be satisfied to run out the clock and try again in the third quarter. But that wasn't Gibbs' style. In the first game against the Raiders, he had called a screen pass in a similar situation and it had worked for 67 yards. Maybe the play would work again and the Redskins could get a big lift from a last-second score.

But Charlie Sumner, the Raiders' defensive coach, had remembered that play, too. As a precaution, he replaced Millen—who was at his best against the run—with Jack Squirek, a better pass defender for a linebacker. When the ball was snapped, Lyle Alzado, the defensive lineman slipped between Theismann and Joe Washington, the intended receiver on the screen pass.

Theismann did not see Squirek coming up to defend against Washington. His pass was thrown high and softly to get over Alzado's outstretched arms. It enabled Squirek to intercept it and return for an easy touchdown. In a shocking turn of events, the Raiders had taken a 21–3 halftime lead.

A second Super Bowl crown for ex-Raider quarterback Tom Flores.

UPI

That would make the Redskins' task so much more difficult. But they did not give up. They took the second-half kickoff and drove 70 yards for a touchdown, John Riggins plunging over from the one. The conversion attempt was blocked, but the Redskins were back in the game, 21-9.

Now it was time for the Raiders to regain the impetus. Plunkett and the offense had been quiet except for one drive. It was their turn. They moved 70 yards in methodical fashion, relying on Allen's slashing runs and short passes by Plunkett. The drive ended at its destination when Allen scored from 5 yards out. It was 28-9, Raiders.

On their next possession, Plunkett decided to stick with the running game. The ball was on the Raiders'

26-yard line when the quarterback handed off to Allen, who started wide, then cut back inside and accelerated. In a split second, he had broken free and was unescorted as he ran 74 yards for a touchdown. "I kind of cut back and they kind of missed me." Allen said. "It was all a reaction. No thinking involved."

The touchdown gave the Raiders an insurmountable 35–9 lead. And the anticipated closely played rematch never materialized. Chris Bahr added a 21-yard field goal to make it 38–9. Theismann, Riggins, and the Redskins were hardly the Fun Bunch this time as the game ended and the Raiders had become Super Bowl champions for the third time.

Allen, who gave the offense that extra dimension, was named the Most Valuable Player. He gained 191 yards on 20 carries, a Super Bowl record that broke the mark Riggins had established a year earlier. And a happy Al Davis contemplated even more success. "This is the greatest team we ever had," he said. "And next year, God, wait 'til next year. The depth we'll have on this team will be something."

MARCUS ALLEN
Records for
"Young Juice"

In both style and performance, Marcus Allen often reminded people of O. J. Simpson, and in college his teammates called him "Young Juice."

Allen, like his illustrious friend well spoken and with an outgoing personality, is a total team player who runs, blocks, catches the ball, and throws it well. He has been a sensation wherever he's performed, starting at Lincoln High School in San Diego when, in his senior year, he passed for 1,434 yards and 9 touchdowns, rushed for 1,098 yards and 12 TDs, and also starred on defense.

Moving on to USC, he received little opportunity to display his talents his first two years. Nevertheless, upon his graduation, Allen took with him twelve NCAA records and a share of a thirteenth. As a senior in 1981, Allen became the first collegian to rush for more than 2,000 yards in a season, totaling 2,342, and he registered five consecutive 200-yard games as he also carried away the Heisman Trophy.

Despite these credentials, Allen was thought to be neither big enough nor fast enough to be a superstar in the pros, and as a result he was only the tenth player chosen in the 1982 draft. Allen, who contends, "I'm faster than most people think I am," wasted no time proving his detractors wrong.

In his NFL debut he rushed for 116 yards against San Francisco, and he went on to lead the NFL in scoring, the first rookie to do so since Gale Sayers in 1965. Allen was chosen Rookie of the Year and was also selected for the Pro Bowl.

Allen provided an appropriate encore the following year, earning the MVP award in Super Bowl XVIII with his record running performance as the Los Angeles Raiders routed Washington, 38–9.

Adopting a common-sense approach to his accomplishments, Allen said, "I'm very fortunate, but I realize that what I have today can be gone tomorrow. I always remember that."

Scoring Summary

	1	2	3	4	
Washington Redskins (NFC)..	0	3	6	0	—9
Los Angeles Raiders (AFC) ..	7	14	14	3	—38

Los Angeles—Jensen, recovered blocked punt in end zone (Bahr kick)

Los Angeles—Branch, pass from Plunkett 12 (Bahr kick)

Washington—Moseley (FG) 24

Los Angeles—Squirek, interception 5

Washington—Riggins, run 1

Los Angeles—Allen, run 5 (Bahr kick)

Los Angeles—Allen, run 74 (Bahr kick)

Los Angeles—Bahr (FG) 21

SUPER BOWL XIX

GROUNDING THE DOLPHIN FLIPPER

San Francisco's Joe Montana ran as well as passed on the way to his second MVP award in Super Bowl XIX.

Wide World

Participants—Miami Dolphins, champions of the American Football Conference, and San Francisco 49ers, champions of the National Football Conference.

Date—January 20, 1985.

Site—Stanford Stadium, Stanford, California.

Time—3:00 P.M., PST.

Attendance—84,059.

Radio and TV—American Broadcasting Company (TV); Columbia Broadcasting System (radio).

Regular-Season Records—Miami, 14–2; San Francisco, 15–1.

Playoff Records—Miami defeated Seattle Seahawks, 31–10, and Pittsburgh Steelers, 45–28, for AFC title; San Francisco defeated New York Giants, 21–10, and Chicago Bears, 23–10, for NFC title.

Players' Shares—$36,000 to each member of winning team; $18,000 to each member of losing team.

Coaches—Don Shula, Miami; Bill Walsh, San Francisco.

GROUNDING THE DOLPHIN

No one could explain why it happened. If the Super Bowl did not bring together the two best teams in pro football, then it was certainly a matchup of good teams that had capitalized on a well-timed hot streak or good fortune. Why, then, had this showcase game so rarely lived up to expectations? Why had all but a handful of the celebrated matchups ended in defensive tugs-of-war or one-sided contests?

Perhaps the publicity preceding the Super Bowl made it almost impossible for one game to meet the demands of the fans. Perhaps if the Super Bowl were a best two-of-three series, or four-of-seven, it would unfold like a book with several chapters, building to a climax. Instead, the Super Bowl lasted sixty minutes, and fans wanted all of them to be like a highlight film.

Past disappointments and Super letdowns, though, did not spoil the anticipation for the next Super Bowl. And Super Bowl XIX promised to be everything most of its predecessors weren't. Even the most recent matchup between the Los Angeles Raiders and Washington Redskins, which had turned Super Bowl XVIII into a rout by halftime, was forgotten as the fans eagerly waited for the meeting of the two most dashing and exciting quarterbacks in the NFL—Joe Montana of the San Francisco 49ers and Dan Marino of the Miami Dolphins.

Super Bowl XIX promised to be an offensive carnival no matter what had occurred in the past. How was the Dolphins' suspect defense going to stop Montana and the versatile 49ers offense devised by that resident silver-haired genius, coach Bill Walsh?

And how were the 49ers going to stymie the most prolific single-season passer in NFL history? No team had been able to contain the curly-haired Marino in sixteen regular-season and two playoff games in 1984, as coach Don Shula abandoned his conservative, run-first, pass-later offense that characterized his five previous Super Bowl teams, for an all-out air show that left opposing teams dizzy from looking up.

"Marino," said Tom Flores, coach of the Raiders who defeated the Dolphins in a high-scoring game late in the season, "is simply frightening."

Thus, the final score of Super Bowl XIX promised to be the equivalent of a halftime score in a National Basketball Association game. Marino was a husky twenty-three-year-old second-year player who won the starting job early in his rookie season and played like an old pro.

As a collegian, Marino in his hometown at the University of Pittsburgh led the Panthers to four major bowl games but still incurred the wrath of fans who wanted a national championship. When Jackie Sherrill, the Pittsburgh coach, left after Marino's junior year to become head coach at Texas A&M, the Panthers were left without a direction on offense.

Marino slumped during his senior year, and there were rumors that he had a sore arm and was taking drugs. In part, that is why five other quarterbacks were selected ahead of him on the first round of the NFL's college draft. Shula, the opportunist, took one look at Marino's strong arm and quick release and selected him for the Dolphins.

In a relatively low-key atmosphere in Miami, Marino learned to relax. He was tanned and healthy-looking, and his own confidence was bolstered by Shula's faith in him. Marino replaced David Woodley at quarterback, and after Marino's superb rookie season, Shula traded Woodley to the Pittsburgh Steelers, a team that bypassed Marino in the draft.

But even Shula had not anticipated what 1984 would be like. Because of the death of running back David

Overstreet in an off-season automobile accident, and injuries to the other runners, the Dolphins were forced to rely on the passing game.

Marino made it a devastating force. He threw an NFL record 48 touchdown passes during the regular season. Including playoff games, he had passed for 5,767 yards and 55 touchdowns. He completed 64 percent of his passes. His favorite receivers were Mark Clayton, who had 73 receptions, and Mark Duper, who had 71. Mark I and Mark II, they were called in Miami.

In sixteen of eighteen games, the Dolphins had scored 4 or more touchdowns; in 10 games, Marino passed for 300 yards or more. Placekicker Ewe von Schamann was mired in a season-long slump and hardly anyone knew. It really didn't matter with Marino around.

The subject of all this attention was rather nonchalant about his success. After all the negative publicity in Pittsburgh when he was a collegian, Marino began to shy away from the limelight. "It's hard for me to describe myself," he said. "What do you want me to say? I find it hard talking about myself and explaining the way I am."

In contrast, Montana warmed to the spotlight. He had led the 49ers to victory in Super Bowl XVI, survived a disappointing season the next year, then recaptured the spirit and winning touch as the 49ers reasserted themselves as a playoff team in 1983. In the 1984 regular season, they finished with a 15–1 record, then added two more victories in the playoffs for a 17–1 record. In Super Bowl XIX, the 49ers had a chance to establish an NFL record for most victories in a single season.

Montana was twenty-eight years old now. Unlike Marino, who was a classic dropback passer, Montana was one of the new generation of quarterbacks, quick on his feet, agile, and most effective when throwing on the run. He didn't have the strongest arm in the league, but he completed 63 percent of his passes and threw for 32 touchdowns, a pretty good year compared to anyone except Marino.

"He's a great competitor," Walsh said. "A born leader,

a champion. He can make the spontaneous play as well as anyone who ever played the game."

The 49ers were considered a more well-rounded team than the Dolphins, which was why they were installed as the favorites. In addition to Montana, Roger Craig and Wendell Tyler gave them a running tandem they didn't have when they won their first Super Bowl game. Craig was also an excellent receiver and caught 75 passes to lead the team. Tyler had overcome a reputation for being a fumbler.

The 49ers also had a more dependable defense. The defensive backfield of Ronnie Lott, Eric Wright, Dwight Hicks, and Carlton Williamson all had been named to the NFC Pro Bowl team. They would provide the toughest test yet for Marino.

An added bonus for the 49ers was that Super Bowl XIX was being played in Palo Alto, California, on the campus of Stanford University, just twenty miles from San Francisco. Thus, the 49ers were only the second team in Super Bowl history to enjoy a home-field advantage. They had also played their last two regular-season games and two preceding playoff games at home, thus the 49ers had not been on the road since November.

Yet all these advantages could be for naught if Marino had one of his typically spectacular games. "No one has ever done these things before," an appreciative Shula said of his quarterback.

When Marino eclipsed Bob Griese's Dolphin passing records by midseason, Shula shrugged and said, "He just sort of tipped his wings and continued on."

What added to this matchup of Marino and Montana was that both were getting married shortly after the Super Bowl.

This only added to the upbeat feeling in the Bay Area during Super Bowl week. Fans enjoyed the attractions in San Francisco, the day trips to wine country, and the serenity of the Stanford campus. The only thing that spoiled the events preceding the game was a counterfeit ticket scam that left hundreds of ticket buyers disappointed and poorer.

On January 20, as the sun burned through the lingering morning fog, Super Bowl XIX—the great passing fancy—began before a crowd of 84,059 in Stanford Stadium.

The Dolphins quickly struck for a field goal in the opening quarter as Marino moved them 45 yards in 7 plays. The big play was a 25-yard pass from Marino to running back Tony Nathan. Von Schamann kicked a 37-yarder to put Miami in front, 3–0.

It didn't take Montana long to show what he could do. The 49ers began a 79-yard march of their own in which the quarterback effectively mixed his plays. Montana kept the drive alive with a 15-yard scramble on third down and then capped it with a 33-yard scoring pass to reserve back Carl Monroe. Now it was 7–3, San Francisco.

Perhaps Shula realized at this point that his inconsistent defense was not going to be able to contain Montana. If the Dolphins were to win, they would simply have to outscore the 49ers. So on the ensuing kickoff, Marino threw a challenge at the San Francisco defense: he operated without a huddle as if it were a 2-minute drill.

The action left the fans and the 49ers breathless. In just 2 minutes and 17 seconds, the Dolphins drove 70 yards in 6 plays, scoring on a 42-yard touchdown pass from Marino to tight end Dan Johnson. Miami led again, 10–7.

But that drive actually might have helped San Francisco in the long run. The 49ers were unable to make substitutions, for instance, sending more defensive backs into the game in passing situations.

So Walsh and his defensive coaches decided they would use a version of the Nickel Defense for the rest of the game. Instead of three linebackers, the 49ers used only one and had six defensive backs. Perhaps it would make it more difficult for Marino to throw.

Montana was having no such difficulty. A poor punt by Miami's Reggie Roby gave the 49ers good field position, and Montana led them on a 47-yard drive for a touchdown. He gained 19 yards on a quarterback draw, then passed 16 yards to Dwight Clark to set up

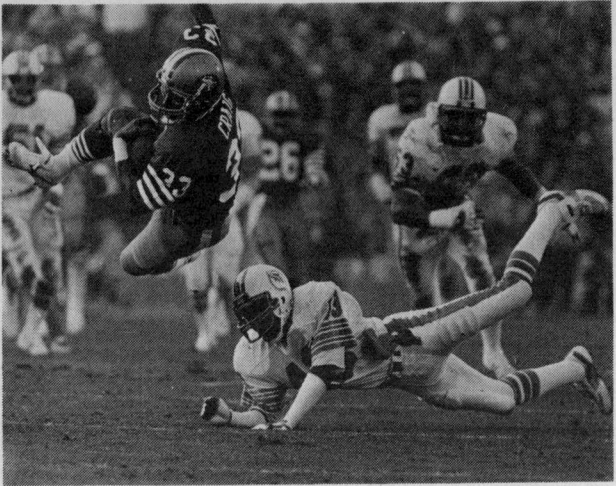

49er Roger Craig goes airborne as he crosses the goal line for one of his 2 first-half touchdowns.
Wide World

an eight-yard touchdown pass to Roger Craig for a 14–10 lead.

Later in the quarter, Montana scored again on a 6-yard run, making it 21–10. By now, the 49ers' defensive line was applying pressure to Marino, and the six defensive backs and linebacker were blanketing the receivers. Roby continued to punt poorly, and the 49ers continued to score. A 52-yard drive resulted in another touchdown as Craig ran over from the 2. Once again, Montana provided a key play—a 7-yard run.

Marino struggled as he hadn't all season. Von Schamann provided 2 more field goals as the first half ended, but San Francisco appeared in command with a 28–16 lead. When the Dolphin flipper was sacked three times early in the third quarter, the situation began to look desperate.

Meanwhile, Montana was toying with the Dolphins' defense. Ray Wersching kicked a 27-yard field goal to make it 31–16, and then the 49ers drove 70 yards in only 5 plays, with Montana throwing a 16-yard touchdown pass to Craig. It was difficult to believe, but Super Bowl XIX had become a rout. The 49ers led, 38–16.

Marino spent the remainder of the game adding to his passing totals but not the Dolphins' point totals. The 4–1–6 defense effectively took away the long pass, and Marino was under constant pressure from the four-man rush. It was an education for a young quarterback who had been playing the role of teacher all season.

Dan Marino, Miami's record-setting quarterback, endures the agony of frustration.

Wide World

When the game ended, the score was still 38–16, and the 49ers had won their second Super Bowl. Montana, who completed 24 passes for 331 yards and 3 touchdowns, and who had run for 59 more yards, was named Most Valuable Player for the second time.

"I haven't seen anything like that since I've been playing this game," Dolphin linebacker Bob Brudzinski said in praise of the 49ers. "They were awesome."

ROGER CRAIG
Setting a
Super Mark

One of the more important lessons Roger Craig learned in college was how to contain his ego.

For most of his career at Nebraska, Craig served as a backup to Jarvis Redwine and Mike Rozier, playing both tailback and fullback, and he adjusted so well to his role that he finished as the school's number-four all-time rusher with 2,446 yards. In addition, he ranked sixth in touchdowns (26) and eighth in total points (158).

Craig was selected in the second round of the 1983 draft, the first choice of San Francisco, and once again had to subvert any ambition he might have nourished to be the big star. But he is well able to accept his role, saying, "I'm just a spoke in a wheel."

Perhaps he is a bit more essential than a handy cog. A swift and powerful runner, Craig has become a key all-purpose back who is just as dangerous catching the ball as he is running with it.

He set a club rookie record in 1983 with 12 touchdowns and 72 points; 8 of his touchdowns came rushing, 2 more than the entire team total during the strike-shortened 1982 season.

Although he had little experience catching the ball, with only 16 receptions at Nebraska, where the pass was not a favored weapon, Craig had 83 receptions for 788 yards in regular-season and playoff games in 1984. As the club's number-two fullback, he also ranked second to Wendell Tyler in rushing with 785 yards.

Even in his most notable game, Craig wasn't the top star. In Super Bowl XIX, he scored 3 touchdowns, 2 on pass receptions of 8 and 16 yards and the other on a 2-yard run, as San Francisco crushed Miami, 38–16. But even though Craig was the first player to score 3 touchdowns in a Super Bowl game, it was quarterback Joe Montana who was selected as MVP.

"I'm more of a team player," Craig said of his role. "I'm not into being the individual player. That's not to say I couldn't take on that role, being the main man. I just try to play all my angles."

Scoring Summary

Miami Dolphins (AFC)	10	6	0	0—16
San Francisco 49ers (NFC) ..	7	21	10	0—38

Miami—von Schamann (FG) 37
San Francisco—Monroe, pass from Montana 33 (Wersching kick)
Miami—D. Johnson, pass from Marino 2 (von Schamann kick)
San Francisco—Craig, pass from Montana 8 (Wersching kick)
San Francisco—Montana, run 6 (Wersching kick)
San Francisco—Craig, run 2 (Wersching kick)
Miami—von Schamann (FG) 31
Miami—von Schamann (FG) 30
San Francisco—Wersching (FG) 27
San Francisco—Craig, pass from Montana 16 (Wersching kick)

SUPER BOWL TRIVIA QUIZ

(Answers start on page 252)

In the Beginning

1. What was the Super Bowl called before it was called the Super Bowl?
2. There were two different footballs used in Super Bowl I. Who made them, and what were their differences?
3. How much did the television rights to the first Super Bowl cost?
4. Who were the four announcers who covered the game for CBS?
5. Who were the three announcers who covered the game for NBC?
6. How much did each of the winning Packers receive for their Super Bowl efforts?
7. How much did each winning 49er receive after Super Bowl XIX?
8. True or false: The AFL's two-point conversion was in effect for Super Bowl I.
9. In Super Bowl I, only two of the Kansas City Chief players had NFL experience. Who were they?
10. Who was the only Green Bay Packer in uniform not to get into the first game?

Firsts

11. Who made the first Super Bowl tackle?
12. Who picked off the first pass interception in Super Bowl play?

13. Who was the first defender to return an intercepted pass for a touchdown?

14. Who was the first back to rush for 100 yards in the Super Bowl?

15. Which was the first Super Bowl to be played on artificial turf?

16. Which was the first Super Bowl to be played indoors?

17. Which was the first Super Bowl to be played in the Snow Belt?

18. Which was the first "wild card" team to play in the Super Bowl?

19. Which was the first "wild card" team to win the Super Bowl?

20. Who is the only head coach to win a Super Bowl in his first season as head coach?

Alma Mater

21. Match the Raider Super Bowl performers on the left with the colleges, on the right, where they played ball.
    1. Mike Eischeid   a. Villanova
    2. Gene Upshaw   b. Upper Iowa
    3. Ray Guy   c. Yankton
    4. Howie Long   d. Texas A&I
    5. Lyle Alzado   e. Southern Mississippi

22. Match these Dolphin Super Bowl performers with their schools.
    1. Doug Swift   a. Central College (Iowa)
    2. Lloyd Mumphord   b. Utah
    3. Manny Fernandez   c. Kentucky
    4. Vern Den Herder   d. Texas Southern
    5. Larry Seiple   e. Amherst

23. Penn State is often called Linebacker U., and true to this reputation, seven former Nittany Lions have played linebacker for Super Bowl teams. How many can you name?

24. Name four former Alabama quarterbacks who played in the Super Bowl.

25. Match these Viking Super Bowl performers with their schools.
    1. Grady Alderman
    2. Stu Voight
    3. Carl Eller
    4. Doug Sutherland
    5. Bob Lurtsema
    a. Western Michican
    b. Minnesota
    c. Wisconsin-Superior
    d. U. of Wisconsin
    e. Detroit

26. The Packers assembled their two Super Bowl teams from a variety of schools. Match the Super Bowl performers on the left with their colleges on the right.
    1. Elijah Pitts
    2. Fuzzy Thurston
    3. Max McGee
    4. Jerry Kramer
    5. Ron Kostelnik
    a. Idaho
    b. Tulane
    c. Cincinnati
    d. Philander Smith
    e. Valparaiso

27. Name six Super Bowl running backs who played their college ball for the Southern California Trojans.

28. Otis Sistrunk of the Raiders didn't play football in college, but which mythical school did he often claim as his *alma mater*?

29. The Dallas Cowboy scouting system often turned up pro prospects at small schools. Match the Dallas Super Bowl players on the left with the schools they attended.
    1. Rayfield Wright
    2. Cliff Harris
    3. Jethro Pugh
    4. Doug Dennison
    5. George Andrie
    a. Kutztown State
    b. Marquette
    c. Ouachita
    d. Fort Valley State
    e. Elizabeth City State

30. The Pittsburgh Steeler Super Bowl teams were built primarily through the draft. Match the players on the left with the schools from which they were taken on the right.
    1. Rocky Bleier
    2. Dwight White
    3. Terry Bradshaw
    4. Jack Deloplaine
    5. Steve Courson
    a. South Carolina
    b. Louisiana Tech
    c. Notre Dame
    d. East Texas State
    e. Salem College

Oops!

31. Who missed the most field-goal attempts in one game?
32. Who missed more field-goal attempts, 5, than anyone else in Super Bowl history?
33. Who was the first kicker to have an extra-point try blocked in Super Bowl competition?
34. Only one kicker has missed 2 extra-point attempts in the Super Bowl. Name him.
35. Who is the only punter to have a kick blocked for a safety?
36. Who has thrown more interceptions, 7, than any other passer in the Super Bowl?
37. Who is the all-time leading fumbler in Super Bowl history with 5?
38. Which offensive line allowed its quarterbacks to get sacked a record 7 times?
39. One of the sloppiest games ever—10 fumbles, 3 missed field goals, 4 interceptions—also produced the most penalties by two teams, 20. Who were the teams involved?
40. The record for the most turnovers by two teams in a Super Bowl is 11. Who set it?
41. Five times in the Super Bowl a quarterback was intercepted 3 or more times and each time his team lost the game. Name the harried passers.

Name Games

42. Supply the real first names for these Super Bowl performers.
    - a.) Mercury Morris
    - b.) Cris Collinsworth
    - c.) Ray Guy
    - d.) Tony Hill
43. Sixteen men named Brown have played in the Super Bowl, nine of them appearing more than once. How many of the nine can you name?
44. Although they really do have given names, these Super Bowl players are best known by their initials. Fill in the blanks.

A_____ J_____ Duhe
D_____ D_____ Lewis
E_____ J_____ Holub

45. What Super Bowl running back has the same name as a former pro basketball player and coach who is now coaching in the college ranks?

46. What Super Bowl backup quarterback had the same name as a well-traveled basketball player who played with nine different teams in the ABA and NBA?

47. What Super Bowl defensive end had the same name as a Brooklyn Dodger outfielder who once committed three errors in a World Series game?

48. What Super Bowl offensive lineman had the same name as the Olympic high jump champion who won the first medal of the 1936 Olympics?

49. What Super Bowl rusher had the same name as a major-league pitcher who twice lost 20 games in a season?

50. What Super Bowl player had the same name as a one-time manager of the Chicago Cubs in the mid-1970s?

51. Although Jones is one of the most common names, only four men with that name have played in the Super Bowl. Can you name them?

52. Match the teams on the left with their Super Bowl defenses on the right.
    1. Dallas   a. Orange Crush
    2. Pittsburgh   b. Doomsday Defense
    3. Miami   c. Purple People Eaters
    4. Denver   d. Steel Curtain
    5. Minnesota   e. No-Name Defense

53. True or false: A man named John Smith has never played in the Super Bowl.

54. Match the eight individuals on the left with the teams with which they appeared in the Super Bowl on the right.
    1. Jim Jensen   a. Cincinnati
    2. Jim Jensen   b. Denver
    3. Jim Hargrove   c. Kansas City
    4. Jim Hargrove   d. L.A. Raiders
    5. Larry Brown   e. Miami
    6. Larry Brown   f. Minnesota
    7. Johnny Robinson   g. Pittsburgh
    8. Johnny Robinson   h. Washington

Just for Kicks

55. Until Ray Wersching scored his 21st point in Super Bowl XIX, who was the all-time leading scorer among kickers with 20?
56. Who kicked the first field goal in Super Bowl history?
57. Who holds the record for the longest field goal in the Super Bowl?
58. The longest punt in Super Bowl history is 61 yards. Who kicked it?
59. True or false: There has never been a Super Bowl game without at least 1 field goal being attempted.
60. The single-game record for most punt attempts is 9. Who holds it?
61. Who has punted more, 17 times, than anyone else in the Super Bowl?
62. The highest punting average in a Super Bowl game is 48.5 yards per kick. Who holds the record?
63. Jim O'Brien kicked the only field goal that ever decided a Super Bowl back in III. Who was the holder? Who snapped the ball?

Defensive Troops

64. The Green Bay Packers started the same set of linebackers in both their Super Bowl victories. Name the trio.
65. What defensive lineman is credited with the first safety in Super Bowl competition?
66. What defensive lineman is credited with the last safety in Super Bowl competition?
67. Who were the three starting linebackers in the Cowboys' "Doomsday Defense" in Super Bowl VI?
68. One of the Super Bowl's more memorable plays is Garo Yepremian's fumbled pass attempt recovered by Mike Bass, who rambled 49 yards for a touchdown. What Redskin blocked the field goal attempt and forced Yepremian's error?
69. In the biggest upset in Super Bowl history, the Jets' defense held Baltimore scoreless until late

in the fourth quarter. Who were the New York linebackers who anchored the defense?

70. In Super Bowl IX, Pittsburgh's defense limited Minnesota to a total of 199 yards on offense. Who were the starting Steeler linebackers in that game?

71. Only four times has the team that scored first failed to win the Super Bowl. Name the teams and the Super Bowls.

72. Who were the four defensive linemen who started both Super Bowl I and Super Bowl IV for the Kansas City Chiefs?

73. The fewest points scored by two teams in one half is 2. How did the points come about?

74. Of these defensive backs, who is the only one to intercept a pass in the Super Bowl?
   a. George Atkinson
   b. Paul Krause
   c. Charlie Waters
   d. Jack Tatum
   e. Pat Fischer

Grabbers

75. One man holds the record for most yards gained on receptions and most receptions in Super Bowl competition. Name him.

76. Half of these receivers have never scored a Super Bowl TD. Which Three?
   a. Preston Pearson
   b. Drew Pearson
   c. Stu Voigt
   d. Paul Warfield
   e. Chuck Foreman
   f. Billy Joe DuPree

77. When Cincinnati's Dan Ross grabbed 11 passes in Super Bowl XVI, he broke the single-game record set by whom?

78. The longest scoring pass in Super Bowl history came in XV to a receiver who had not notched a TD reception all season. Name him.

79. Whose first, last, and only NFL reception came in the Super Bowl and was good for a touchdown?
80. True or false: No wide receiver has ever been named Super Bowl MVP.
81. Who has more TD receptions than anyone else in Super Bowl history?

Who Said?

82. "If the Super Bowl is the ultimate, how come they're playing it again next year?"
83. "If they want to protect the Super Bowl quarterback, put a dress on him."

Bowl Potpourri

84. What stadium has been the site of more Super Bowl games than any other?
85. All three Super Bowls that drew more than 100,000 attendance were played in the Rose Bowl. Which non-Pasadena game attracted the largest crowd under 100,000?
86. Which team holds the record for most consecutive Super Bowl appearances, at three?
87. Only five teams have appeared in the Super Bowl and never returned. Name them.
88. With the Raiders counting as one franchise, who is the only player to appear in the Super Bowl with three different teams?
89. Thirteen of the current twenty-eight NFL teams have never played in the Super Bowl. How many can you name?
90. Super Bowl V was the first game in which former Super Bowl teammates returned to the big game to line up against each other. Who were these players, and what was their former affiliation?

Run to Glory

91. Jim O'Brien's field goal won Super Bowl V for the Colts, but who was Baltimore's leading ground-gainer in that game with 33 yards on 10 carries?

92. Name the eight Heisman Trophy winners who have played in the Super Bowl.

93. In Super Bowl X, the Dallas Cowboys uncharac-teristically ran a reverse on a kickoff. Who trav-eled 48 yards with the ball before being tackled?

94. Who is the first running back to be named MVP in the Super Bowl?

95. Which of these running backs failed to score a TD in a Super Bowl?
    - a. Paul Hornung
    - b. Mercury Morris
    - c. Robert Newhouse
    - d. Mark van Eeghen
    - e. Chuck Foreman

96. When Fulton Walker returned a kickoff 98 yards for a TD, whose record of 67 yards on a nonscoring return did he break?

97. Miami is the only team ever to fail to score a touchdown in a single Super Bowl. The Dolphins managed only 3 points against Dallas in VI. Who was the Dolphins' "offensive" star, returning 4 kickoffs for a total of 90 yards?

Switches

98. One Super Bowl team had a quarterback who played on an NCAA championship *basketball* team and a coach who played on an NBA champion-ship team. Name them.

99. Speaking of basketball, who is the only player to appear in an ABA championship game as well as in two Super Bowls?

100. What star of an Emmy Award-winning televi-sion show played twice in the Super Bowl?

101. Who was the first athlete to perform in the Olym-pics and then play in a Super Bowl?

102. Who is the only man to play in the Super Bowl and box professionally?

103. Who was the injured Dolphin player moonlighting as a sportswriter who upset Redskin coach George Allen by interviewing his players prior to Super Bowl VII?

104. With the exception of special teams' personnel, only two men have started on offense and defense in Super Bowl games. Who are they?

105. Who was the first running back to complete a halfback option pass in the Super Bowl?

Field General

106. Which quarterback has been on the most Super Bowl teams?
     a. Earl Morrall
     b. Terry Bradshaw
     c. Roger Staubach

107. Which Super Bowl quarterback threw more passes than anyone else without connecting for a touchdown?

108. What quarterback started a Super Bowl game against the NFL team that originally drafted him?

109. In the New York Jets' upset victory in Super Bowl III, Joe Namath was at quarterback for all but one drive. Who replaced him then?

110. Who are the only two quarterbacks to score Super Bowl touchdowns?

111. Who has attempted the most passes, 98, in Super Bowl competition?

112. What two quarterbacks share the record of completing 8 consecutive passes in a Super Bowl?

113. What three quarterbacks have thrown more than 25 passes in Super Bowl play without an interception?

114. More than a dozen quarterbacks have been to the Super Bowl but not gotten to play. Name the half dozen who sat out two or more whole games.

Up and Down the Field

115. Which of these teams never scored more than 30 points in a winning Super Bowl effort?
     a. Dallas
     b. Green Bay
     c. Raiders
     d. Steelers
     e. Dolphins

116. The L.A. Raiders blew out Washington, 38–9, in Super Bowl XVIII. What was the next most-lopsided margin of victory?

117. Three teams have won the Super Bowl in January, but by the end of the following season have had losing records. Name them.

118. What is the shortest time between the first year a team competed and the year it first played in the Super Bowl?

119. Which two players had the longest time span—thirteen years—between their first and their last Super Bowl appearances?

120. Who is the only player from a losing team to be named MVP?

121. Who is the only man to play on an undefeated Super Bowl championship team and also play on an NFL team that didn't win a single game all season?

122. What owner created a stir when he offered to pay for wives to accompany their husbands to the Super Bowl city, but refused to pick up the tab for mothers, fiancées, or girlfriends of single players?

123. What two Super Bowl quarterbacks attended the same high school, Woodlawn High in Shreveport, Louisiana?

124. Match these Super Bowl performers with the degrees they earned in college.
     1. Dwight Clark   a. Geological engineering
     2. Mel Owens   b. History
     3. Joe Pellegrini   c. Literature
     4. Randy Hughes   d. Real Estate

125. What is the earliest date in January that a Super Bowl game has been played?

SUPER BOWL
TRIVIA ANSWERS

In the Beginning

1. The AFL-NFL World Championship Game
2. The AFL football was made by Spalding, the NFL's by Wilson. The AFL version was a quarter-inch longer, had ends that were slightly more pointed and was tackier to the touch.
3. CBS and NBC each paid $1 million to televise the game on their respective networks simultaneously.
4. Jack Whitaker, Ray Scott, Frank Gifford, Pat Summerall
5. Curt Gowdy, Paul Christman, Charlie Jones
6. $15,000
7. $36,000
8. False
9. Lenny Dawson, with Pittsburgh and Cleveland; Mike Mercer, with Minnesota
10. Paul Hornung

Firsts

11. Jim Weatherwax, Green Bay Packers
12. Willie Wood, Super Bowl I
13. Herb Adderley, Super Bowl II
14. Tom Matte, Baltimore (who hit the century mark in Super Bowl III slightly ahead of the Jets' Matt Snell)
15. Super Bowl V in Miami's Orange Bowl, Baltimore vs. Dallas

16. Super Bowl XII, Dallas vs. Denver, at the New Orleans Superdome
17. Super Bowl XVI, Cincinnati vs. San Francisco, Pontiac, Michigan
18. Dallas, Super Bowl X
19. Oakland Raiders, Super Bowl XV
20. Don McCafferty, Baltimore Colts, Super Bowl V

Alma Mater

21. 1-b, 2-d, 3-e, 4-a, 5-c
22. 1-e, 2-d, 3-b, 4-a, 5-c
23. Ralph Baker, New York Jets; Bruce Bannon, Miami; Matt Millen, Raiders; Jack Ham, Pittsburgh; Larry Kubin, Washington; Rich Milot, Washington; Dave Robinson, Green Bay
24. Joe Namath, Jeff Rutledge, Ken Stabler, Bart Starr
25. 1-e, 2-d, 3-b, 4-c, 5-a
26. 1-d, 2-e, 3-b, 4-a, 5-c
27. Marcus Allen, Raiders; Clarence Davis, Raiders; Mike Garrett, Chiefs; Mike Hull, Washington; Manfred Moore, Raiders; Ben Wilson, Packers
28. The University of Mars
29. 1-d, 2-c, 3-e, 4-a, 5-b
30. 1-c, 2-d, 3-b, 4-e, 5-a

Oops!

31. Efren Herrera, Dallas, Super Bowl XII
32. Roy Gerela, Pittsburgh, 2 of 7
33. Jim O'Brien, Baltimore, Super Bowl III
34. Errol Mann, Oakland, Super Bowl XI
35. Mitch Hoopes, Dallas, Super Bowl X
36. Craig Morton
37. Roger Staubach, Dallas
38. Dallas, Super Bowl X (vs. Pittsburgh)
39. Dallas vs. Denver, Super Bowl XII
40. Baltimore vs. Dallas, Super Bowl V
41. Earl Morrall, Baltimore, Super Bowl III; Craig

Morton, Dallas, Super Bowl V and Denver, Super Bowl XII; Billy Kilmer, Washington, Super Bowl VII; Fran Tarkenton, Minnesota, Super Bowl IX

Name Games

42. a. Eugene; b. Anthony; c. William; d. Leroy
43. Aaron Brown, Kansas City; Bill Brown, Minnesota; Bob Brown, Green Bay; Charlie Brown, Washington; Guy Brown, Dallas; Larry Brown, Pittsburgh; Terry Brown, Minnesota; Tom Brown, Green Bay; Willie Brown, Oakland
44. Adam Joseph Duhe, Dwight Douglas Lewis, Emil Joseph Holub
45. Larry Brown, Washington
46. Tom Owen, San Francisco
47. Willie Davis, Green Bay
48. Cornelius Johnson, Baltimore
49. Roger Craig
50. Jim Marshall
51. Clint Jones, Minnesota; Ed Jones, Dallas; Jimmie Jones, Washington; Willie Jones, Oakland
52. 1-b, 2-d, 3-e, 4-a, 5-c
53. True
54. 1-b or e; 2-b or e; 3-f or a; 4-f or a; 5-g or h; 6-g or h; 7-c or d; 8-c or d

Just for Kicks

55. Don Chandler, Green Bay
56. Mike Mercer, Kansas City, Super Bowl I
57. Jan Stenerud, Kansas City, 48 yards, Super Bowl IV
58. Jerrell Wilson, Kansas City, Super Bowl I
59. True
60. Ron Widby, Dallas, Super Bowl V
61. Mike Eischeid, Oakland and Minnesota
62. Jerrell Wilson, Kansas City, Super Bowl IV
63. Earl Morrall and Tom Goode, respectively

Defensive Troops

64. Dave Robinson, Ray Nitschke, Lee Roy Caffey

65. Dwight White, Pittsburgh
66. Reggie Harrison, Pittsburgh
67. Dave Edwards, Lee Roy Jordan, Chuck Howley
68. Bill Brundige
69. Ralph Baker, Al Atkinson, Larry Grantham
70. Jack Ham, Jack Lambert, Andy Russell
71. Dallas in Super Bowl V and X; Miami in Super Bowl XVII and XIX
72. Jerry Mays, Curly Culp, Buck Buchanan, Aaron Brown
73. In Super Bowl IX, Viking QB Fran Tarkenton fell on a ball in his own end zone for a Pittsburgh safety, credited to Dwight White
74. b

Grabbers

75. Lynn Swann
76. a, d, and e
77. George Sauer of the New York Jets in Super Bowl III
78. Kenny King, Oakland
79. Percy Howard, Dallas, Super Bowl X
80. False: Fred Biletnikoff, Oakland, XI MVP
81. John Stallworth, three

Who Said?

82. Duane Thomas, Dallas Cowboys
83. Jack Lambert, Pittsburgh Steeleers

Bowl Potpourri

84. Orange Bowl, five
85. Super Bowl VII, Washington vs. Miami in the Los Angeles Coliseum, 90,182
86. Miami
87. Jets, Broncos, Rams, Eagles, Bengals

88. Preston Pearson, Baltimore, Pittsburgh, Dallas
89. Browns, Oilers, Patriots, Falcons, Seahawks, Chargers, Cardinals, Bears, Lions, Buccaneers, Giants, Bills, and Saints
90. Bill Curry of the Colts and Herb Adderley of the Cowboys had been teammates with the Green Bay Packers in the first two Super Bowls.

Run to Glory

91. Tom Nowatzke
92. Paul Hornung, Billy Cannon, Roger Staubach, Mike Garrett, Jim Plunkett, Tony Dorsett, Archie Griffin, Marcus Allen
93. Thomas "Hollywood" Henderson
94. Larry Csonka
95. None of them scored a TD in the Super Bowl
96. Rick Upchurch's, Denver, Super Bowl XII
97. Mercury Morris

Switches

98. Joe Kapp and Bud Grant, Minnesota, Super Bowl IV
99. Ron Widby, Dallas Cowboys and, in the ABA, New Orleans Buccaneers (1968)
100. *Hill Street Blues'* Ed Marinaro, Minnesota, Super Bowl VIII and IX
101. Bob Hayes, Dallas
102. Ed "Too Tall" Jones
103. Tim Foley
104. Bill Curry, Green Bay and Baltimore; E. J. Holub, Kansas City; both played center and linebacker
105. Sam Havrilak, Baltimore, Super Bowl V

Field General

106. c—All played in four games, but Staubach, though injured, was on the squad in a fifth game.

107. Earl Morrall (32)
108. Daryle Lamonica, Oakland vs. Green Bay, Super Bowl II
109. Babe Parilli
110. Fran Tarkenton and Joe Montana (twice)
111. Roger Staubach
112. Len Dawson, Kansas City, Super Bowl II; and Joe Theismann, Washington, Super Bowl XVII
113. Joe Montana, Jim Plunkett, and Joe Namath
114. Bob Berry, Minnesota; Glenn Carano, Dallas; Joe Gilliam, Mike Kruczek, and Cliff Stoudt, all Pittsburgh; and Bob Holly, Washington
115. a and e
116. Super Bowl I when Green Bay beat Kansas City, 35–10
117. Packers, 1968; Raiders, 1981; 49ers, 1982
118. Six years, Miami
119. Gene Upshaw, Super Bowl II and XV; Ted Hendricks, Super Bowl V and XVIII
120. Chuck Howley, Dallas, Super Bowl V
121. Larry Ball, Miami Dolphins, 1972, and Tampa Bay Buccaneers, 1976
122. Joe Robbie of Miami
123. Terry Bradshaw (Pittsburgh) and David Woodley (Miami)
124. 1-b, 2-c, 3-a, 4-d
125. January 9, 1977 (Super Bowl XI)

SUPER BOWL CHAMPIONS

I—Green Bay Packers
II—Green Bay Packers
III—New York Jets
IV—Kansas City Chiefs
V—Baltimore Colts
VI—Dallas Cowboys
VII—Miami Dolphins
VIII—Miami Dolphins
IX—Pittsburgh Steelers
X—Pittsburgh Steelers

XI—Oakland Raiders
XII—Dallas Cowboys
XIII—Pittsburgh Steelers
XIV—Pittsburgh Steelers
XV—Oakland Raiders
XVI—San Francisco 49ers
XVII—Washington Redskins
XVIII—Los Angeles Raiders
XIX—San Francisco 49ers

MISCELLANEOUS
SUPER BOWL RECORDS
(Source: Elias Sports Bureau)

INDIVIDUAL

Service

Most Games
5   Marv Fleming, Green Bay, 1967, 1968; Miami, 1972, 1973,1974
    Larry Cole, Dallas, 1971, 1972, 1976, 1978, 1979
    Cliff Harris, Dallas, 1971, 1972, 1976, 1978, 1979
    D.D. Lewis, Dallas, 1971, 1972, 1976, 1978, 1979
    Preston Pearson, Baltimore, 1969; Pittsburgh, 1975; Dallas, 1976, 1978, 1979
    Charlie Waters, Dallas, 1971, 1972, 1976, 1978, 1979
    Rayfield Wright, Dallas, 1971, 1972, 1976, 1978, 1979

Most Games, Coach
6   Don Shula, Baltimore 1969; Miami, 1972, 1973, 1974, 1983, 1985

Most Games, Winning Team, Coach
4   Chuck Noll, Pittsburgh, 1975, 1976, 1979, 1980

Scoring

POINTS
Most Points, Career
24   Franco Harris, Pittsburgh, 4 games (4 TD)

Most Points, Game
18   Roger Craig, San Francisco vs. Miami, 1985 (3 TD)

TOUCHDOWNS
Most Touchdowns, Career
4   Franco Harris, Pittsburgh, 4 games (4 r)

Most Touchdowns, Game
3   Roger Craig, San Francisco vs. Miami, 1985 (2 p, 1 r)

POINTS AFTER TOUCHDOWN
Most Points After Touchdown, Career
8   Don Chandler, Green Bay, 2 games (8 att)
     Roy Gerela, Pittsburgh, 3 games (9 att)
     Chris Bahr, Oakland-L.A. Raiders, 2 games (8 att)

Most Points After Touchdown, Game
5   Don Chandler, Green Bay vs. Kansas City, 1967 (5 att)
     Roy Gerela, Pittsburgh vs. Dallas, 1979 (5 att)
     Chris Bahr, L.A. Raiders vs. Washington, 1984 (5 att)
     Ray Wersching, San Francisco vs. Miami, 1985 (5 att)

FIELD GOALS
Field Goals Attempted, Career
7   Roy Gerela, Pittsburgh, 3 games

Most Field Goals Attempted, Game
5   Jim Turner, N.Y. Jets vs. Baltimore, 1969
     Efren Herrera, Dallas vs. Denver, 1978

Most Field Goals, Career
5   Ray Wersching, San Francisco, 2 games (5 att)

Most Field Goals, Game
4   Don Chandler, Green Bay vs. Oakland, 1968
     Ray Wersching, San Francisco vs. Cincinnati, 1982

Longest Field Goal
48   Jan Stenerud, Kansas City vs. Minnesota, 1970

SAFETIES
Most Safeties, Game
1   Dwight White, Pittsburgh vs. Minnesota, 1975
     Reggie Harrison, Pittsburgh vs. Dallas, 1976

RUSHING

ATTEMPTS
Most Attempts, Career
101   Franco Harris, Pittsburgh, 4 games

Most Attempts, Game
38   John Riggins, Washington vs. Miami, 1983

YARDS GAINED

Most Yards Gained, Career
354   Franco Harris, Pittsburgh, 4 games

Most Yards Gained, Game
191   Marcus Allen, L.A. Raiders vs. Washington, 1984

Longest Run from Scrimmage
74   Marcus Allen, L.A. Raiders vs. Washington, 1984
     (TD)

TOUCHDOWNS
Most Touchdowns, Career
4   Franco Harris, Pittsburgh, 4 games

Most Touchdowns, Game
2   Elijah Pitts, Green Bay vs. Kansas City, 1967
    Larry Csonka, Miami vs. Minnesota, 1974
    Pete Banaszak, Oakland vs. Minnesota, 1977
    Franco Harris, Pittsburgh vs. Los Angeles, 1980
    Marcus Allen, L.A. Raiders vs. Washington, 1984

PASSING

ATTEMPTS
Most Passes Attempted, Career
98   Roger Staubach, Dallas, 4 games

Most Passes Attempted, Game
50   Dan Marino, Miami vs. San Francisco, 1985

COMPLETIONS
Most Passes Completed, Career
61   Roger Staubach, Dallas, 4 games

Most Passes Completed, Game
29   Dan Marino, Miami vs. San Francisco, 1985

Most Consecutive Completions, Game
8   Len Dawson, Kansas City vs. Green Bay, 1967
    Joe Theismann, Washington vs. Miami, 1983

COMPLETION PERCENTAGE
Highest Completion Percentage, Career (40 attempts)
66.7   Joe Montana, San Francisco, 2 games (57–38)

Highest Completion Percentage, Game (20 attempts)
73.5   Ken Anderson, Cincinnati vs. San Francisco, 1982 (34–25)

YARDS GAINED
Most Yards Gained, Career
932   Terry Bradshaw, Pittsburgh (4 games)

Most Yards Gained, Game
331   Joe Montana, San Francisco vs. Miami, 1985

Longest Pass Completion
80   Jim Plunkett (to Kenny King), Oakland vs. Philadelphia, 1981 (TD)

TOUCHDOWNS
Most Touchdown Passes, Career
9   Terry Bradshaw, Pittsburgh, 4 games

Most Touchdown Passes, Game
4   Terry Bradshaw, Pittsburgh vs. Dallas, 1979

HAD INTERCEPTED
Lowest Percentage, Passes Had Intercepted Career (40 attempts)
0.00   Jim Plunkett, Oakland-L.A. Raiders, 2 games (46–0)
0.00   Joe Montana, San Francisco, 2 games (57–0)

Most Attempts, Without Interception, Game
35   Joe Montana, San Francisco vs. Miami, 1985

Most Passes Had Intercepted, Career
7   Craig Morton, Dallas-Denver, 2 games

Most Passes Had Intercepted, Game
4   Craig Morton, Denver vs. Dallas, 1978

PASS RECEIVING

RECEPTIONS
Most Receptions, Career
16   Lynn Swann, Pittsburgh, 4 games

Most Receptions, Game
11   Dan Ross, Cincinnati vs. San Francisco, 1982

YARDS GAINED
Most Yards Gained, Career
364   Lynn Swann, Pittsburgh, 4 games

Most Yards Gained, Game
161   Lynn Swann, Pittsburgh vs. Dallas, 1976

Longest Reception
80   Kenny King (from Jim Plunkett), Oakland vs. Philadelphia, 1981 (TD)

TOUCHDOWNS

Most Touchdowns, Career
3   John Stallworth, Pittsburgh, 4 games.

Most Touchdowns, Game
2   Max McGee, Green Bay vs. Kansas City, 1967
    Bill Miller, Oakland vs. Green Bay, 1968
    John Stallworth, Pittsburgh vs. Dallas, 1979
    Cliff Branch, Oakland vs. Philadelphia, 1981
    Dan Ross, Cincinnati vs. San Francisco, 1982
    Roger Craig, San Francisco vs. Miami, 1985

INTERCEPTIONS BY

Most Interceptions By, Career
3   Chuck Howley, Dallas, 2 games
    Rod Martin, Oakland-L.A. Raiders, 2 games

Most Interceptions By, Game
3   Rod Martin, Oakland vs. Philadelphia, 1981

YARDS GAINED
Most Yards Gained, Career
75   Willie Brown, Oakland, 2 games

Most Yards Gained, Game
75   Willie Brown, Oakland vs. Minnesota, 1977

Longest Return
75   Willie Brown, Oakland vs. Minnesota, 1977 (TD)

TOUCHDOWNS
Most Touchdowns, Game
1   Herb Adderley, Green Bay vs. Oakland, 1968
     Willie Brown, Oakland vs. Minnesota, 1977
     Jack Squirek, L.A. Raiders vs. Washington, 1984

PUNTING

Most Punts, Career
17   Mike Eischeid, Oakland-Minnesota, 3 games

Most Punts, Game
9   Ron Widby, Dallas vs. Baltimore, 1971

Longest Punt
61   Jerrel Wilson, Kansas City vs. Green Bay, 1967

AVERAGE YARDAGE
Highest Average, Punting, Career (10 punts)
46.5   Jerrel Wilson, Kansas City, 2 games (11–151)

Highest Average, Punting, Game (4 punts)
48.5   Jerrel Wilson, Kansas City vs. Minnesota, 1970
        (4–194)

PUNT RETURNS

Most Punt Returns, Career
6   Willie Wood, Green Bay, 2 games
     Jake Scott, Miami, 3 games
     Theo Bell, Pittsburgh, 2 games
     Mike Nelms, Washington, 1 game

Most Punt Returns, Game
6   Mike Nelms, Washington vs. Miami, 1983

Most Fair Catches, Game
3   Ron Gardin, Baltimore vs. Dallas, 1971
     Golden Richards, Dallas vs. Pittsburgh, 1976
     Greg Pruitt, L.A. Raiders vs. Washington, 1984

YARDS GAINED
Most Yards Gained, Career
52   Mike Nelms, Washington, 1 game

Most Yards Gained, Game
52 Mike Nelms, Washington vs. Miami, 1983

Longest Return
34 Darrell Green, Washington vs. L.A. Raiders, 1984

AVERAGE YARDAGE
Highest Average, Career (4 returns)
10.8 Neal Colzie, Oakland, 1 game (4–43)

Highest Average, Game (3 returns)
11.3 Lynn Swann, Pittsburgh vs. Minnesota, 1975 (3–34)

KICKOFF RETURNS

Most Kickoff Returns, Career
Larry Anderson, Pittsburgh, 2 games

Most Kickoff Returns, Game
5 Larry Anderson, Pittsburgh vs. Los Angeles, 1980
   Billy Campfield, Philladelphia vs. Oakland, 1981
   David Verser, Cincinnati vs. San Francisco, 1982
   Alvin Garrett, Washington vs. L.A. Raiders, 1984

YARDS GAINED
Most Yards Gained, Career
283 Fulton Walker, Miami, 2 games

Most Yards Gained, Game
190 Fulton Walker, Miami vs. Washington, 1983

Longest Return
98 Fulton Walker, Miami vs. Washington, 1983 (TD)

AVERAGE YARDAGE
Highest Yardage, Career (4 returns)
35.4 Fulton Walker, Miami, 2 games (8–283)

Highest Average, Game (3 returns)
47.5 Fulton Walker, Miami vs. Washington, 1983 (4–190)

TOUCHDOWNS
Most Touchdowns, Game
1 Fulton Walker, Miami vs. Washington, 1983

FUMBLES

Most Fumbles, Career
5   Roger Staubach, Dallas, 4 games

Most Fumbles, Game
3   Roger Staubach, Dallas vs. Pittsburgh, 1976

YARDS GAINED
Most Yards Gained, Game
49   Mike Bass, Washington vs. Miami, 1973 (opp)

Longest Return
49   Mike Bass, Washington vs. Miami, 1973 (TD)

Combined Net Yards Gained

ATTEMPTS
Most Attempts, Career
108   Franco Harris, Pittsburgh, 4 games

Most Attempts, Game
39   John Riggins, Washington vs. Miami, 1983

YARDS GAINED
Most Yards Gained, Career
468   Franco Harris, Pittsburgh, 4 games

Most Yards Gained, Game
209   Marcus Allen, L.A. Raiders vs. Washington, 1984

TEAM

GAMES, VICTORIES, DEFEATS

Most Games
5   Dallas, 1971, 1972, 1976, 1978, 1979
    Miami, 1972, 1973, 1974, 1983, 1985

Most Consecutive Games
3   Miami, 1972, 1973, 1974

Most Games Won
4   Pittsburgh, 1975, 1976, 1979, 1980

Most Consecutive Games Won
2   Green Bay, 1967–68
    Miami, 1973–74
    Pittsburgh, 1975–76, 1979–80

Most Games Lost
4   Minnesota, 1970, 1974, 1975, 1977

Most Consecutive Games Lost
2   Minnesota, 1974–75

SCORING

Most Points, Game
38   L.A. Raiders vs. Washington, 1984
     San Francisco vs. Miami, 1985

Fewest Points, Game
3   Miami vs. Dallas, 1972

Most Points, Both Teams, Game
66   Pittsburgh (35) vs. Dallas (31), 1979

Fewest Points, Both Teams, Game
21   Washington (7) vs. Miami (14), 1973

Largest Margin of Victory, Game
29   L.A. Raiders vs. Washington, 1984 (38–9)

TOUCHDOWNS
Most Touchdowns, Game
5   Green Bay vs. Kansas City, 1967
    Pittsburgh vs. Dallas, 1979
    L.A. Raiders vs. Washington, 1984
    San Francisco vs. Miami, 1985

Fewest Touchdowns, Game
0   Miami vs. Dallas, 1972

Most Touchdowns, Both Teams, Game
9   Pittsburgh (5) vs. Dallas (4), 1979

Fewest Touchdowns, Both Teams, Game
2   Baltimore (1) vs. N.Y. Jets (1), 1969

POINTS AFTER TOUCHDOWN
Most Points After Touchdown, Game
5   Green Bay vs. Kansas City, 1967
    Pittsburgh vs. Dallas, 1979
    L.A. Raiders vs. Washington, 1984
    San Francisco vs. Miami, 1985

Most Points After Touchdown, Both Teams, Game
9   Pittsburgh (5) vs. Dallas (4), 1979

Fewest Points After Touchdown, Both Teams, Game
2   Baltimore (1) vs. N.Y. Jets (1), 1969
    Baltimore (1) vs. Dallas (1), 1971
    Minnesota (0) vs. Pittsburgh (2), 1975

FIELD GOALS
Most Field Goals Attempted, Game
5   N.Y. Jets vs. Baltimore, 1969
    Dallas vs. Denver, 1978

Most Field Goals Attempted, Both Teams, Game
7   N.Y. Jets (5) vs. Baltimore (2), 1969

Fewest Field Goals Attempted, Both Teams, Game
1   Minnesota (0) vs. Miami (1), 1974

Most Field Goals, Game
4   Green Bay vs. Oakland, 1968
    San Francisco vs. Cincinnati, 1982

Most Field Goals, Both Teams, Game
4   Green Bay (4) vs. Oakland (0), 1968
    San Francisco (4) vs. Cincinnati (0), 1982
    San Francisco (1) vs. Miami (3), 1985

SAFETIES
Most Safeties, Game
1   Pittsburgh vs. Minnesota, 1975; vs. Dallas, 1976

FIRST DOWNS

Most First Downs, Game
31   San Francisco vs. Miami, 1985

Fewest First Downs, Game
9   Minnesota vs. Pittsburgh, 1975
    Miami vs. Washington, 1983

Most First Downs, Both Teams, Game
50   San Francisco (31) vs. Miami (19), 1985

Fewest First Downs, Both Teams, Game
24   Dallas (10) vs. Baltimore (14), 1971

RUSHING
Most First Downs, Rushing, Game
16   San Francisco vs. Miami, 1985

PASSING
Most First Downs, Passing, Game
17   Miami vs. San Francisco, 1985

NET YARDS RUSHING AND PASSING

Most Yards Gained, Game
537   San Francisco vs. Miami, 1985

Most Yards Gained, Both Teams, One Game
851   San Francisco (537) vs. Miami (314), 1985

RUSHING

ATTEMPTS
Most Attempts, Game
57   Pittsburgh vs. Minnesota, 1975

YARDS GAINED
Most Yards Gained, Game
276   Washington vs. Miami, 1983

AVERAGE GAIN
Highest Average Gain, Game
7.00   L.A. Raiders vs. Washington, 1984 (33–231)

TOUCHDOWNS
Most Touchdowns, Game
3   Green Bay vs. Kansas City, 1967
    Miami vs. Minnesota, 1974

PASSING

ATTEMPTS
Most Passes Attempted, Game
50   Miami vs. San Francisco, 1985

Most Passes Attempted, Both Teams, Game
85   San Francisco (35) vs. Miami (50), 1985

COMPLETIONS
Most Passes Completed, Game
29   Miami vs. San Francisco, 1985

Most Passes Completed, Both Teams, Game
53   Miami (29) vs. San Francisco (24), 1985

COMPLETION PERCENTAGE
Highest Completion Percentage, Game (20 attempts)
73.5   Cincinnati vs. San Francisco, 1982 (34–25)

YARDS GAINED
Most Yards Gained, Game
326   San Francisco vs. Miami, 1985

Most Yards Gained, Both Teams, Game
615   San Francisco (326) vs. Miami (289), 1985

TIMES SACKED
Most Times Sacked, Game
7   Dallas vs. Pittsburgh, 1976

TOUCHDOWNS
Most Touchdowns, Game
4   Pittsburgh vs. Dallas, 1979

Most Touchdowns, Both Teams, Game
7   Pittsburgh (4) vs. Dallas (3), 1979

INTERCEPTIONS BY

Most Interceptions By, Game
4   N.Y. Jets vs. Baltimore, 1969
    Dallas vs. Denver, 1978

TOUCHDOWNS
Most Touchdowns, Game
1   Green Bay vs. Oakland, 1968
    Oakland vs. Minnesota, 1977
    L.A. Raiders vs. Washington, 1984

PUNTING

Most Punts, Game
9   Dallas vs. Baltimore, 1971

AVERAGE YARDAGE
Highest Average, Game (4 punts)
48.50   Kansas City vs. Minnesota, 1970 (4–194)

PUNT RETURNS

Most Punt Returns, Game
6   Washington vs. Miami, 1983

Most Punt Returns, Both Teams, Game
9   Pittsburgh (5) vs. Minnesota (4), 1975

YARDS GAINED
Most Yards Gained, Game
52   Washington vs. Miami, 1983

Most Yards Gained, Both Teams, Game
74   Washington (52) vs. Miami (22), 1983

AVERAGE RETURN
Highest Average, Game (3 returns)
10.8   Oakland vs. Minnesota, 1977 (4–43)

KICKOFF RETURNS

Most Kickoff Returns, Game
7   Oakland vs. Green Bay, 1968
    Minnesota vs. Oakland, 1977
    Cincinnati vs. San Francisco, 1982
    Washington vs. L.A. Raiders, 1984
    Miami vs. San Francisco, 1985

YARDS GAINED
Most Yards Gained, Game
222   Miami vs. Washington, 1983

AVERAGE GAIN
Highest Average, Game (3 returns)
37.0   Miami vs. Washington, 1983 (6–222)

TOUCHDOWNS
Most Touchdowns, Game
1   Miami vs. Washington, 1983

PENALTIES

Most Penalties, Game
12   Dallas vs. Denver, 1978

Most Penalties, Both Teams, Game
20   Dallas (12) vs. Denver (8), 1978

YARDS PENALIZED
Most Yards Penalized, Game
133   Dallas vs. Baltimore, 1971

Most Yards Penalized, Both Teams, Game
164   Dallas (133) vs. Baltimore (31), 1971

FUMBLES

Most Fumbles, Game
6 Dallas vs. Denver, 1978

Most Fumbles, Both Teams, Game
10   Dallas (6) vs. Denver (4), 1978

Most Fumbles Recovered, Game
8 Dallas vs. Denver (4 own, 4 opp)

TURNOVERS

Most Turnovers, Game
8 Denver vs. Dallas, 1978

Most Turnovers, Both Teams, Game
11   Baltimore (7) vs. Dallas (4), 1967

ALL-TIME SUPER BOWL
PLAYER ROSTER

What follows is a complete alphabetical listing of every man on a Super Bowl roster. Asterisks indicate the player did not play in the game noted.

Name	Team	Game	Position	College
Abell, Bud	Kansas City	I	LB	Missouri
Adderley, Herb	Green Bay, Dallas	I,II,V,VI	DB	Michigan State
Alderman, Grady	Minnesota	IV,VII,IX	OT	Detroit
Aldridge, Lionel	Green Bay	I,II	DE	Utah State
Alexander, Charles	Cincinnati	XVI	RB	LSU
Allen, Jimmy	Pittsburgh	IX,X	DB	UCLA
Allen, Marcus	L.A. Raiders	XVIII	RB	USC
Allen, Nate	Minnesota	XI	CB	Texas Southern
Allison, Henry	Denver	XII	T	San Diego State
Alston, Mack	Washington	VII	TE	Maryland State
Alworth, Lance	Dallas	VI	WR	Arkansas
Alzado, Lyle	Denver, L.A. Raiders	XII,XVIII	DE	Yankton College

Name	Team	Game	Position	College
Anderson, Anthony	Pittsburgh	XIV	RB	Temple
Anderson, Bill	Green Bay	I	TE	Tennessee
Anderson, Dick	Miami	VI,VII,VIII	DB	Colorado
Anderson, Donny	Green Bay	I,II	RB-P	Texas Tech
Anderson, Fred	Pittsburgh	XIII	DE-DT	Prairie View A&M
Anderson, Ken	Cincinnati	XVI	QB	Augustana (Ill.)
Anderson, Larry	Pittsburgh	XIII,XIV	CB-KR	Louisiana Tech
Anderson, Scott	Minnesota	IX	C	Missouri
Anderson, Stuart	Washington	XVIII	LB	Virginia
Andrews, George	L.A. Rams	XIV	LB	Nebraska
Andrie, George	Dallas	V,VI	DE	Marquette
Arbanas, Fred	Kansas City	I,IV	TE	Michigan State
Archer, Dan	Oakland	II	OT	Oregon
Armstrong, Otis	Denver	XII	RB	Purdue
Asher, Bob	Dallas	V	OT	Vanderbilt
Atkinson, Al	N.Y. Jets	III	LB	Villanova
Atkinson, George	Oakland	XI	DB	Morris Brown
Audick, Dan	San Francisco	XVI	T	Hawaii
Austin, Ocie	Baltimore	III	DB	Utah State
Ayers, John	San Francisco	XVI,XIX	G	West Texas State
Babb, Charles	Miami	VII,VIII	S	Memphis State
Bahr, Chris	Oakland, L.A. Raiders	XV, XVIII	K	Penn State
Bahr, Matt	Pittsburgh	XIV	K	Penn State

274

Name	Team	Super Bowl	Pos.	College
Bain, Bill	L.A. Rams	XIV	G	USC
Baird, Bill	N.Y. Jets	III	DB	San Francisco State
Baker, Ralph	N.Y. Jets	III	LB	Penn State
Baker, Ron	Philadelphia	XV	G	Oklahoma State
Ball, Larry	Miami	VII,VIII	LB	Louisville
Ball, Sam	Baltimore	III,V	OT	Kentucky
Ballman, Gary	Minnesota	VIII	TE	Michigan State
Banaszak, John	Pittsburgh	X,XIII,XIV	DE-DT	Eastern Michigan
Banaszak, Pete	Oakland	II,XI	RB	Miami
Bankston, Warren	Oakland	XI	RB-TE	Tulane
Bannon, Bruce	Miami	VII	LB	Penn State
Barnes, Benny	Dallas	X,XII,XIII	CB	Stanford
Barnes, Jeff	Oakland, L.A. Raiders	XV,XVIII	LB	California
Barnes, Rodrigo	Oakland	XI	LB	Rice
Barnett, Bill	Miami	XIX	NT-DE	Nebraska
Barnwell, Malcolm	L.A. Raiders	XVIII	WR	Virginia Union
Bass, Don	Cincinnati	XVI	WR-TE	Houston
Bass, Mike	Washington	VII	BC	Michigan
Baumhower, Bob	Miami	XVII,XIX	NT	Alabama
Beamon, Autry	Minnesota	XI	S	East Texas State
Beasley, John	Minnesota	IV	TE	California
Beasley, Tom	Pittsburgh	XIII,XIV	DT	Virginia Tech
Beathard, Pete	Kansas City	I	QB	USC
Bell, Bobby	Kansas City	I,IV	LB	Minnesota

Name	Team	Game	Position	College
Bell, Theo	Pittsburgh	XIII,XIV	WR-KR	Arizona
Belser, Ceaser	Kansas City	IV	DB	Arkansas AM&N
Benjamin, Guy	San Francisco	XVI*	QB	Stanford
Bennett, Woody	Miami	XVII,XIX	RB	Miami
Benson, Charles	Miami	XIX	DE	Baylor
Benson, Duane	Oakland	II	LB	Hamline
Bergey, Bill	Philadelphia	XV	LB	Arkansas State
Berry, Bob	Minnesota	VII*,IX*,XI*	QB	Oregon
Bethea, Larry	Dallas	XIII	DT	Michigan State
Betters, Doug	Miami	XVII,XIX	DE	Nevada-Reno
Beverly, Randy	N.Y. Jets	III	DB	Colorado State
Biggs, Verlon	N.Y. Jets, Washington	III,VII	DE	Jackson State
Biletnikoff, Fred	Oakland	II,XI	WR	Florida State
Biodrowski, Dennis	Kansas City	I	G	Memphis State
Bird, Rodger	Oakland	II	DB	Kentucky
Birdwell, Dan	Oakland	II	DT	Houston
Bishop, Richard	Miami	XVII*	NT	Louisville
Blackmore, Richard	Philadelphia	XV	CB	Mississippi State
Blackwell, Alois	Dallas	XIII	RB	Houston
Blackwood, Glenn	Miami	XVII,XIX	S	Texas
Blackwood, Lyle	Miami	XVII,XIX	S	TCU
Blahak, Joe	Minnesota	IX*	CB-S	Nebraska
Blair, Matt	Minnesota	IX,XI	LB	Iowa State

Name	Team		Pos.	College
Blanda, George	Oakland	II	K	Kentucky
Bleier, Rocky	Pittsburgh	IX,X,XIII,XIV	RB	Notre Dame
Blount, Mel	Pittsburgh	IX,X,XIII,XIV	CB	Southern
Board, Dwaine	San Francisco	XVI,XIX	DE	North Carolina A&T
Bokamper, Kim	Miami	XVII,XIX	DE	San Jose State
Bonness, Rik	Oakland	XI	LB	Nebraska
Boone, Dave	Minnesota	IX*	DE	Eastern Michigan
Boozer, Emerson	N.Y. Jets	III	RB	Maryland State
Bostic, Jeff	Washington	XVII,XVIII	C	Clemson
Bowman, Ken	Green Bay	I,II	C	Wisconsin
Bowser, Charles	Miami	XVII,XIX	LB	Duke
Boyd, Bob	Baltimore	III	DB	Oklahoma
Braase, Ordell	Baltimore	III	DE	South Dakota
Bradley, Ed	Pittsburgh	IX,X	LB	Wake Forest
Bradshaw, Morris	Oakland	XI, XV	WR	Ohio State
Bradshaw, Terry	Pittsburgh	IX,X,XIII,XIV	QB	Louisiana Tech
Bragg, Mike	Washington	VII	P	Kansas State
Branch, Cliff	Oakland, L.A.Raiders	XI,XV,XVIII	WR	Colorado
Bratkowski, Zeke	Green Bay	I,II	QB	Georgia
Breech, Jim	Cincinnati	XVI	K	California
Breeden, Louis	Cincinnati	XVI	CB	North Carolina Central
Breunig, Bob	Dallas	X,XII,XIII	LB	Arizona State
Brinson, Larry	Dallas	XII,XIII	RB	Florida
Briscoe, Marlin	Miami	VII,VIII	WR	Omaha

Name	Team	Game	Position	College
Brooks, Larry	L.A. Rams	XIV	DT	Virginia State-Petersburg
Brooks, Perry	Washington	XVII,XVIII	DT	Southern
Brophy, Jay	Miami	XIX	LB	Miami
Brown, Aaron	Kansas City	I,IV	DE	Minnesota
Brown, Bill	Minnesota	IV,VIII,IX	RB	Illinois
Brown, Bob	Green Bay	I,II	DE	Arkansas AM&N
Brown, Bud	Miami	XIX	S	Southern Mississippi
Brown, Charlie	Washington	XVII,XVIII	WR	South Carolina State
Brown, Dave	Pittsburgh	X	DB	Michigan
Brown, Eddie	L.A. Rams	XIV	S-KR	Tennessee
Brown, Guy	Dallas	XII,XIII	LB	Houston
Brown, Larry	Pittsburgh	IX,X,XIII,XIV	TE-T	Kansas
Brown, Larry	Washington	VII	RB	Kansas State
Brown, Mark	Miami	XIX	LB	Purdue
Brown, Terry	Minnesota	VII,IX	S	Oklahoma State
Brown, Thomas	Philadelphia	XV	DE	Baylor
Brown, Tim	Baltimore	III	RB	Ball State
Brown, Tom	Green Bay	I,II	DB	Maryland
Brown, Willie	Oakland	II,XI	DB	Grambling
Browner, Ross	Cincinnati	XVI	DE	Notre Dame
Browning, Dave	Oakland	XV	DE	Washington
Brudzinski, Bob	L.A. Rams, Miami	XIV,XVII,XIX	LB	Ohio State
Brundige, Bill	Washington	VII	DT	Colorado

278

Name	Team		Pos.	College
Brunet, Bob	Washington	VII	RB	Louisiana Tech
Bryant, Bobby	Minnesota	VIII,XI	CB	South Carolina
Bryant, Cullen	L.A. Rams	XIV	RB	Colorado
Buchanan, Buck	Kansas City	I,IV	DT	Grambling
Budde, Ed	Kansas City	I,IV	G	Michigan State
Budness, Bill	Oakland	II	LB	Boston
Buehler, George	Oakland	XI	G	Stanford
Buetow, Bart	Minnesota	XI	T	Minnesota
Bujnoch, Glenn	Cincinnati	XVI*	G	Texas A&M
Bulaich, Norm	Baltimore	V	RB	TCU
Bunting, John	Philadelphia	XV	LB	North Carolina
Bunz, Dan	San Francisco	XVI,XIX	LB	Long Beach State
Buoniconti, Nick	Miami	VI,VII,VIII	LB	Notre Dame
Burford, Chris	Kansas City	I	WR	Stanford
Burley, Gary	Cincinnati	XVI	DE	Pittsburgh
Burman, George	Washington	VII	C-G	Northwestern
Bush, Blair	Cincinnati	XVI	C	Washington
Butz, Dave	Washington	XVII,XVIII	DT	Purdue
Byrd, Darryl	L.A. Raiders	XVIII	LB	Illinois
Caffey, Lee Roy	Green Bay	I,II	LB	Texas A&M
Caldwell, Tony	L.A. Raiders	XVIII	LB	Washington
Cameron, Glenn	Cincinnati	XVI	LB	Florida
Campbell, Joe	Oakland	XV	DE-NT	Maryland
Campfield, Billy	Philadelphia	XV	RB	Kansas

Name	Team	Game	Position	College
Cannon, Billy	Oakland	II	RB	LSU
Capone, Warren	Dallas	X	LB	LSU
Capp, Dick	Green Bay	II	TE-LB	Boston College
Carano, Glenn	Dallas	XII,XIII*	QB	Nevada-Las Vegas
Carmichael, Harold	Philadelphia	XV	WR	Southern
Carolan, Reg	Kansas City	I	TE	Idaho
Carpenter, Brian	Washington	XVIII	CB	Michigan
Carter, Joe	Miami	XIX	RB	Alabama
Carter, Michael	San Francisco	XIX	NT	SMU
Carter, Rubin	Denver	XII	DT	Miami
Casper, Dave	Oakland	XI	TE	Notre Dame
Caster, Richard	Washington	XVII*	TE	Jackson State
Cavanaugh, Matt	San Francisco	XIX*	QB	Pittsburgh
Cefalo, Jimmy	Miami	XVII,XIX	WR	Penn State
Celotto, Mario	Oakland	XV	LB	USC
Chandler, Bob	Oakland	XV	WR	USC
Chandler, Don	Green Bay	I,II	K	Florida
Charles, Mike	Miami	XIX	DE	Syracuse
Chavous, Barney	Denver	XII	DE	South Carolina State
Chesley, Al	Philadelphia	XV	LB	Pittsburgh
Chester, Raymond	Oakland	XV	TE	Morgan State
Choma, John	San Francisco	XVI	G-T	Virginia
Christensen, Todd	Oakland, L.A. Raiders	XV,XVIII	TE-RB	Brigham Young

Name	Team	Super Bowls	Position	College
Christy, Earl	N.Y. Jets	III	DB	Maryland State
Clabo, Neil	Minnesota	XI	P	Tennessee
Clack, Jim	Pittsburgh	IX,X	G-C	Wake Forest
Clark, Dwight	San Francisco	XVI,XIX	WR	Clemson
Clark, Ken	L.A. Rams	XIV	P	St. Mary's (Nova Scotia)
Clark, Mario	San Francisco	XIX*	CB	Oregon
Clark, Mike	Dallas	V,VI	K	Texas A&M
Clarke, Steve	Miami	XVII*,XIX	DE-G	Utah
Clarke, Ken	Philadelphia	XV	NT	Syracuse
Clayton, Mark	Miami	XIX	WR	Louisville
Coan, Bert	Kansas City	I	RB	Kansas
Coffey, Ken	Washington	XVIII	S	Southwest Texas State
Cole, Larry	Dallas	V,VI,X,XII,XIII	DE-DT	Hawaii
Cole, Robin	Pittsburgh	XIII,XIV	LB	New Mexico
Cole, Terry	Baltimore, Miami	III,VI	RB	Indiana
Coleman, Monte	Washington	XVII,XVIII	LB	Central Arkansas
Collier, Mike	Pittsburgh	X	RB	Morgan State
Collinsworth, Cris	Cincinnati	XVI	WR	Florida
Colquitt, Craig	Pittsburgh	XIII,XIV	P	Tennessee
Colzie, Neal	Oakland	XI	DB	Ohio State
Conn, Dick	Pittsburgh	IX	S	Georgia
Conners, Dan	Oakland	II	LB	Miami
Cooper, Earl	San Francisco	XVI,XIX	TE-RB	Rice
Cooper, Jim	Dallas	XII,XIII	T-G-C	Temple

Name	Team	Game	Position	College
Corey, Walt	Kansas City	I	LB	Miami
Cornish, Frank	Miami	VI	DT	Grambling
Corral, Frank	L.A. Rams	XIV	K	UCLA
Courson, Steve	Pittsburgh	XIII,XIV	G	South Carolina
Cox, Fred	Minnesota	IV,VIII,IX,XI	K	Pittsburgh
Craig, Roger	San Francisco	XIX	RB	Nebraska
Craig, Steve	Minnesota	IX,XI	TE	Northwestern
Crane, Paul	N.Y. Jets	III	LB-C	Alabama
Cromwell, Nolan	L.A. Rams	XIV	S-CB	Kansas
Cronan, Pete	Washington	XVII,XVIII	LB	Boston College
Cross, Randy	San Francisco	XVI,XIX	G	UCLA
Crusan, Doug	Miami	VI,VII,VIII	OT	Indiana
Crutcher, Tommy	Green Bay	I,II	LB	TCU
Csonka, Larry	Miami	VI,VII,VIII	RB	Syracuse
Culp, Curly	Kansas City	IV	DT	Arizona State
Cunningham, Bennie	Pittsburgh	XIII*,XIV	TE	Clemson
Cuozzo, Gary	Minnesota	IV	QB	Virginia
Curry, Bill	Green Bay, Baltimore	I,III,V	C-LB	Georgia Tech
Curtis, Isaac	Cincinnati	XVI	WR	San Diego State
Curtis, Mike	Baltimore	III,V	LB	Duke
Dalby, Dave	Oakland, L.A. Raiders	XI,XV,XVIII	C	UCLA
Dale, Carroll	Green Bay, Minnesota	I,II,VIII	WR	Virginia Tech
D'Amato, Mike	N.Y. Jets	III	DB	Hofstra

Name	Team	Super Bowl	Pos.	College
Daney, George	Kansas City	IV	G	Texas-El Paso
Davidson, Ben	Oakland	II	DE	Washington
Davis, Bruce	Oakland, L.A. Raiders	XV,XVIII	G-T	UCLA
Davis, Charlie	Pittsburgh	IX	DT	TCU
Davis, Clarence	Oakland	XI	RB	USC
Davis, Doug	Minnesota	IV*	T	Kentucky
Davis, James	L.A. Raiders	XVIII	CB	Southern
Davis, Johnny	San Francisco	XVI	RB	Alabama
Davis, Kyle	Dallas	X	C	Oklahoma
Davis, Mike	Oakland, L.A. Raiders	XV,XVIII	S	Colorado
Davis, Oliver	Cincinnati	XVI	S	Tennessee
Davis, Sam	Pittsburgh	IX,X,XIII,XIV	G	Allen
Davis, Steve	Pittsburgh	IX	RB	Delaware State
Davis, Willie	Green Bay	I,II	DE	Grambling
Dawson, Len	Kansas City	I,IV	QB	Purdue
Dean, Fred	San Francisco	XVI, XIX	DE	Louisiana Tech
Dean, Fred	Washington	XVII	G	Texas Southern
Dean, Vernon	Washington	XVII,XVIII	CB	San Diego State
DelGaizo, Jim	Miami	VII*	QB	Tampa
Deloplaine, Jack	Pittsburgh	XIII	RB-KR	Salem College
DeMarco, Bob	Miami	VI	C	Dayton
Den Herder, Vern	Miami	VI,VII,VIII,XVII	DE	Central College (Iowa)
Dennard, Mark	Miami	XVII	C	Texas A&M
Dennard, Preston	L.A. Rams	XIV	WR	New Mexico

Name	Team	Game	Position	College
Dennison, Doug	Dallas	X,XII	RB	Kutztown State
Diana, Rich	Miami	XVII	RB	Yale
Dickson, Paul	Minnesota	IV	DT	Baylor
Didier, Clint	Washington	XVII,XVIII	TE	Portland State
Dilts, Bucky	Denver	XII	P	Georgia
DiMidio, Tony	Kansas City	I	OT	West Chester State
Dinkel, Tom	Cincinnati	XVI	LB	Kansas
Ditka, Mike	Dallas	V,VI	TE	Pittsburgh
Dixon, Hewritt	Oakland	II	RB	Florida A&M
Dockery, John	N.Y. Jets	III	DB	Harvard
Dolbin, Jack	Denver	XII	WR	Wake Forest
Donovan, Pat	Dallas	X,XII,XIII	T	Stanford
Dornbrook, Thom	Pittsburgh	XIV	C-G	Kentucky
Dorsett, Tony	Dallas	XII,XIII	RB	Pittsburgh
Doss, Reggie	L.A. Rams	XIV	DE	Hampton Institute
Dowler, Boyd	Green Bay	I,II	WR	Colorado
Downing, Walt	San Francisco	XVI	C-G	Michigan
Druschel, Rick	Pittsburgh	IX	G-T	North Carolina State
Dryer, Fred	L.A. Rams	XIV	DE	San Diego State
Duhe, A. J.	Miami	XVII,XIX	LB	LSU
Dumler, Doug	Minnesota	XI	C	Nebraska
Dunaway, Jim	Miami	VII*	DT	Mississippi
Duncan, Jim	Baltimore	V	DB	Maryland State

Duncan, Les	Washington	VII*	S	Jackson State
Dungy, Tony	Pittsburgh	XIII	S	Minnesota
Dunn, Gary	Pittsburgh	XIII,XIV	DT	Miami
Duper, Mark	Miami	XVII*,XIX	WR	Northwestern State (La.)
DuPree, Billy Joe	Dallas	X,XII,XIII	TE	Michigan State
Easley, Walt	San Francisco	XVI*	RB	West Virginia
East, Ron	Dallas	V	DT	Montana State
Edwards, Dave	Dallas	V,VI,X	LB	Auburn
Edwards, Eddie	Cincinnati	XVI	DE	Miami
Edwards, Glen	Pittsburgh	IX,X	S	Florida A&M
Edwards, Herman	Philadelphia	XV	CB	San Diego State
Egloff, Ron	Denver	XII	TE	Wisconsin
Eischeid, Mike	Oakland, Minnesota	II,VIII,IX	P	Upper Iowa
Eller, Carl	Minnesota	IV,VIII,IX,XI	DE	Minnesota
Elliott, John	N.Y. Jets	III	DT	Texas
Elliott, Lenvil	San Francisco	XVI*	RB	Northeast Missouri State
Ellis, Ken	San Francisco	XIV*	CB	Southern
Ellison, Riki	San Francisco	XIX	LB	USC
Elmendorf, Dave	L.A. Rams	XIV	S	Texas A&M
Evans, Larry	Denver	XII	LB	Mississippi College
Evans, Norm	Miami	VI,VII,VIII	OT	TCU
Evans, Reggie	Washington	XVIII	RB	Richmond
Fahnhorst, Keith	San Francisco	XVI,XIX	T	Minnesota
Fanning, Mike	L.A. Rams	XIV	DT	Notre Dame

Name	Team	Game	Position	College
Fanucci, Mike	Washington	VII	DE	Arizona State
Fernandez, Manny	Miami	VI,VII,VIII	DT	Utah
Ferragamo, Vince	L.A. Rams	XIV	QB	Nebraska
Fischer, Pat	Washington	VII	CB	Nebraska
Fitzgerald, John	Dallas	VI,X,XII,XIII	C	Boston College
Flanigan, Jim	Green Bay	II	LB	Pittsburgh
Fleming, Marv	Green Bay, Miami	I,II,VI,VII,VIII	TE	Utah
Flores, Tom	Kansas City	IV*	QB	Pacific
Flowers; Richmond	Dallas	V	WR	Tennessee
Foley, Steve	Denver	XII	CB	Tulane
Foley, Tim	Miami	VI,VIII	DB	Purdue
Foreman, Chuck	Minnesota	VIII,IX,XI	RB	Miami
Foster, Roy	Miami	XVII,XIX	G-T	USC
France, Doug	L.A. Rams	XIV	T	Ohio State
Francis, Russ	San Francisco	XIX	TE	Oregon
Frank, John	San Francisco	XIX*	TE	Ohio State
Franklin, Andra	Miami	XVII	RB	Nebraska
Franklin, Tony	Philadelphia	XV	K	Texas A&M
Frazier, Guy	Cincinnati	XVI	LB	Wyoming
Frazier, Wayne	Kansas City	I	C	Auburn
Frederick, Andy	Dallas	XII,XIII	T	New Mexico
Fritsch, Toni	Dallas	X	K	None
Fugett, Jean	Dallas	X	TE-WR	Amherst

Name	Team		Position	College
Fuller, Jeff	San Francisco	XIX	S	Texas A&M
Fuller, Mike	Cincinnati	XVI	S	Auburn
Fuqua, John	Pittsburgh	X	RB	Morgan State
Furness, Steve	Pittsburgh	IX,X,XIII,XIV	DT-DE	Rhode Island
Gallagher, Frank	Minnesota	VIII	G	North Carolina
Gardin, Ron	Baltimore	V	DB	Arizona
Garrett, Alvin	Washington	XVII,XVIII	WR	Angelo State
Garrett, Carl	Oakland	XI	RB	New Mexico Highlands
Garrett, Mike	Kansas City	I,IV	RB	USC
Garrett, Reggie	Pittsburgh	IX,X	WR	Eastern Michigan
Garrison, Walt	Dallas	V,VI	RB	Oklahoma State
Gaubatz, Dennis	Baltimore	III	LB	LSU
Gerela, Roy	Pittsburgh	IX,X,XIII	K	New Mexico State
Gervais, Rick	San Francisco	XVI	S	Stanford
Giammona, Louie	Philadelphia	XV	RB-KR	Utah State
Giaquinto, Nick	Washington	XVII,XVIII	RB	Connecticut
Giesler, Jon	Miami	XVII,XIX	T	Michigan
Gilliam, Joe	Pittsburgh	IX*,X*	QB	Tennessee State
Gilliam, John	Minnesota	VIII,IX	WR	South Carolina State
Gilliam, Jon	Kansas City	I	C	East Texas State
Gillingham, Gale	Green Bay	I,II	G	Minnesota
Ginn, Hubert	Miami, Oakland	VI,VII,XI	RB	Florida A&M
Glassic, Tom	Denver	XII	G	Virginia
Goode, Irv	Miami	VIII	C-G	Kentucky

287

Name	Team	Game	Position	College
Goode, Tom	Baltimore	V	C	Mississippi State
Goodrum, Charles	Minnesota	VIII,IX,XI	T-G	Florida A&M
Gordon, Cornell	N.Y. Jets	III	DB	North Carolina A&T
Gordon, Larry	Miami	XVII	LB	Arizona State
Grabowski, Jim	Green Bay	I,II*	RB	Illinois
Grandishar, Randy	Denver	XII	LB	Ohio State
Grant, Bob	Baltimore	V	LB	Wake Forest
Grant, Darryl	Washington	XVII,XVIII	DT	Rice
Grant, John	Denver	XII	DT	USC
Grantham, Larry	N.Y. Jets	III	LB	Mississippi
Gravelle, Gordon	Pittsburgh, L.A. Rams	IX,X,XIV	G-T	Brigham Young
Graves, Tom	Pittsburgh	XIV	LB	Michigan State
Grayson, Dave	Oakland	II	DB	Oregon
Green, Cleveland	Miami	XVII,XIX	T	Southern
Green, Cornell	Dallas	V,VI	DB	Utah State
Green, Darrell	Washington	XVIII	CB-KR	Texas A&I
Greene, Joe	Pittsburgh	IX,X,XIII,XIV	DT	North Texas State
Greenwood, L. C.	Pittsburgh	IX,X,XIII,XIV	DE	Arkansas AM&N
Gregg, Forrest	Green Bay, Dallas	I,II,VI*	T-G	SMU
Gregory, Bill	Dallas	VI,X,XII	DT	Wisconsin
Griese, Bob	Miami	VI,VII,VIII	QB	Purdue
Griffin, Archie	Cincinnati	XVI	RB	Ohio State
Griffin, Ray	Cincinnati	XVI	CB	Ohio State

Name	Team	SB	Pos	College
Grim, Bob	Minnesota	IV,XI	WR	Oregon State
Grimm, Russ	Washington	XVII,XVIII	C-G	Pittsburgh
Groce, Ron	Minnesota	XI	RB	Macalester
Grossman, Randy	Pittsburgh	IX,X,XIII,XIV	TE	Temple
Guy, Ray	Oakland, L.A. Rams	XI,XV,XVIII	K-P	Southern Mississippi
Hackbart, Dale	Minnesota	IV	DB	Wisconsin
Hagberg, Roger	Oakland	II	RB	Minnesota
Hairston, Carl	Philadelphia	XV	DE	Maryland State
Hall, Willie	Oakland	XI	LB	USC
Hall, Windlan	Minnesota	XI	S	Arizona State
Ham, Jack	Pittsburgh	IX,X,XIII,XIV*	LB	Penn State
Hamilton, Wes	Minnesota	XI	G	Tulsa
Hanburger, Chris	Washington	VII	LB	North Carolina
Hannah, Charley	L.A. Raiders	XVIII	G	Alabama
Hanratty, Terry	Pittsburgh	IX*,X	QB	Notre Dame
Hardman, Cedrick	Oakland	XV	DE	North Texas State
Hardy, Bruce	Miami	XVII,XIX	TE	Arizona State
Hargrove, Jim	Minnesota	IV	LB	Howard Payne
Hargrove, Jim	Cincinnati	XVI	RB	Wake Forest
Harmon, Clarence	Washington	XVII	RB	Mississippi State
Harmon, Derrick	San Francisco	XIX	RB	Cornell
Harper, Willie	San Francisco	XVI	LB	Nebraska
Harrah, Dennis	L.A. Rams	XIV	G	Miami
Harraway, Charley	Washington	VII	RB	San José State

289

Name	Team	Game	Position	College
Harrington, Perry	Philadelphia	XV	RB	Jackson State
Harris, Bill	Minnesota	IV	RB	Colorado
Harris, Bo	Cincinnati	XVI	LB	LSU
Harris, Cliff	Dallas	V,VI,X,XII,XIII	DB-S	Ouachita
Harris, Duriel	Miami	XVII	WR	New Mexico State
Harris, Franco	Pittsburgh	IX,X,XIII,XIV	RB	Penn State
Harris, Joe	L.A. Rams	XIV	LB	Georgia Tech
Harris, Leroy	Philadelphia	XV	RB	Arkansas State
Harris, M. L.	Cincinnati	XVI	TE	Kansas State
Harrison, Dennis	Philadelphia	XV	DE	Vanderbilt
Harrison, Reggie	Pittsburgh	IX,X	RB	Cincinnati
Hart, Doug	Green Bay	I,II	DB	Arlington State
Harty, John	San Francisco	XVI	NT	Iowa
Harvey, Jim	Oakland	II	G	Mississippi
Hasselbeck, Don	L.A. Raiders	XVIII	TE	Colorado
Hathcock, Dave	Green Bay	I	DB	Memphis State
Hauss, Len	Washington	VII	C	Georgia
Havrilak, Sam	Baltimore	V	RB	Bucknell
Hawkins, Alex	Baltimore	III	WR	South Carolina
Hawkins, Frank	L.A. Raiders	XVIII	RB	Nevada-Reno
Hawkins, Wayne	Oakland	II	G	Pacific
Hawthorne, Greg	Pittsburg	XIV	RB	Baylor
Hayes, Bob	Dallas	V,VI	WR	Florida A&M

Name	Team		Pos	College
Hayes, Jeff	Washington	XVII,XVIII	P	North Carolina
Hayes, Lester	Oakland, L.A. Raiders	XV,XVIII	CB	Texas A&M
Hayes, Wendell	Kansas City	IV	RB	Humboldt State
Haymond, Alvin	Washington	VII	S	Southern
Haynes, Mike	L.A. Raiders	XVIII	CB	Arizona State
Headrick, Sherrill	Kansas City	I	LB	TCU
Heflin, Vince	Miami	XVII,XIX	WR	Central State (Ohio)
Hegman, Mike	Dallas	XII,XIII	LB	Tennessee State
Heinz, Bob	Miami	VI,VII,VIII	DT-DE	Pacific
Henderson, John	Minnesota	IV	WR	Michigan
Henderson, Thomas	Dallas	X,XII,XIII	LB	Langston
Henderson, Zac	Philadelphia	XV	S	Oklahoma
Hendricks, Ted	Baltimore, Oakland, L.A. Raiders	V,XI,XV,XVIII	LB	Miami
Henry, Wally	Philadelphia	XV	WR-KR	UCLA
Herman, Dave	N.Y. Jets	III	TE	Michigan State
Hermeling, Terry	Washington	VII	T	Nevada-Reno
Herock, Ken	Oakland	II	OT	West Virginia
Herrera, Efren	Dallas	XII	K	UCLA
Hertel, Rob	Philadelphia	XV*	QB	USC
Hester, Ron	Miami	XVII	LB	Florida State
Hicks, Bryan	Cincinnati	XVI	S	McNeese State
Hicks, Dwight	San Francisco	XVI,XIX	S-CB	Michigan
Hilgenberg, Wally	Minnesota	IV,VIII,IX,XI	LB	Iowa

Name	Team	Game	Position	College
Hill, Calvin	Dallas	V,VI	RB	Yale
Hill, Dave	Kansas City	I,IV	OT	Auburn
Hill, Drew	L.A. Rams	XIV	WR-KR	Georgia Tech
Hill, Eddie	L.A. Rams, Miami	XIV,XVII,XIX	RB-KR	Memphis State
Hill, Jerry	Baltimore	III,V	RB	Wyoming
Hill, Kenny	L.A. Raiders	XVIII	S	Yale
Hill, Kent	L.A. Rams	XIV	G	Georgia Tech
Hill, Tony	Dallas	XII,XIII	WR	Stanford
Hill, Winston	N.Y. Jets	III	OT	Texas Southern
Hilton, Roy	Baltimore	III,V	DE	Jackson State
Hinton, Eddie	Baltimore	V	WR	Oklahoma
Holland, John	Minnesota	IX*	WR	Tennessee State
Holly, Bob	Washington	XVII*, XVIII*	QB	Princeton
Holmes, Ernie	Pittsburgh	IX,X	DT	Texas Southern
Holmes, Robert	Kansas City	IV	RB	Southern
Holmoe, Tom	San Francisco	XIX	S	Brigham Young
Holub, E. J.	Kansas City	I,IV	LB-C	Texas Tech
Homan, Dennis	Dallas	V	WR	Alabama
Hoopes, Mitch	Dallas	X	P	Arizona
Horn, Don	Green Bay	II*	QB	San Diego State
Horn, Rod	Cincinnati	XVI	NT	Nebraska
Hornung, Paul	Green Bay	I*	RB	Notre Dame
Howard, Paul	Denver	XII	G	Brigham Young

292

Name	Team		Pos.	College
Howard, Percy	Dallas	X	WR	Austin Peay
Howard, Ron	Dallas	X	TE	Seattle
Howley, Chuck	Dallas	V,VI	LB	West Virginia
Hudson, Jim	N.Y. Jets	III	DB	Texas
Huff, Ken	Washington	XVIII	G	North Carolina
Hughes, Randy	Dallas	X,XII,XIII	S	Oklahoma
Hull, Mike	Washington	VII	RB	USC
Humm, David	Oakland, L.A. Raiders	XI,XVIII	QB	Nebraska
Humphrey, Claude	Philadelphia	XV	DE	Tennessee State
Hunt, Bobby	Kansas City	I	DB	Auburn
Hurston, Chuck	Kansas City	I,IV	DE-LB	Auburn
Huther, Bruce	Dallas	XII,XIII	LB	New Hampshire
Hyde, Glenn	Denver	XII	T	Pittsburgh
Hyland, Bob	Green Bay	I	C	Boston College
Jackson, Bernard	Denver	XII	S	Washington State
Jackson, Monte	Oakland	XV	CB	San Diego State
Jackson, Tom	Denver	XII	LB	Louisville
Jackson, Wilbur	Washington	XVII	RB	Alabama
Jacoby, Joe	Washington	XVII,XVIII	T	Louisville
Jaqua, Jon	Washington	VII	S	Lewis & Clark
Jaworski, Ron	Philadelphia	XV	QB	Youngstown State
Jefferson, Roy	Baltimore, Washington	V,VII	WR	Utah
Jenkins, Al	Miami	VII*	G-T	Tulsa
Jenkins, Ed	Miami	VII	RB	Holy Cross

Name	Team	Game	Position	College
Jensen, Derrick	Oakland, L.A. Raiders	XV,XVIII	RB-TE	Texas Arlington
Jensen, Jim	Denver	XII	RB	Iowa
Jensen, Jim	Miami	XVII,XIX	QB-WR	Boston
Jeter, Bob	Green Bay	I,II	DB	Iowa
Jodat, Jim	L.A. Rams	XIV	RB	Carthage
Johnson, Butch	Dallas	XII,XIII	WR	California-Riverside
Johnson, Charlie	Philadelphia	XV	NT	Colorado
Johnson, Cornelius	Baltimore	III,V	G	Virginia Union
Johnson, Curley	N.Y. Jets	III	P	Houston
Johnson, Curtis	Miami	VI,VII,VIII	DB	Toledo
Johnson, Dan	Miami	XIX	TE	Iowa State
Johnson, Gary	San Francisco	XIX	DE	Grambling
Johnson, Mitch	Washington	VII*	T	UCLA
Johnson, Monte	Oakland	XI	LB	Nebraska
Johnson, Pete	Cincinnati, Miami	XVI,XIX*	RB	Ohio State
Johnson, Ron	Pittsburgh	XIII,XIV	CB	Eastern Michigan
Johnson, Sammy	Minnesota	XI	RB	North Carolina
Jones, Clint	Minnesota	IV	RB	Michigan
Jones, Ed	Dallas	X,XII,XIII	DE	Tennessee State
Jones, Jimmie	Washington	VII*	DE	Wichita State
Jones, Willie	Oakland	XV	DE	Florida State
Jordan, Curtis	Washington	XVII,XVIII	S	Texas Tech
Jordan, Henry	Green Bay	I,II	DT	Virginia

Name	Team		Pos.	College
Jordan, Lee Roy	Dallas	V,VI,X	LB	Alabama
Jordan, Shelby	L.A. Raiders	XVIII	T	Washington (Mo.)
Judson, William	Miami	XVII,XIX	CB	South Carolina State
Kadish, Mike	Miami	VII*	DT	Notre Dame
Kapp, Joe	Minnesota	IV	QB	California
Kassulke, Karl	Minnesota	IV	DB	Drake
Kaufman, Mel	Washington	XVII,XVIII	LB	Cal Poly-San Luis Obispo
Kearney, Jim	Kansas City	IV	DB	Prairie View
Keating, Tom	Oakland	II	DT	Michigan
Kelcher, Louie	San Francisco	XIX	NT	SMU
Kellum, Marv	Pittsburgh	IX,X	LB	Wichita State
Kemp, Bobby	Cincinnati	XVI	S	Cal State-Fullerton
Kennedy, Allan	San Francisco	XVI,XIX	T	Washington State
Kenney, Steve	Philadelphia	XV	T	Clemson
Keyworth, Jon	Denver	XII	RB	Colorado
Klick, Jim	Miami	VI,VII,VIII	RB	Wyoming
Kilmer, Billy	Washington	VII	QB	UCLA
Kimball, Bruce	Washington	XVIII	G	Massachusetts
Kindig, Howard	Miami	VII	T-C	Cal State-L.A.
Kiner, State	Dallas	V	LB	Tennessee
King, Kenny	Oakland, L.A. Raiders	XV,XVIII	RB	Oklahoma
Kingsriter, Doug	Minnesota	VIII,IX	TE	Minnesota
Kinlaw, Reggie	Oakland, L.A. Raiders	XV,XVIII	NT	Oklahoma
Knight, Curt	Washington	VII	K	Coast Guard Academy

Name	Team	Game	Position	College
Kocourek, Dave	Oakland	II	TE	Wisconsin
Kolb, Jon	Pittsburgh	IX,X,XIII,XIV	T	Oklahoma State
Kolen, Mike	Miami	VI, VII,VIII	LB	Auburn
Kostelnik, Ron	Green Bay	I,II	DT	Cincinnati
Kozlowski, Mike	Miami	XVII,XIX	S	Colorado
Kramer, Jerry	Green Bay	I,II	G	Idaho
Kramer, Kent	Minnesota	IV	TE	Minnesota
Krause, Paul	Minnesota	IV,VIII,IX,XI	S	Iowa
Kreider, Steve	Cincinnati	XVI	WR	Lehigh
Krepfle, Keith	Philadelphia	XV	TE	Iowa State
Kruczek, Mike	Pittsburgh	XIII*,XIV*	QB	Boston College
Kruse, Bob	Oakland	II	G	Wayne State
Kubin, Larry	Washington	XVII,XVIII	LB	Penn State
Kuechenberg, Bob	Miami	VI,VII,VIII,XVII	G	Notre Dame
Kyle, Aaron	Dallas	XII,XIII	CB	Wyoming
Laakso, Eric	Miami	XVII	T	Tulane
Laaveg, Paul	Washington	VII	G	Iowa
Laidlaw, Scott	Dallas	XII,XIII	RB	Stanford
Lambert, Jack	Pittsburgh	IX,X,XIII,XIV	LB	Kent State
Lammons, Pete	N.Y. Jets	III	TE	Texas
Lamonica, Daryle	Oakland	II	QB	Notre Dame
Langer, Jim	Miami	VI,VII,VIII	G	South Dakota State
Lanier, Willie	Kansas City	IV	LB	Morgan State

Name	Team	Super Bowls	Pos.	College
Lankford, Paul	Miami	XVII,XIX	CB-S	Penn State
Lapham, Dave	Cincinnati	XVI	G	Syracuse
Larsen, Gary	Minnesota	IV,VIII,IX	DT	Concordia (Minn.)
Lash, Jim	Minnesota	VIII,IX	WR	Northwestern
Laskey, Bill	Oakland	II	LB	Michigan
Lassiter, Ike	Oakland	II	DE	St. Augustine
Laster, Donald	Washington	XVII	T	Tennessee State
Laufenberg, Babe	Washington	XVIII*	QB	Indiana
Lavender, Joe	Washington	XVII	CB	San Diego State
Lawless, Burton	Dallas	X,XII,XIII	G	Florida
Lawrence, Amos	San Francisco	XVI	RB	North Carolina
Lawrence, Henry	Oakland, L.A. Raiders	XI,XV,XVIII	T	Florida A&M
Lawson, Steve	Minnesota	VIII*,IX	G	Kansas
LeClair, Jim	Cincinnati	XVI	LB	North Dakota
Lee, Bob	Minnesota, L.A. Rams	IV,XI,XIV*	QB-P	Pacific
Lee, David	Baltimore	III,V	P	Louisiana Tech
Lee, Ronnie	Miami	XVII,XIX	TE-T	Baylor
Leigh, Charles	Miami	VII,VIII	RB	None
LeMaster, Frank	Philadelphia	XV	LB	Kentucky
Leopold, Bobby	San Francisco	XVI	LB	Notre Dame
Lewis, D. D.	Dallas	V,VI,X,XII,XIII	LB	Mississippi State
Lewis, Frank	Pittsburgh	IX,X	WR	Grambling
Liebenstein, Todd	Washington	XVII,XVIII	DE	Nevada-Las Vegas
Lilly, Bob	Dallas	V,VI	DT	TCU

Name	Team	Game	Position	College
Lindsey, Jim	Minnesota	IV	RB	Arkansas
Liscio, Tony	Dallas	V*,VI	OT	Tulsa
Little, Larry	Miami	VI,VII,VIII	G	Bethune-Cookman
Livingston, Mike	Kansas City	IV	QB	SMU
Logan, Jerry	Baltimore	III,V	DB	West Texas State
Logan, Randy	Philadelphia	XV	S	Michigan
Long, Bob	Green Bay	I,II	WR	Wichita
Long, Howie	L.A. Raiders	XVIII	DE	Villanova
Longley, Clint	Dallas	X*	QB	Abilene Christian
Lothamer, Ed	Kansas City	IV	DT	Michigan State
Lothridge, Billy	Miami	VII*	P	Georgia
Lott, Ronnie	San Francisco	XVI,XIX	CB-S	USC
Lowry, Quentin	Washington	XVII	LB	Youngstown State
Lurtsema, Bob	Minnesota	VIII,IX	DT-DE	Western Michigan
Lyles, Lenny	Baltimore	III	DB	Louisville
Lynch, Jim	Kansas City	IV	LB	Notre Dame
Lytle, Rob	Denver	XII	RB	Michigan
Mack, Red	Green Bay	I	WR	Notre Dame
Mackbee, Earsell	Minnesota	IV	DB	Utah State
Mackey, John	Baltimore	III,V	TE	Syracuse
Maitland, Jack	Baltimore	V	RB	Williams
Manders, Dave	Dallas	V,VI	C	Michigan State
Mandich, Jim	Miami, Pittsburgh	VI,VII,VIII,XIII	TE	Michigan

Name	Team		Pos	College
Manley, Dexter	Washington	XVII,XVIII	DE	Oklahoma State
Mann, Charles	Washington	XVIII	DE	Nevada-Reno
Mann, Errol	Oakland	XI	K	North Dakota
Manor, Brison	Denver	XII	DE	Arkansas
Mansfield, Ray	Pittsburgh	IX,X	C	Washington
Maples, Bobby	Denver	XII	C	Baylor
Marinaro, Ed	Minnesota	VIII,IX	RB	Cornell
Marino, Dan	Miami	XIX	QB	Pittsburgh
Marsalis, Jim	Kansas City	IV	DB	Tennessee State
Marshall, Jim	Minnesota	IV,VIII,IX,XI	DE	Ohio State
Martin, Amos	Minnesota	VIII,IX,XI	LB	Louisville
Martin, Harvey	Dallas	X,XII,XIII	DE	East Texas State
Martin, Rod	Oakland, L.A. Raiders	XV,XVIII	LB	USC
Martin, Saladin	San Francisco	XVI*	CB	San Diego State
Martini, Rich	Oakland	XV	WR	California-Davis
Marvin, Mickey	Oakland, L.A. Raiders	XV,XVIII	G	Tennessee
Mason, Lindsey	Oakland	XV	T-G	Kansas
Matheson, Bob	Miami	VI,VII,VIII	LB	Duke
Mathis, Bill	N.Y. Jets	III	RB	Clemson
Matte, Tom	Baltimore	III	RB	Ohio State
Matthews, Ira	Oakland	XV	KR-WR-RB	Wisconsin
Matuszak, John	Oakland	XI,XV	DE	Tampa
Maurer, Andy	Minnesota, Dallas	IX,XII	G-T	Oregon
Maxwell, Tom	Baltimore	V	DB	Texas A&M

299

Name	Team	Game	Position	College
May, Mark	Washington	XVII,XVIII	G	Pittsburgh
May, Ray	Baltimore	V	LB	USC
Maynard, Don	N.Y. Jets	III	WR	Texas Western
Mays, Jerry	Kansas City	I,IV	DE	SMU
McAdams, Carl	N.Y. Jets	III	DT-LB	Oklahoma
McClanahan, Brent	Minnesota	IX,XI	RB	Arizona State
McClanahan, Randy	Oakland	XV	LB	Southwestern Louisiana
McClinton, Curtis	Kansas City	I,IV	RB-TE	Kansas
McCloughan, Kent	Oakland	II	DB	Nebraska
McColl, Milt	San Francisco	XVI,XIX	LB	Stanford
McCullum, Sam	Minnesota	IX	WR	UCLA
McCutcheon, Lawrence	L.A. Rams	XIV	RB	Colorado State
McDaniel, LeCharls	Washington	XVII	CB	Cal Poly-San Luis Obispo
McDole, Ron	Washington	VII	DE	Nebraska
McElroy, Vann	L.A. Raiders	XVIII	S	Baylor
McGee, Max	Green Bay	I,II	WR	Tulane
McGee, Tony	Washington	XVII,XVIII	DE	Bishop (Tex.)
McGill, Mike	Minnesota	IV	LB	Notre Dame
McGrath, Mark	Washington	XVIII*	WR	Montana State
McInally, Pat	Cincinnati	XVI	P-WR	Harvard
McIntyre, Guy	San Francisco	XIX	G	Georgia
McKinney, Odis	Oakland, L.A. Raiders	XV,XVIII	CB-S	Colorado
McLemore, Dana	San Francisco	XIX	CB-KR	Hawaii

300

Name	Team		Pos.	College
McLinton, Harold	Washington	VII	LB	Southern
McMakin, John	Pittsburgh	IX	TE	Clemson
McMath, Herb	Oakland	XI	DE	Morningside
McNeal, Don	Miami	XVII,XIX	CB	Alabama
McNeil, Clifton	Washington	VII	WR	Grambling
NcNeil, Fred	Minnesota	IX,XI	LB	UCLA
McVea, Warren	Kansas City	IV	RB	Houston
Medlin, Dan	Oakland	XI	G	North Carolina State
Mendenhall, Mat	Washington	XVII	DE	Brigham Young
Mercein, Chuck	Green Bay	II	RB	Yale
Mercer, Mike	Kansas City	I	K	Arizona State
Merz, Curt	Kansas City	I	G	Iowa
Michaels, Lou	Baltimore	III	DE-K	Kentucky
Millen, Matt	Oakland, L.A. Raiders	XV,XVIII	LB	Penn State
Miller, Bill	Oakland	II	WR	Miami
Miller, Fred	Baltimore	III,V	DT	LSU
Miller, Jim	San Francisco	XVI	P	Mississippi
Miller, Robert	Minnesota	XI	RB	Kansas
Milot, Rich	Washington	XVII,XVIII	LB	Penn State
Minor, Claudie	Denver	XII	T	San Diego State
Mira, George	Miami	VI*	QB	Miami
Mitchell, Tom	Baltimore	III,V	TE	Bucknell
Mitchell, Willie	Kansas City	I,IV	DB	Tennessee State
Monk, Art	Washington	XVIII	WR	Syracuse

301

Name	Team	Game	Position	College
Monroe, Carl	San Francisco	XIX	RB-KR	Utah
Montana, Joe	San Francisco	XVI,XIX	QB	Notre Dame
Montgomery, Blanchard	San Francisco	XIX	LB	UCLA
Montgomery, Cle	L.A. Raiders	XVIII	WR-KR	Abilene Christian
Montgomery, Wilbert	Philadelphia	XV	RB	Abilene Christian
Montler, Mike	Denver	XII	C	Colorado
Montoya, Max	Cincinnati	XVI	G	UCLA
Moody, Keith	Oakland	XV	CB-KR	Syracuse
Moore, Blake	Cincinnati	XVI	C-T	Wooster
Moore, Manfred	Oakland	XI	RB	USC
Moore, Maulty	Miami	VII,VIII	DT	Bethune-Cookman
Moore, Nat	Miami	XVII,XIX	WR	Florida
Moore, Wayne	Miami	VI,VII,VIII	OT	Lamar Tech
Moorman, Mo	Kansas City	IV	G	Texas A&M
Morrall, Earl	Baltimore, Miami	III,V,VII,VIII	QB	Michigan State
Morris, Mercury	Miami	VI,VII,VIII	RB	West Texas State
Morriss, Guy	Philadelphia	XV	C	TCU
Morton, Craig	Dallas, Denver	V,VI*,XII	QB	California
Mosebar, Don	L.A. Raiders	XVIII	G	USC
Moseley, Mark	Washington	XVII,XVIII	K	Stephen F. Austin
Moser, Rick	Pittsburgh	XIII,XIV	RB-KR	Rhode Island
Moses, Haven	Denver	XII	WR	San Diego State
Muhammad, Calvin	L.A. Raiders	XVIII	WR	Texas Southern

302

Name	Team		Position	College
Mul-Key, Herb	Washington	VII	RB	None
Mullaney, Mark	Minnesota	XI	DE	Colorado State
Mullins, Gerry	Pittsburgh	IX,X,XIII,XIV	G-T	USC
Mumphord, Lloyd	Miami	VI,VII,VIII	DB	Texas Southern
Munoz, Anthony	Cincinnati	XVI	T	USC
Murphy, Mark	Washington	XVII,XVIII	S	Colgate
Nairne, Rob	Denver	XII	LB	Oregon State
Namath, Joe	N.Y. Jets	III	QB	Alabama
Nathan, Tony	Miami	XVII,XIX	RB	Alabama
Neely, Ralph	Dallas	V,X,XII	G-T	Oklahoma
Nehemiah, Renaldo	San Francisco	XIX	WR	Maryland
Neidert, John	N.Y. Jets	III	LB	Louisville
Nelms, Mike	Washington	XVII,XVIII	S-KR-WR	Baylor
Nelson, Bob	Oakland, L.A. Raiders	XV,XVIII	LB	Nebraska
Nelson, Terry	L.A. Rams	XIV	TE	Arkansas-Pine Bluff
Newhouse, Robert	Dallas	X,XII,XIII	RB	Houston
Newman, Ed	Miami	VIII,XIX	G	Duke
Newsome, Billy	Baltimore	V	DE	Grambling
Nichols, Robbie	Baltimore	V	LB	Tulsa
Niland, John	Dallas	V,VI	G	Iowa
Nitschke, Ray	Green Bay	I,II	LB	Illinois
Nock, George	Washington	VII*	RB	Morgan State
Noonan, Karl	Miami	VI	WR	Iowa
Norman, Pettis	Dallas	V	TE	Johnson C. Smith

303

Name	Team	Game	Position	College
Nottingham, Don	Miami	VIII	RB	Kent State
Nowatzke, Tom	Baltimore	V	RB	Indiana
Nye, Blaine	Dallas	V,VI,X	G	Stanford
Oates, Carleton	Oakland	II	DE	Florida A&M
O'Brien, Jim	Baltimore	V	K	Cincinnati
Obrovac, Mike	Cincinnati	XVI	G	Bowling Green
Odoms, Riley	Denver	XII	TE	Houston
Oldham, Ray	Pittsburgh	XIII	S	Middle Tennessee State
Oikewicz, Neal	Washington	XVII,XVIII	LB	Maryland
Orosz, Tom	Miami	XVII	P	Ohio State
Orr, Jimmy	Baltimore	III,V*	WR	Georgia
Osborn, Dave	Minnesota	IV,VIII,IX	RB	North Dakota
O'Steen, Dwayne	L.A. Rams, Oakland	XIV,XV	CB	San José State
Otto, Gus	Oakland	II	LB	Missouri
Otto, Jim	Oakland	II	C	Miami
Owen, Tom	Washington	XVII*	QB	Wichita State
Owens, Brig	Washington	VII	S	Cincinnati
Owens, Burgess	Oakland	XV	S	Miami
Page, Alan	Minnesota	IV,VIII,IX,XI	DT	Notre Dame
Pardee, Jack	Washington	VII	LB	Texas A&M
Parilli, Babe	N.Y. Jets	III	QB	Kentucky
Paris, Bubba	San Francisco	XIX	T	Michigan
Parker, Rodney	Philadephia	XV	WR	Tennessee State

304

Name	Team	Games	College
Patton, Ricky	San Francisco	XVI	RB	Jackson State
Pear, Dave	Oakland	XV	NT	Washington
Pearson, Drew	Dallas	X,XII,XIII	WR	Tulsa
Pearson, Preston	Baltimore, Pittsburgh, Dallas	III,IX,X,XII,XIII	RB	Illinois
Penrose, Craig	Denver	XII*	QB	San Diego State
Peoples, Woody	Philadelphia	XV	G	Grambling
Perkins, Ray	Baltimore	III,V	WR	Alabama
Perot, Petey	Philadelphia	XV	G	Northwestern Louisiana
Perrin, Lonnie	Denver	XII	RB	Illinois
Perry, Rod	L.A. Rams	XIV	CB	Colorado
Peters, Tony	Washington	XVII	S	Oklahoma
Peterson, Cal	Dallas	X	LB	UCLA
Peterson, Ted	Pittsburgh	XIII,XIV	C-T	Eastern Illinois
Petitbon, Richie	Washington	VII*	S	Tulane
Petrella, Bob	Miami	VI	DB	Tennessee
Philbin, Gerry	N.Y. Jets	III	DE	Buffalo
Phillips, Charles	Oakland	XI	DB	USC
Phillips, Ray	Philadelphia	XV	LB	Nebraska
Philyaw, Charles	Oakland	XI	DE	Texas Southern
Pickel, Bill	L.A. Raiders	XVIII	DE	Rutgers
Pillers, Lawrence	San Francisco	XVI,XIX	DE	Alcorn A&M
Pinney, Ray	Pittsburgh	XIII	T-C	Washington
Pisarcik, Joe	Philadelphia	XV*	QB	New Mexico State

Name	Team	Game	Position	College
Pitts, Elijah	Green Bay	I, IV	RB	Philander Smith
Pitts, Frank	Kansas City	I, IV	WR	Southern
Plunkett, Jim	Oakland, L.A. Raiders	XV, XVIII	QB	Stanford
Ply, Bobby	Kansas City	—	DB	Baylor
Podolak, Ed	Kansas City	IV	RB	Iowa
Poltl, Randy	Minnesota, Denver	IX, XII	CB-S	Stanford
Porter, Ron	Baltimore, Minnesota	III, VIII	LB	Idaho
Potter, Steve	Miami	XVII	LB	Virginia
Pottios, Myron	Washington	VII	LB	Notre Dame
Powell, Jesse	Miami	VI, VII	LB	West Texas State
Powers, Warren	Oakland	II	DB	Nebraska
Prudhomme, Remi	Kansas City	IV	C	LSU
Pruitt, Greg	L.A. Raiders	XVIII	RB-KR	Oklahoma
Puetz, Garry	Washington	XVII*	T	Valparaiso
Pugh, Jethro	Dallas	V, VI, X, XII, XIII*	DT	Elizabeth City State
Puki, Craig	San Francisco	XVI	LB	Tennessee
Quillan, Fred	San Francisco	XVI, XIX	C	Oregon
Rademacher, Bill	N.Y. Jets	III	WR	Northern Michigan
Rae, Mike	Oakland	XI	QB	USC
Rafferty, Tom	Dallas	XII, XIII	G-C	Penn State
Ramsey, Derrick	Oakland	XV	TE	Kentucky
Ramson, Eason	San Francisco	XVI	TE	Washington State
Randall, Tom	Dallas	XIII	G	Iowa State

Name	Team		Pos.	College
Randolph, Al	Minnesota	VIII*	S	Iowa
Rashad, Ahmad	Minnesota	XI	WR	Oregon
Rasmussen, Randy	N.Y. Jets	III	G	Kearney State
Rather, Bo	Miami	VIII*	WR	Michigan
Razzano, Rick	Cincinnati	XVI	LB	Virginia Tech
Reavis, Dave	Pittsburgh	IX,X	T	Arkansas
Reed, Oscar	Minnesota	IV,VIII,IX	RB	Colorado State
Reese, Archie	San Francisco	XVI	NT	Clemson
Reeves, Dan	Dallas	V,VI	RB	South Carolina
Reilly, Mike	Minnesota	IV*	LB	Iowa
Renfro, Mel	Dallas	V,VI,X,XII	DB-CB	Oregon
Ressler, Glenn	Baltimore	III,V	G	Penn State
Reynolds, Al	Kansas City	I	G	Tarkio (Mo.)
Reynolds, Jack	L.A. Rams, San Francisco	XIV,XVI,XIX	LB	Tennessee
Rhone, Earnie	Miami	XVII,XIX	LB	Henderson (Ark.)
Rice, Andy	Kansas City	I	DT	Texas Southern
Rice, Floyd	Oakland	XI	LB	Alcorn A&M
Rich, Randy	Denver	XII	S	New Mexico
Richards, Golden	Dallas	X,XII	WR	Hawaii
Richards, Jim	N.Y. Jets	III	DB	Virginia Tech
Richardson, Gloster	Kansas City, Dallas	IV,VI*	WR	Jackson State
Richardson, Jeff	N.Y. Jets	III	OT-C	Michigan State
Richardson, John	Miami	VI	DT	UCLA

Name	Team	Game	Position	College
Richardson, Willie	Baltimore	III	WR	Jackson State
Riggins, John	Washington	XVII,XVIII	RB	Kansas
Riley, Larry	Denver	XII*	CB	Salem College
Riley, Jim	Miami	VI	DE	Oklahoma
Riley, Ken	Cincinnati	XVI	CB	Florida A&M
Riley, Steve	Minnesota	IX*,XI	T	USC
Ring, Bill	San Francisco	XVI,XIX	RB-KR	Brigham Young
Rizzo, Joe	Denver	XII	LB	Merchant Marine Academy
Robinson, Dave	Green Bay	I,II	LB	Penn State
Robinson, Jerry	Philadelphia	XV	LB	UCLA
Robinson, Johnny	Kansas City	I,IV	DB	LSU
Robinson, Johnny	L.A. Raiders	XVIII	NT	Louisiana Tech
Roby, Reggie	Miami	XIX	P	Iowa
Rochester, Paul	N.Y. Jets	III	DT	Michigan State
Rock, Walter	Washington	VII	T	Maryland
Rose, Joe	Miami	XVII,XIX	TE	California
Ross, Dan	Cincinnati	XVI	TE	Northeastern
Rowe, Dave	Oakland	XI	DT	Penn State
Rowser, John	Green Bay	II	DB	Michigan
Rucker, Reggie	Dallas	V	WR	Boston
Runager, Max	Philadelphia, San Francisco	XV,XIX	P	South Carolina
Russell, Andy	Pittsburgh	IX,X	LB	Missouri

308

Name	Team	Super Bowl	Pos.	College
Rutledge, Jeff	L.A. Rams	XIV*	QB	Alabama
Ryczek, Dan	L.A. Rams	XIV	C-G	Virginia
St. Clair, Mike	Cincinnati	XVI	DE	Grambling
Saldi, Jay	Dallas	XII*	TE	South Carolina
Sample, Johnny	N.Y. Jets	III	DB	Maryland State
Sauer, George	N.Y. Jets	III	WR	Texas
Saul, Rich	L.A. Rams	XIV	C	Michigan State
Schindler, Steve	Denver	XII*	G	Boston College
Schmitt, John	N.Y. Jets	III	C	Hofstra
Schoenke, Ray	Washington	VII*	T	SMU
Schonert, Turk	Cincinnati	XVI*	QB	Stanford
Schuh, Harry	Oakland	II	OT	Memphis State
Schultz, John	Denver	XII	WR	Maryland
Sciarra, John	Philadelphia	XV	S-KR	UCLA
Scott, Herbert	Dallas	X,XII,XIII	G	Virginia Union
Scott, Jake	Miami	VI,VII,VIII	DB	Georgia
Seay, Virgil	Washington	XVII,XVIII*	KR-WR	Troy State
Seiple, Larry	Miami	VI,VII,VIII	TE-P	Kentucky
Sellers, Goldie	Kansas City	IV	DB	Grambling
Sellers, Ron	Miami	VIII*	WR	Florida State
Septien, Rafael	Dallas	XIII	K	Southwestern Louisiana
Severson, Jeff	Washington	VII	DB	Cal State-Long Beach
Shanklin, Ron	Pittsburgh	IX	WR	North Texas State
Sharockman, Ed	Minnesota	IV	DB	Pittsburgh

Name	Team	Game	Position	College
Shell, Art	Oakland	XI,XV	T	Maryland-E. S.
Shell, Donnie	Pittsburgh	IX,X,XIII,XIV	S-CB-DB	South Carolina State
Shell, Todd	San Francisco	XIX	LB	Brigham Young
Sherman, Rod	Oakland	II*	WR	USC
Shields, Billy	San Francisco	XIX	T	Georgia Tech
Shinnick, Don	Baltimore	III	LB	UCLA
Shipp, Jackie	Miami	XIX	LB	Oklahoma
Shiver, Sanders	Miami	XIX	LB	Carson-Newman
Shull, Steve	Miami	XVII	LB	William & Mary
Shumann, Mike	San Francisco	XVI	WR	Florida State
Siani, Mike	Oakland	XI	WR	Villanova
Siemon, Jeff	Minnesota	VIII,IX,XI	LB	Stanford
Simmons, John	Cincinnati	XVI	CB	SMU
Simmons, Roy	Washington	XVIII	G	Georgia Tech
Sisemore, Jerry	Philadelphia	XV	T	Texas
Sistrunk, Manny	Washington	VII	DT	Arkansas AM&N
Sistrunk, Otis	Oakland	XI	DE	None
Skoronski, Bob	Green Bay	I,II	OT	Indiana
Slater, Jackie	L.A. Rams	XIV	T	Jackson State
Slater, Mark	Philadelphia	XV	C	Minnesota
Sligh, Richard	Oakland	II	DT	North Carolina College
Small, Gerald	Miami	XVII	CB	San José State
Smiley, Larry	Minnesota	VIII*	DT	Texas Southern

Name	Team		Position	College
Smith, Billy Ray	Baltimore	III,V	OT	Arkansas
Smith, Bubba	Baltimore	III,V	DE	Michigan State
Smith, Charles	Philadelphia	XV	WR	Grambling
Smith, Fletcher	Kansas City	I	DB	Tennessee A&I
Smith, Jackie	Dallas	XIII	TE	Northwestern Louisiana
Smith, Jerry	Washington	VII	TE	Arizona State
Smith, Jim	Pittsburgh	XIII,XIV	WR-KR	Michigan
Smith, Paul	Denver	XII	DT	New Mexico
Smith, Ron	L.A. Rams	XIV	WR	San Diego State
Smith, Steve	Minnesota	IV	DE	Michigan
Smith, Tody	Dallas	VI	DE	USC
Smith, Tom	Miami	VIII*	RB	Miami
Smolinski, Mark	N.Y. Jets	III	RB	Wyoming
Snell, Matt	N.Y. Jets	III	RB	Ohio State
Solomon, Freddie	San Francisco	XVI,XIX	WR-KR	Tampa
Sowell, Robert	Miami	XIX	CB	Howard
Spagnola, John	Philadelphia	XV	TE	Yale
Squirek, Jack	L.A. Raiders	XVIII	LB	Illinois
Stabler, Ken	Oakland	XI	QB	Alabama
Stalls, Dave	Dallas, L.A. Raiders	XII,XIII,XVIII	DT-DE-NT	Northern Colorado
Stallworth, John	Pittsburgh	IX,X,XIII,XIV	WR	Alabama A&M
Stanfill, Bill	Miami	VI,VII,VIII	DE	Georgia
Starke, George	Washington	XVII,XVIII	T	Columbia

311

Name	Team	Game	Position	College
Starr, Bart	Green Bay	I,II	QB	Alabama
Staubach, Roger	Dallas	V*,VI,X,XII,XIII	QB	Navy
Steele, Robert	Dallas	XIII	WR	North Alabama
Stein, Bob	Kansas City	IV	LB	Minnesota
Stenerud, Jan	Kansas City	IV	K	Montana State
Stephenson, Dwight	Miami	XVII,XIX	C	Alabama
Stincic, Tom	Dallas	V,VI	LB	Michigan
Stoudt, Cliff	Pittsburgh	XIII*,XIV*	QB	Youngstown State
Stover, Jeff	San Francisco	XIX	DE	Oregon
Stover, Smokey	Kansas City	I	LB	Northeast Louisiana
Stowe, Otto	Miami	VI,VII*	WR	Iowa State
Strock, Don	Miami	VIII,XVII,XIX	QB	Virginia Tech
Stuckey, Henry	Miami	VII,VIII	DB	Missouri
Stuckey, Jim	San Francisco	XVI,XIX	DE	Clemson
Stukes, Charles	Baltimore	III,V	DB	Maryland State
Sullivan, Dan	Baltimore	III,V	G	Boston College
Sully, Ivory	L.A. Rams	XIV	S-CB	Delaware
Sunde, Milt	Minnesota	IV,IX	G	Minnesota
Sutherland, Doug	Minnesota	VIII,IX,XI	DT	Wisconsin State-Superior
Svihus, Bob	Oakland	II	OT	USC
Swann, Lynn	Pittsburgh	IX,X,XIII,XIV	WR	USC
Swenson, Bob	Denver	XII	LB	California
Swift, Doug	Miami	VI,VII,VIII	LB	Amherst

Name	Team	Super Bowls	Pos.	College
Sylvester, Steve	Oakland, L.A. Raiders	XI,XV,XVIII	C-G	Notre Dame
Szymanski, Dick	Baltimore	III	C	Notre Dame
Talamini, Bob	N.Y. Jets	III	G	Kentucky
Talbert, Diron	Washington	VII	DT	Texas
Taliaferro, Mike	Washington	VII*	QB	Illinois
Tarkenton, Fran	Minnesota	VIII,IX,XI	QB	Georgia
Tatum, Jack	Oakland	XI	DB	Ohio State
Taylor, Charley	Washington	VII	WR	Arizona State
Taylor, Jim	Green Bay	I	RB	LSU
Taylor, Otis	Kansas City	I,IV	WR	Prairie View
Taylor, Roosevelt	Washington	VII	S	Grambling
Theismann, Joe	Washington	XVII,XVIII	QB	Notre Dame
Thomas, Duane	Dallas	V,VI	RB	West Texas State
Thomas, Emmitt	Kansas City	I,IV	DB	Bishop College
Thomas, Gene	Kansas City	I	RB	Florida A&M
Thomas, Isaac	Dallas	VI	DB	Bishop College
Thomas, J. T.	Pittsburgh	IX,X,XIV	CB-S	Florida State
Thomas, Lynn	San Francisco	XVI	CB	Pittsburgh
Thomas, Pat	L.A. Rams	XIV	CB	Texas A&M
Thomas, Skip	Oakland	XI	DB	USC
Thompson, Bill	Denver	XII	S	Maryland State
Thompson, Jack	Cincinnati	XVI*	QB	Washington State
Thompson, Steve	N.Y. Jets	III	DE	Washington

313

Name	Team	Game	Position	College
Thornton, Sidney	Pittsburgh	XIII,XIV	RB	Northwestern Louisiana
Thurman, Dennis	Dallas	XIII	CB	USC
Thurston, Fred (Fuzzy)	Green Bay	I,II	G	Valparaiso
Tillman, Rusty	Washington	VII	LB	Northern Arizona
Tingelhoff, Mick	Minnesota	IV,VIII,IX,XI	C	Nebraska
Todd, Larry	Oakland	II	RB	Arizona State
Toews, Jeff	Miami	XVII,XIX	C-G	Washington
Toews, Loren	Pittsburgh	IX,X,XIII,XIV	LB	California
Toomay, Pat	Dallas	V,VI	DE	Vanderbilt
Torrey, Bob	Philadelphia	XV*	RB	Penn State
Townsend, Greg	L.A. Raiders	XVIII	DE	TCU
Trosch, Gene	Kansas City	IV	DE	Miami
Truax, Bill	Dallas	VI	TE	LSU
Tuiasosopo, Manu	San Francisco	XIX	NT	UCLA
Turk, Godwin	Denver	XII	LB	Southern
Turner, Bake	N.Y. Jets	III	WR	Texas Tech
Turner, Jim	N.Y. Jets, Denver	III,XII	K	Utah State
Turner, Keena	San Franscisco	XVI,XIX	LB	Purdue
Twilley, Howard	Miami	VI,VII,VIII	WR	Tulsa
Tyler, Wendell	L.A. Rams, San Francisco	XIV,XIX	RB	UCLA
Tyrer, Jim	Kansas City	I,IV	OT	Ohio State
Unitas, Johnny	Baltimore	III,V	QB	Louisville

Name	Team		Pos.	College
Upchurch, Rick	Denver	XII	WR	Minnesota
Upshaw, Gene	Oakland	II,XI,XV	G	Texas A&I
Vactor, Ted	Washington	VII	CB	Nebraska
Valentine, Zach	Pittsburgh	XIV	LB	East Carolina
Vandersea, Phil	Green Bay	I	RB	Massachusetts
van Eeghen, Mark	Oakland	XI,XV	RB	Colgate
Vella, John	Oakland	XI	T	USC
Vellone, Jim	Minnesota	IV	G	South Carolina
Verser, David	Cincinnati	XVI	WR	Kansas
Vigorito, Tom	Miami	XVII	RB-KR	Virginia
Villapiano, Phil	Oakland	XI	LB	Bowling Green
Vogel, Bob	Baltimore	III,V	OT	Ohio State
Voigt, Stu	Minnesota	VIII,IX,XI	TE	Wisconsin
Volk, Rick	Baltimore	III,V	DB	Michigan
von Schamann, Uwe	Miami	XVII,XIX	K	Oklahoma
Waddy, Billy	L.A. Rams	XIV	WR	Colorado
Wade, Charley	Miami	VII*	WR	Tennessee State
Wagner, Mike	Pittsburgh	IX,X,XIII	S	Western Illinois
Walden, Bobby	Pittsburgh	IX,X	P	Georgia
Walker, Fulton	Miami	XVII,XIX	CB-KR	West Virginia
Walker, Rick	Washington	XVII,XVIII	TE	UCLA
Wallace, Jackie	Minnesota, L.A. Rams	IX,XIV	CB-S	Arizona
Walter, Mike	San Francisco	XIX	LB	Oregon
Walters, Stan	Philadelphia	XV	T	Syracuse

315

Name	Team	Game	Position	College
Walton, Bruce	Dallas	X*	T	UCLA
Walton, Sam	N.Y. Jets	III	OT	East Texas State
Ward, Jim	Baltimore	III*	QB	Gettysburg
Warfield, Paul	Miami	VI,VII,VIII	WR	Ohio State
Warren, Don	Washington	XVII,XVIII	TE	San Diego State
Warwick, Lonnie	Minnesota	IV	LB	Tennessee Tech
Washington, Anthony	Washington	XVIII	CB	Fresno State
Washington, Gene	Minnesota	IV	WR	Michigan State
Washington, Joe	Washington	XVII*,XVIII	RB	Oklahoma
Washington, Mark	Dallas	V,X,XII,XIII*	DB-CB	Morgan State
Waters, Charlie	Dallas	V,VI,X,XII,XIII	DB-S	Clemson
Watts, Ted	L.A. Raiders	XVIII	CB	Texas Tech
Weatherwax, Jim	Green Bay	I,II	DE-DT	Los Angeles State
Webster, Mike	Pittsburgh	IX,X,XIII,XIV	C-G	Wisconsin
Weese, Norris	Denver	XII	QB	Mississippi
Welch, Claxton	Dallas	V,VI	RB	Oregon
Wells, Mike	Minnesota	VIII*	QB	Illinois
Wells, Warren	Oakland	II	WR	Texas Southern
Wersching, Ray	San Francisco	XVI,XIX	K	California
West, Charlie	Minnesota	IV,VIII	DB	Texas-El Paso
Westbrooks, Greg	L.A. Rams	XIV	LB	Colorado
White, Danny	Dallas	XII,XIII	QB-P	Arizona State
White, Dwight	Pittsburgh	IX,X,XIII,XIV	DE	East Texas State

316

Name	Team	Game	Position	College
Willis, Len	Minnesota	XI	WR	Ohio State
Wilson, Ben	Green Bay	II	RB	USC
Wilson, Brenard	Philadelphia	XV	S	Vanderbilt
Wilson, Jerrell	Kansas City	I,IV	P	Southern Mississippi
Wilson, Marc	Oakland,	XV*,XVIII	QB	Brigham Young
	L.A. Raiders			
Wilson, Mike	San Francisco	XVI,XIX	WR	Washington State
Wilson, Mike	Cincinnati	XVI	T	Georgia
Winston, Dennis	Pittsburgh	XIII,XIV	LB	Arkansas
Winston, Roy	Minnesota	IV,VIII,IX,XI	LB	LSU
Wolf, Jim	Pittsburgh	IX*	DE	Prairie View
Wonsley, Otis	Washington	XVII,XVIII	RB	Alcorn State
Wood, Willie	Green Bay	I,II	DB	USC
Woodley, David	Miami	XVII	QB	LSU
Woodruff, Dwayne	Pittsburgh	XIV	CB	Louisville
Woods, Larry	Miami	VIII*	DT	Tennessee State
Woolsey, Rolly	Dallas	X	DB	Boise State
Wright, Eric	San Francisco	XVI,XIX	CB	Missouri
Wright, George	Baltimore	V*	DT	Sam Houston
Wright, Jeff	Minnesota	VIII,IX,XI	S	Minnesota
Wright, Louis	Denver	XII	CB	San José State
Wright, Nate	Minnesota	VIII,IX,XI	CB	San Diego State
Wright, Rayfield	Dallas	V,VI,X,XII,XIII	T	Fort Valley State

Name	Team		Pos.	College
Wright, Steve	Green Bay	I,II*	T	Alabama
Wyche, Sam	Washington	VII	QB	Furman
Yary, Ron	Minnesota	IV,VIII,IX,XI	T	USC
Yepremian, Garo	Miami	VI,VII,VIII	K	None
Young, Charle	L.A. Rams, San Francisco	XIV,XVI	TE	USC
Young, Charley	Dallas	X	RB	North Carolina State
Young, Roynell	Philadelphia	XV	CB	Alcorn State
Young, Willie	Miami	VIII*	T	Alcorn A&M
Youngblood, Jack	L.A.Rams	XIV	DE	Florida
Youngblood, Jim	L.A. Rams	XIV	LB	Tennessee Tech
Zaunbrecher, Godfrey	Minnesota	VIII*	C	LSU